PHEROZESHAH MEHTA

Socio-Political Ideology

Indian Freedom Fighters Series—14

Pherozeshah Mehta

Socio-Political Ideology

S.R. BAKSHI

Anmol Publications

ANMOL PUBLICATIONS
4378/4B, Ansari Road,
Darya Ganj, New Delhi-110002.

Pherozeshah Mehta : *Socio-Political Ideology*

ISBN 81-7041-427-X

PRINTED IN INDIA

Published by J.L. Kumar for Anmol Publications and Printed at Sangita Printers Delhi-53.

Preface

Pherozeshah Mehta was a remarkable Congress leader for about three decades. As one of the prominent founders of this organization, he was honoured to chair its session which indeed was an unique honour. He was an able legal expert and earned much fame in the profession. He was a prominent Member and Chairman of the Bombay Municipal Corporation, Member, Bombay Legislative Council and Member, Imperial Council. He took deep interest in the development of the Bombay University and always suggested that education should be made a universal phenomenon. He fought for the welfare and upliftment of the youth of our country and recommended to the Raj for holding Civil Service examination in India, thus facilitating numerically more number of Indians who otherwise would have faced financial hazards.

I have weaved the whole career of Pherozeshah Mehta into a few Chapters dealing with his early career, social ideology, Congress President, Indian Nationalism and a brief assessment. In the end I have mentioned the sources in the Bibliography.

I have consulted the material in the Nehru Memorial Museum and Library, Sapru House Library and the Indian Council of Historical Research Library. I am thankful to the authorities of these institutions for helping me during my researches.

S.R. Bakshi

[illegible] and [illegible]

[illegible]

[illegible] world [illegible] material [illegible].

My [illegible] a few Central [illegible] with the early Christian [illegible] in the [illegible] Library [illegible] in the [illegible].

I [illegible] Library, [illegible] Centre of the [illegible] Research Library [illegible] the authorities of these institutions for [illegible] research.

[illegible] S.P. [illegible]

Contents

1

Early Career

Pherozeshah Mehta was born in a merchant family in Bombay on 4 August 1845. His father was a man of means and was able to bring up his children in comfort. His early education was in Ayrton's School and the Branch School, and after High School he joined the Elphinstone College. Indeed he was a diligent student of History and English Literature.

The culture imparted in those days was in many respects sounder, and took deeper root than modern conditions allow. The pupils were few and they came closely and directly under the influence of singularly able and conscientious teachers. Pherozeshah made the most of his opportunities. In the annual reports which were sent to his father over the signature of Sir Alexander, his conduct and progress were described as excellent. He was quick at grasping the salient points of the subject before him, but avoided the short cuts to knowledge which such facility often encourages. He belonged to that somewhat rare type of men in whom great natural advantages are found allied with a capacity for taking pains.

While the cultivation of the mind was promoted in every way, the development of the body was not neglected. Though little inclined to any vigorous physical exertion, Pherozeshah was fond of cricket, and played a great deal of what was then a little known game. He is said to have played in characteristic

fashion, never knowing when he was defeated. Sir Alexander was himself fond of the game, and encourged its pursuit among his pupils. On one occasion, he even took a team with him to the Deccan, Pherozeshah forming one of the Eleven. In after years, at College and other convivial gatherings, when old days were recalled with affection, Pherozeshah took a whimsical delight in claiming that he was one of the pioneers of the game, and in disputing with the late Mr. Jamsetjee Patel, his title as the Father of Indian Cricket, contending that long before the latter emerged on the scene, he and his contemporaries, proud of their bats and stumps which had been made by a native carpenter, used to indulge in the game in the *maidan* outside the ramparts of the Old Fort, which had guarded the little town for generations, and which later had to be demolished with the rise of modern Bombay.

Those years at College were well spent. They taught the young man to stand upright, they certainly fostered no "slave mentality." They were devoted to the cultivation of a mind which was very receptive, and to the pursuit of a healthy outdoor life. The opportunities for the acquisition of culture which existed in those days, the attention that it was possible to bestow on each student, and the sympathetic understanding which existed between the professors and their pupils, all contributed to bring out the best that was in a man, and in such an atmosphere Pherozeshah's intellect ripened early. He had the rare advantage, besides, of coming under the influence of Sir Alexander Grant's inspiring personality, and the value of this early association he repeatedly acknowledge in after years.

In 1864, Pherozeshah passed his B.A. examination, and was awarded a Dakshina Fellowship by Sir Alexander, who was anxious to retain his connection with the College. About this time, he received a compliment which was as rare as it was gratifying in those days. Sir Bartle Frere, having heard about him, was desirous of meeting him, and asked him to an interview at Government House. Whether or not, the future

greatness of the man was already stamped on his youthful features, there is no doubt he must have deeply impressed the Governor, as he did every one else who came in contact with him. What transpired at the interview is not known.

A few months later, an event of far-reaching importance took place in the life of Pherozeshah. The late Mr. Rustumji Jamsetjee Jejeebhoy, the second son of the first Parsi Baronet, and a man of remarkably enlightened views and catholic philanthropy, had offered in December, 1863, a sum of Rs. 1,50,000 in trust "to enable five natives of India to proceed to England for the purpose of qualifying themselves for practice at the Bar in India." The benefits of the proposal were to be open to a Parsi, a Hindu and a Portuguese in Bombay, and a Mohamedan and a Hindu or East Indian from Calcutta or Madras, "all of good family connections, occupying a respectable position in society." The donor had further laid down that in making the selection, "the good moral character of the respective parties must be an indispensable qualification, and not merely abilities alone." For each selected candidate the handsome provision of Rs. 30,000 was made, which included a sum of Rs. 10,000 to be presented to him on his qualifying himself as a barrister, and producing a certificate of his good moral conduct during his residence in England. Such were the terms of the generous offer made by Mr. Rustumji Jamsetjee, a man whose charity was as wide and catholic as that of his illustrious father—as an instance of which might be mentioned his magnificent donation for the relief of Lancashire operatives at the time of the American Civil War—and who, it is related, had in the hey-day of his prosperity set apart the princely sum of Rs. 51 lacs for the benefit of the poor of his community. The downfall of this singularly enlightened and large-hearted citizen was one of the greatest tragedies of the Share Mania of 1865.

When applications were invited for the scholarship, Sir Alexander induced Pherozeshah to put forward his candidature, though his father had some misgivings about the propriety of his son accepting the benefit of a charitable trust, and wanted him to adopt a commercial career. Sir Alexander pointed out that it was in fact an honour to be selected as a candidate, and the elder Mehta gave in. It is interesting to note, as throwing a side-light on the early conditions of Indian life, that not one Hindu came forward in Bombay to take the benefit of this magnificent provision. As Pherozeshah said some three years later in the course of a lecture before the East India Association, "the uneducated were withheld by the prejudices of caste and country, and the educated did not care to break abruptly some of the most sacred social and family ties, especially when the means of enlightenment were, to a certain extent, near at their hands." In forwarding his gifted pupil's application, the eminent educationist wrote in terms of warm appreciation of his talents and character:

"I have great pleasure in testifying that Mr. Pherozeshah Merwanji is in every way worthy of the benefaction which he seeks. He is on the whole best student of all I have had to do with in the Elphinstone College. He has good abilities, industry, good sense, modesty, an excellent moral character, and remarkably gentlemanly and pleasing manners. From much association with him on the cricket field as well as in the lecture room, I can testify to his manliness and courage, which I think the committee will consider valuable qualifications. I beg you will lay before them this letter, and say to them with all respect that should their choice fall upon Mr. Pherozeshah Metha, I should cordially congratulate the honourable founder of this benefaction on the worthy character of the young man selected to represent himself and the Parsee community in England."

The choice of the committee happily fell upon Pherozeshah —in Calcutta the late Mr. W.C. Bonnerji was selected—and as Sir Alexander was going to England in December, 1864, and was desirous of taking his pupil with him, the latter was allowed as a special grace to appear for his M.A. within six months of his passing the B.A. examination. The task was not an easy one, but those who knew him felt sure of his success.

Their confidence was speedily justified, and Pherozeshah became one of the first M.A.'s of the Bombay University. More exciting than the examination, however, was the prospect of his impending departure. He was going out to a new and wonderful world about which he had read and dreamt a great deal. The gifts with which he had been so amply endowed by Nature were to find the fullest scope for development, and the future seemed bright and full of hope. After weeks of preparation befitting the importance of the occasion—a visit to Eurcpe was looked on as a bit of an adventure in those days—Pherozeshah sailed for England in December, 1864. Accompanying him was another Elphinstonian, Mr., now Sir, Hormasji Wadya, whose success as a lawyer in the mofussil later brought him in frequent contact with his old friend, with whom he fought many a legal battle in Kathiawar and other places. On the eve of their departure, their fellow-students at the College presented them with a farewell address. It was an unpretentious document written on a plain sheet of paper, and couched in simple language, but it bore the names of many who in after years attained to eminence in various walks of life, such as Mahadeo Govind Ranade, Bal Mangesh Wagle, Rahimtulla Mohamed Sayani and Goculdas Kahandas Parekh. The address referred to the brilliant career of the two young men, and expressed a hope that as the Benefaction had attracted candidates from Madras and Calcutta, they would carry themselves not only as Elphinstonians, but as representing the whole of the Presidency. The presentation of the address with its simple but stimulating message was a happy idea, and the document enshrining it was preserved by Pherozeshah with loving care. Amidst the triumphs of after years, this little token of good-will extended to him by the associates of his early life remained a pleasant and ineffaceable memory. (H.P. Mody)

He spent about four years in England i.e., 1865 to 1868. Apart from legal studies, he devoted some time to the study of French. In social life, he became friendly with D.D. Cama's family and several other Parsi and non-Parsi families. He was also inspired by writings of Carlyle, Ruskin, Mill, Darwin,

Herbert Spencer, Mazzini, Victor Hugo and several others.

He had been called to the Bar in Easter Term in 1868 and had been received at the Benchers' Table. A bill for £1 1s. made out by "John Punt, second butler", for proportionate contribution to the expenses of a wine party affords evidence that the occasion was duly celebrated. As he had completed his training, his father was desirous that he should return at the earliest opportunity, preferably with Sir Alexander, who was coming out in July. The failure of Mr. Rustumji Jamsetjee, shortly after Pherozeshah's departure for England, had deprived the latter of the benefit of the scholarship, and had thrown on the elder Mehta a burden of which he was anxious to be relieved. His son with his extravagant habits had spent quite a small fortune during his three and a half years' stay in England. Pherozeshah delayed his departure, however, as he wanted to give a few finishing touches to his education. Ultimately, with the good wishes of those who were taking a sympathetic interest in his career, and to the regret of his intimate associates, who felt that life was losing much of its savour by his departure, Pherozeshah sailed for India in September, 1868. Those four years which he had spent in England had been among the happiest in his life, and had equipped him with much that went to the making of his remarkable public career. (H.P. Mody)

As a member of the bar, young Pherozeshah did well and became a prominent lawyer by dint of hard and painstaking efforts. Indeed he showed remarkable regularity in attending the courts and dealt with legal cases with 'full' preparation. His powers of exposition and skill in cross-examination were remarkable and these qualities greatly impressed his clients as well to as the judges. His reputation as an intelligent advocate travelled to the neighbouring state, Gujarat where the clients began to engage him for several important and intricate cases. He also did very well in the High Court.

With the passage of time, he began to show interest in

the socio-economic and political problems of the Presidency as well as other provinces. He was one of the founders of the Indian National Congress, and till the last breath of his life, he participated in its deliberations by suggesting several innovations in this organisation. In fact at that point of time, Gandhi had not arrived at the political stage of India, and Gokhale and Mehta, along with several other leaders, guided the destiny of the country by negotiating, discussion and arguments with the bureaucracy of the Raj.

2

Social Ideology

Pherozeshah Mehta picked up several social issues which touched upon the problems being faced by our society. At this point of time he had gained much prominence as a public figure by his consistent efforts which had deep linkage with the socio-economic and cultural development of our society.[1] He showed much interest in holding the Civil Service Examination in India as well so that youngmen aspiring for this service might not incur much financial burden on their parents.[2] He greatly evlogised the services rendered in this regard by no less a prominent leader than Dadabhai Naoroji. Whereas he took part in several protest meetings from time to time, he fought for the development of school and university education in the Bombay Presidency. He was in favour of separation of judiciary and executive in regard to their functions, urged for the in area of personnel in the Bombay police and took up numerous other issues like High Courts in India, reforms in Bombay University, Indian representatives in England and the improvement of socio-economic condition of Indians living in South Africa. In fact these issues were taken up at various levels and he saw to it that these are resolved with the support of the public as well as the Raj.

INDIAN REFORMS SIMULTANEOUS EXAMINATIONS

The third annual Dinner of the Elphinstonians took place

on 18th December 1886 at the Elphinstone Institution when Mr. Dadabhai Naoroji took the Chair. Mr. Pherozeshah in proposing the toast of the Chairman, spoke as follows.

Brother Eliphinstonians,—I am asked to propose the next toast—that of our Chairman. In entrusting this toast to me, one of the most hopeful tasks that could be imagined has been assigned to me. I am asked to say something about a person whose life and career and public services have been once and again described by tongues and pens more eloquent than I could ever hope to wield. If I attempted such a task, I would have to repeat an oft-told tale the tale, of a career which you have all more or less seen and watched with your own eyes, and which has met with general appreciation, not only in Bombay, not only in this Presidency, not only in India, but which has been appreciated throughout the British dominions—in all its noble elements of simplicity. I am, therefore, not going to enter into the details of such a career: I will simply sum it up in the line in which the Poet Laureate has described a noble character, and in proposing the health of our Chairman, I propose the health of one who may be truly described as "a selfless man and stainless gentleman." All his past is before you, but there is perhaps one new incident since you last met to which reference might perhaps be made. But here, I have again to restrain myself. I refer to Mr. Dadabhai's recent visit to England. Gentlemen, we shall soon have a special opportunity to thank him for the good work done by him during his recent stay in that country, as a meeting is called by the Presidency Association early in January for that special purpose. But letting the past to itself, I will ask your permission to say a few words about what Mr. Dadabhai has to do in the immediate future. With several of our well-known public men, many of them Elphinstonians, including my friend Mr. Telang, Mr. Dadabhai proceeds in a few days to Calcutta on what I consider a mission of high enterprize, viz., to represent this Presidency at the National Congress, which is to be held there during the last few days of the year. Gentlemen, it is a matter of very great satisfaction that a great man like Mr. Dadabhai—is going to attend the Congress which is fast becoming an event of high political importance in this country. It is again satisfactory to remember that we, the people of this Presidency, will be represented in that Congress by persons in whose moderation and judgment we can entirely confide. There is very great reason for satisfaction that the voice of this Presidency should be directed by counsels of moderation and of judgment.

Two of the most important questions which will be discussed in the Congress, are the equal admission of natives into the Civil Services of this country, and the reform and extension of the Legislative Councils. These two important questions will be discussed in the Congress, and I hope that when Mr. Dadabhai will go with the representatives of this Presidency, he will deem it fit and proper to place before the Congress the right point of view from which we in the Bombay Presidency are making demands, both as regards the admission into the Civil Service and the extension and reform of the Legislative Councils. It has been alleged that we have been asking for these changes and reforms with the ulterior object of turning out the British from India. You must have read in today's Times of India and the Bombay Gazette a letter signed by F. who takes it for granted that these reforms are sought for to substitute entirely native for British agency in the administration and government of this country, and after that is accomplished, to ask the English to walk out of the country, their task being done and there being nothing left for them to do. Well, gentlemen, we, in this Presidency, are not fond of attempting to gaze too far into the dim and hazy future, and dip into it as far as human eye could see, or, for the matter of that, could not see. We are practical people, and we are content to deal with practical politics and, gentlemen, the point of view from which we demand these reforms and these changes is very different from what the Anglo-Indian press very often delights in representing us to wish for them. Gentlemen, you must have read the letters recently written by Principal Wordsworth in connection with the pamphlet,—"The Star of the East". I agree with him entirely when he says in one of them that the maintenance of British supremacy in India is one of the most important conditions of all political progress in this country When I say that, we are likely to go entirely with him in laying down such a proposition. I certainly should have wished that he had rather presented it from the point of view in which it was put by Lord Rosebery in his speech at St. Andrew's Dinner. I should have added one more thing. I should have said that the maintenance of British supremacy was the most important condition of progress in this country at present, when founded in justice and righteousness as well as in strength. You will remember that Lord Rosebery said that the British in India must be maintained by English strength and English justice—strength without and justice within.

We, in this Presidency, all are earnestly of opinion that the maintenance of such British supremacy is one of the most essential and important things for this country as far as human eyes could dip into the future for the present. When we ask for these reforms in the Civil Service and in the Legislative Councils, it is not for the purpose of turning out the British from India, but we at least in this Presidency ask them from this point of view,—that we are sincerely convinced that these reforms are necessary and essential for securing the stability and permanency of the Rule. We ask for a large infusion of natives into the Civil Service for the purpose of enabling the British to perform work which they cannot perform without asking the natives of the county to freely and loyally co-operate with them. We ask for the reform and expansion of the Legislative Councils, because we also sincerely believe that the British will never be able to achieve rightly the government of this country, till the natives of the land are asked to help them freely and independently with their counsels. I trust then when Mr. Dadabhai leads our representatives in the Congress, he will base the demand for these reforms most distinctly and unhesitatingly on this, that it is not for the purpose of driving out the English bag and baggage from India, but that they are asked for because our aim, our object and our wish, so far as we could see into the dim future, is to maintain that British supremacy—which is, we admit, the indispensable condition of Indian progress. As I am referring to these matters, I should like to make a few remarks on one of the most important questions which ought to be considered at the Congress, namely, the question connected with the appointment of the Civil Service Commission which is now in motion. Now, gentlemen, it has been said that the appointment of the Commission was not received with that cordiality which its authors fully intended it to receive. It might be that suspicion was cast or intemperate words were spoken about the appointment of the Commission, but so far as this Presidency is concerned, we have never imported bad faith. But we may confess that there has been a feeling of nervousness and anxiety as to the scope of the Commission. And the reason of it is this. All the agitation which has taken place with regard to the Civil Service question and which had been carried on under the leadership of our distinguished Chairman—for years and years past, has been based upon one thing.

We have taken our stand with regard to the question upon one of those rights, which we consider has been granted to us forever by charters which are irrevocable. We have always agitated this question upon this basis, that the charters of 1833 and 1858 have irrevocably told us that we natives of India are eligible for all service under the crown without distinction of colour, caste and creed. This is one of our own fundamental charters and it is upon the basis of these charters that we have continued the agitation with regard to the free and equal admission of natives into the Civil Service of the country. That being our position, there was a sentence in the resolution appointing the Commission which seemed to raise doubt on this point, because in one portion of that resolution there was a reference to posts in the service which were to be exclusively reserved for Europeans. It is not to be wondered at that it should be anxiously considered, if this meant that the question, settled by the charters for all time time as to the equal eligibility of natives, was to be reopened, and that the Commission could consider measures utterly inconsistent with the declared policy of the crown.

The words I have referred to in the resolution, besides, sounded unfortunately as if they were taken from the resolutions of a past regime, that of Lord Lytton whose despatches and resolutions are associated in our minds with pretty candid declarations that our charters were like pie-crusts made only to be broken. There was then legitimate room for anxiety. But after the deliberate announcements of the illustrious nobleman[3], who at present rules over us, made at Poona, nothing remains for us but to receive the appointment of the Commission in the same free and cordial spirit in which we have been assured by him it is designed. We must remember, gentlemen, that the Viceroy is not only a distinguished diplomatist, we must also bear in mind that he is a tried and distiguished administrator and statesman, and that he has to maintain a great reputation as an illustrious administrator and as an illustrious statesman. There is an end, therefore, to all doubt and anxiety, reasonable or unreasonable, and the only thing that now remains for us is to gird ourselves to the task of pointing out what we consider to be the only way in which the promise held out would be adequately fulfilled in regard to the appointment of natives to the Civil Service. That course has been over and over described. So far as natives of India are concerned they are entirely at one in that course—a course which was foreshadowed by our Chairman a long while back, and which he, even I go so far back as 1867, suggested before a meeting of the East India Association in London. That course was laid down aftar mature consideration, and we still adhere to the opinion that it is the only one which will satisfy our legitimate aims and just aspirations. That measure, recommended by all economical and political considerations is, that simultaneous examinations of an exactly similar character should be held in India and in England with the proviso that with regard to the natives, after they have passed the examination in India, they should be called upon to finish their education in the country from which we derive our inspiration and our knowledge. I trust in the Congress which is now to be held, all these views will be strongly and adequately represent by Mr. Dadabhai and his associates with that moderation and judgment which characterized the proceedings of the Congress held in

Bombay last year and which I trust will characterize it this year.

I now ask you, gentlemen, to drink to the good health of our Chairman, Mr. Dadabhai Naoroji. May his efforts in the cause of the welfare of India be always crowned with success! (Loud cheers).

QUEEN VICTORIA'S GOLDEN JUBILEE

A Public Meeting of the citizens of Bombay was held on 17th January 1887 to consider the steps which should be taken for celebrating the Golden Jubilee of the reign of Her Majesty Queen Victoria. Sir Charles Sargent, Chief Justice of Bombay, presided Mr. Pherozeshah spoke as follows.

Mr. President and Gentlemen,

The Resolution entrusted to me is this,—"That the form of the proposed public rejoicings and the control of the expenditure thereof, as also the nature of any permanent memorial to be adopted, be entrusted to the General Committee, this Meeting being of opinion that the festivities should include the decoration and illumination of the streets, and the holding of a fair."

In submitting this Proposition to you, gentlemen, you will allow me to make a few very short remarks. I had trusted that some of the previous speakers would have given you a rapid survey of one of the most eventful and glorious reigns in English history, nay, in the history of the world, but their feelings have not allowed them to do so. And I will follow their example and make but one brief remark. There have been greetings and rejoicings over sovereigns who have been great warriors, mighty conquerors, or distinguished statesmen. But on this occasion we have met together to make arrangements for rejoicings over fifty years of the reign of a Sovereign who, as her own Poet Laureate has sung—

"Has a nobler office upon earth
Than arms, or power of brain, or birth,
Could give the warrior kings of old."

Nobly and conscientiously has Queen Victoria performed the duties of that high office for half a century. I trust that whatever form the permanent memorial of the Jubilee may take, it will be commemorative of the triumphs which have distinguished her memorable reign—the peaceful triumphs of arts and morals, of science, literature and laws,—triumphs which have resulted in benefits and blessings to the people of this country in common with her subjects in other parts of her vast Empire. (Loud applause.)

The Proposition was unanimously carried.

THE SERVICES OF LORD REAY AND MR. DADABHAI NAOROJI

The members of the Ripon Club of Bombay entertained Sir D. M. Petit to a dinner on 5th March 1887 in honour of his recent elevation to Kinghthood. Mr. Dossabhoy Framji, C.S.I., presided. Mr. Pherozeshah Mehta, who was received with loud and prolonged cheers, in proposing the toast of the Governor, spoke as follows.

Gentlemen,—It is my proud privilege this evening to give you the toast of His Excellency Lord Reay, the Governor of Bombay. His Excellency has recently given us a very strong proof or token of the great regard in which he holds our small Community. I am alluding to a circumstance which some of the members might think is giving a proof exactly the very contrary of what I am going to say. I refer to the incident which has been now so much talked about, namely, that His Excellency the Governor in his speech on the Jubilee day did not mention the name of the Parsee Community in common with other natives of this land, and the foreigners who reside in this country. Now, it is a well-known thing, gentlemen especially a mongst the Parsees, that when they are about to celebrate some festive occasion and sit down to invite a number of people, they invariably find from experience that they forget the one who has been the nearest in their regard. The same thing appears to have taken place in regard to His Excellency the Governor. It is because the Parsee Community is near in his regard that His Excellency forgot to mention it in his speech. I speak from knowledge and experience and I have not the slightest doubt you will all agree with me that Lord Reay has always dealt with us very fairly and has always had the well-being of the Parsee Community at heart. It is the toast of such a sympathetic Governor that I have the honour of giving you to-night and I am sure you will join with me with all your heart in wishing him a long life and a career as brilliant and as distinguished as that of the most eminent of his predecessors who have ruled over us.

Mr. Pherozeshah then proposed Mr. Dadabhai Naoroji's toast as follows.

Gentlemen,—I now give you the toast of a personage the mention of whose name is ever received as a signal for universal acclamation and which is household throughout the length and breadth of the country,—of the great patriot who has laid India under a deep debt of gratitude by his immeasurable services in her behalf,—of our distinguished guest the Hon. Mr. Dadabhai Naoroji. He is the only eminent visitor ever invited and entertained by our Club, for, you will remember, an entertainment was given in his honour on his departure to England on the last occasion for the purpose of entering into the portals of the House of Commons. He is leaving again these sho es by the next mail—even at his present time of life—to fulfil that high mission and to work for his country to which he has dedicated his noble self,—a work which he has been doing throughout his whole life-time in the most loyal and indefatigable manner. With the sincerest of wishes, therefore, that his noble efforts be fruitful of encouraging results, let us, gentlemen, hold our glasses and wish Mr. Dadabhai Naoroji a happy voyage to the scene of his labours which, let us hope, may be crowned with entire and well-merited success.

SUNDAY MAIL PROTEST MEETING

A Public Meeting of the citizens of Bombay was held on 18th September 1889 to protest against the proposed alteration of the day of despatching English Mails on Sunday. Sir Charles Sargent, Chief Justice of Bombay, presided. Mr. Pherozeshah Mehta, who was received with cheers when he rose to support the Resolution, viz., "That this meeting protests against the proposed despatch of the European Mails from Bombay on Sunday during a large part of the year as a measure fraught with injury to the moral, physical and material well-being of the community in and beyond Bombay", proposed by the Lord Bishop of Bombay and seconded by the Hon. Mr. R.M. Sayani, spoke as follows.

Mr. Chairman and Gentlemen,—I most cordially support the Resolution which has been placed before you so exhaustively by the Bishop of Bombay. It is said that one touch of nature makes the whole world kin; but it seems to me that there is nothing like a common grievance to bring people together. And it is a grievance common to us all that has brought us here together, common to all creeds, all classes, and all the communities of this city. We are all threatened—high and low, official and non-official—with the deprivation of an institution which has worked itself into the common life of the city, and which contributes in no small measure to the preservation of its welfare. Whatever difference of opinion there may exist as to the ways in which Sunday is observed in the different countries of Europe, there can be but one opinion as to the character of the weekly day of rest which English people have introduced in India. The Sunday which they have given us is what has been described by a French writer, and truly described as "the respectable, the beneficent and the humane Sunday of England". It may be said that the despatch of the English mails on Sunday will not affect the whole population of the city. But it is sure in the end to destory the character of Sunday as a common day of rest, in way the poet has described, "like the little rift within the lute, that by and by will make the music mute". I trust, gentlemen, that this our protest will receive the consideration which it so well deserves, though true it is, as we often find to our cost, that it is a far cry from here to India Office. Instances like the present one have the unfortunate tendency of fostering the belief in the public mind that in all questions involving the conflicting interests of England and her sturdy Colonies, India goes to the wall and can cxpect no justice. It may be that many a time and oft this belief is unfounded in particular instances. But that the general belief is not without some justification, is shown by the way in which India has been treated, to mention only a few instances, in the matter of the import duties, the silver plate duty, factory legislation, and home charges. But it is a political blunder to be always throwing the sword ruthlessly in the blance. Let us trust that the Secretary of State will awaken to the sacred duty that lies upon him of protecting the interests of the voiceless peoples over whose destinies he presides, among whom, we may remind him, are English people in no way inferior to the colonists of Australia, and who, perhaps, will now learn to recognise, as I am glad the Lord Bishop has already done, that efforts to secure some small measure of organised representation and power of utterance which may appear to jeopardise the safety of the Empire, may be both reasonable and loyal.

The Resolution was carried unanimously.

CHARLES BRADLAUGH, M.P.

PRESENTATION OF ADDRESSES

On 28th December 1889 a large crowd assembled in the Congress Hall, Bombay, to witness the presentation of addresses to Mr. Charles Bradlaugh. Mr. Pherozeshah Mehta was voted to the Chair and addressed the assembly as follows.

Ladies and Gentlemen,—I stand here to-night in the proud position—I think I can truly say, in the proud position—of being the spokesman of the peoples of India, in formally giving their welcome to our illustrious guest, Mr. Charles Bradlaugh. Many and various have been the ways in which greeting and welcome have poured in from all parts of the country, but we are met here to join in one formal welcome the whole voice of the country. Gentlemen, if you ask me for my credentials I will point to the hundreds of meetings which have been held all over the country, to the telegrams which we have been receiving in shoals, day after day, to the addresses which have poured in upon us from every nook and corner of this vast and various country. And, I think, gentlemen, I can say that I truly represented the feeling of the country the other day, when I said that our hearts were unutterably stirred within us, at finding amongst us Mr. Charles Bradlaugh, restored to health and usefulness. Ladies and gentlemen, I need not tell you—the people assembled here to-day—what it is that promotes this simple and heartfelt welcome to Mr. Bradlaugh. The country, deeply grateful, enthusiastically appreciates the high and unselfish endeavours, by a gentleman who never saw us before and on whom we have no peculiar claim, to promote its welfare, its prosperity, and its best interests. I am not going to give you a long address to-day. I shall be short, for the simple reason that Mr. Bradlaugh may have time to be long. There is a ceremony to be performed. It is impossible, as I have said already, that all the addresses which have poured in upon us, should be read or presented. The utmost that can be done to-night is, that an address representing the joint united feelings of the country, through the mouths of the numerous representatives that have assembled in this city for the purpose of sitting in the Fifth Indian National Cogress, be read. Then all that we can do is to ask the representatives of some of the principal addresses to come up and present them to Mr. Bradlaugh. After that all the other addresses will be taken as having been read and presented.

I will now call upon the much-beloved President of the late Congress, Sir William Wedderburn, to present the address on behalf of the Congress.

Sir William Wedderburn then read the address which was drafted by a Committee consisting of Messrs. John Adam, Pherozeshah Mehta and W.C. Bonnerjee. Mr. Bradlaugh having replied, the proceedings terminated.

PRIMARY EDUCATION IN BOMBAY

At the Meeting of the Bombay Corporation held on 24th November 1890, Mr. T.B. Kirkham, the Government Inspector of Schools moved. "That the Corporation do authorise the Joint Schools' Committee to take over the Sir Mangaldas Nathubhav Gujerati Hindu Girls' School on the terms and conditions of the Trust and henceforth to administer the same as a Municipal School vesting in the Corporation." Mr. G.W. Renghton thereupon moved the followings Amendment:—"That before the Corporation authorised the Joins Schools', Committee to take charge of the Sir Mangaldas Nathubhoy Gujerati Hindu Girls' School a Committee consisting of Messis. Pherozeshah Metha, Wacha, Kirkham, Raughton, Dr. Blaney and Dr. Cawasjee Hormasjee be appointed to consider whether the Corporation has an power to become or authorise the Joint Schools' Committee to become a trustee of the said School and its funds" etc. etc. etc.

Mr. Pherozeshah in seconding the Amendment said that it was extremely necessary to know what responsibility they were about to undertake as Mr. Kirkham might unconciously be asking the Corporation to accept a serious liability in the guist of an endowment. Referring to this question the following letter from the pen of Mr. Pherozeshah, appeared in the Bombay Gazette.

TO THE EDITOR, THE BOMBAY GAZETTE

Sir,—Your today's editorial on the incidental debate on primary education in the Municipal Corporation, enables Mr. Kirkham to see his vindication of Government and the Educational Department placed before the public, while those who challenge it had no opportunity of being heard. I, therefore, trust that you will allow me to say a word on the other side. It has at length dawned upon Mr. Kirkham that his zeal for the promotion of primary education in Bombay has carried him away a little too far, and he has begun to realise that curses, like chicken, come home to roost. His eloquent denunciation regarding the disgraceful and discreditable state of the primary schools in this city, has recoiled on the heads of Government and his own department. These schools were in the charge of Government till last year. And if Mr. Kirkham is correct, they have been kept and maintained by Government all these long years in a condition of which we have reason to be thoroughly ashamed. It is impossible to imagine a more unequivocal condemnation of the way in which Government discharged one of its most important duties. Ever since this unexpected result of his excessive zeal for primary education was brought home to Mr. Kirkham's mind, he has been in search of an apology for Government and his department. Like the immortal Captain Bunsby, he at length delivered himself of it at Monday's debate in the most approved oracular fashion Captain Cuttle could not be more delighted than you are at the profound sagacity of the deliverance. Could a trustee for half a lakh be expected to lay out a lakh, asks Mr. Kirkham triumphantly; and you add that Government simply administered the funds that were placed at their disposal by the Municipality. Mr. Kirkham seems to have deeply studied the Law of Trusts. You must, however, hold with Captain Bunsby that the bearings of the proposition which he has derived from that law "lays in the application on it." Is the allegation on which the analogy is founded a true and correct one? The fact happens, however, to be exactly the contrary of what you assume. Before the present Municipal Act III of 1888 was passed, the duty of maintaining, or contributing to the cost of, primary education in the city did not lie on the Corporation. It only made such voluntary contributions as it pleased. The duty lay entirely on the Government, though it was not precluded from accepting aid from whatever quarter it came. The burden and responsibility of looking after primary education in this city in the manner in which an enlightened Government was bound to do, remained entirely with Government till the present Act was passed, by which they are divided between Government and the Corporation. Surely Mr. Kirkham cannot have forgotten that one of the objects laid down in the local self-government despatches of the Government of India was to transfer this duty from the Provincial Governments to local bodies, subject to the proviso that a sufficient portion of the provincial funds should at the same time be handed over to these bodies for the purpose.

If this fact is carefully borne in mind, Mr. Kirkham's apology, denuded of its false feather, is substantially tantamount to a plea of guilty.

Yours etc.,
Pherozeshah M. Mehta

Mr. Kirkham having replied to the above letter in the Bombay Gazette of 28th November, Mr. Pherozeshah again wrote to that paper as follows.

TO THE EDITOR, THE BOMBAY GAZETTE

Sir,—The subject of the respective obligations of the Government and the Corporation with regard to the primary education in the City of Bombay is of such general public interest that I need make no apology in begging you to allow me to reply briefly to Mr. Kirkham's letter, which appears in your columns today. A very few words will suffice. Mr. Kirkham is a skilful and practised controversialist, and I trust he will permit me to congratulate him upon the admirable gravity with which he dilates upon a number of facts as proving his position, but which not only do nothing of the sort but actually establish the contrary. A close observer cannot however, fail to detect a merry little twinkle in his eyes, while he is devoting two long paragraphs to remove imaginary misapprehensions which have never existed, to impart information about the ways of the Educational Department which though extremely interesting, is not particularly relevant, and to protest against the rise of rhetoric by anybody but himself. He is compelled, however, ultimately to come to one at least of the real points at issue, viz:—Whether this city "has had its fair share of the educational allotments." There is a larger question involved in the controversy which Mr. Kirkham fights shy of, namely, the inadequacy of the educational allotment in itself; but, taking him even on the narrower ground on which he takes his stand, I venture to accept the challenge which he throws out, when he says—"But surely anyone who disputes the fairness of the allotment, assigned to Bombay is bound to state what the amount ought to be, and to show, moreover, the principles by which his result has been reached". Mr. Kirkham says that his own calculation proceeds on the basis of population as the fairest on the whole. But the fairness of this method of calculation involves the assumption that the liability of Government to contribute to the cost of primary education in Bombay was the same as in the rest of the Presidency. But it is however a fact which even Mr. Kirkham cannot deny, and to which the Indian Statute Book testifies, that this liability is different in the one case from what it is in the other and that there is no room for the application of the principle of apportionment at all. Mr. Kirkham has himself told us how this is. Since the Local Cess Act of 1869, the Mofussil Districts have had the obligation imposed upon them by law, of contributing 2 per cent on the rateable value of property for the provision of primary education. In their case, the only liability remaining with Government is to supplement this levy to the point of adequacy. Mr. Kirkham himself is obliged to admit that in the case of Bombay no legal obligation at all was imposed till the passing of the present Municipal Act of 1888. Has Mr. Kirkham asked himself the question why this distinction was allowed to exist for such a length of time? Government had two clear opportunities since 1869 of imposing a similar obligation on this city, firstly, when it passed the Bombay Municipal Act of 1872 and, secondly, when it renewed and revised that Act in 1878. Why then was it not done? Why were Government, anxious as they always are to shift financial burdens from their own shoulders, so unaccountably partial to Bombay that they left a city on which they have not unfrequently cast covetous eyes as the richest city within their jurisdiction, to dole out such voluntary contributions as its Municipal Corporation chose to do in their uncontrolled discretion? Surely the reason is not far to seek. Government had imposed burdens on the city heavier ones by far, which they had not cast on the Mofussil districts and cities. This city alone has had to defray burdens from its local revenues, which were borne by the general revenues with regard to the rest of the Presidency. I will cite only one example, that of the cost of the police. We have had to pay more than two lakhs for police charges every year, while the cost of the entire mofussil police is defrayed out of the Provincial revenues. If Bombay was not saddled with the legal obligation of contributing to the cost of primary education, as in the mofussil, it was simply because other and more onerous burdens were laid on its shoulders. Any attempt at doing so would have been exposed to an inconvenient cry which could scarcely be resisted with any show of justice or fairness; for the adjustment and equalization of other burdens Government prudently made no such attempts in their new Municipal legislation for this city. And thus it is that the liability to adequate provision for primary education in the city, unlike that for a similar provision in the mofussil, continued to rest with Government. It is from this difference in the character and extent of the respective abilities of Government in the two cases that the right of the city arose for a special, and not a proportionate treatment in the allotment and distribution of the Government grant for primary education. I think I have now shown, in answer to Mr. Kirkham's challenge, the principles on which I justify the claim for a separate treatment for this city; and it follows that the duty of Government under such circumstances was to make such a grant as, with the help of fees and the voluntary contributions made by the Municipality, would have sufficed to place primary schools on a progressively satisfactory basis. But what has been the real extent of the grant made by Government year after year? We have Mr. Krikham's emphatic testimony on that point. It has been so grossly inadequate that he cannot find words sufficiently strong to denounce "the discreditable and disgraceful condition" of the primary schools of the city. Am I or am I not justified in saying that Government are judged and condemned out of the mouth of one of their own Educational Officers and that one so well-known for his zeal and ability?

One word more, as not quite inappropriate in this controversy, with regard to the contention which the Corporation has submitted to Government in this matter. Mr. Kirkham, I am sure in perfect good faith, talks as if the Corporation refused and refuses to do its duty in regard to primary education. Nothing can be further from the truth. It is ready and willing, nay, anxious to discharge the function imposed on it by the new Act. It accepts the new obligation cast upon it, but it asks Government to fulfil the distinct and reiterated pledges and declarations which accompanied the new legislation viz., that they should release an equivalent amount of revenue to enable it to discharge the new and additional burden. I hope what I have said above has made it clear that the revenue to be thus released must be something different from the grossly inadequate grant made in previous years.

Pherozeshah M. Mehta

RIPON CLUB ENTERTAINMENT TO PHEROZESHAH, 1890

The Ripon Club of Bombay entertained on 19th December, 1890 Mr. Pherozeshah Mehta in taken of his grant services to the City and to the Country generally and in view of his departure to Calcutta to preside at the 6th Sessions of the Indian National Congress. Mr. Sorabjee Patel, who took the Chair, proposed the toast of the evening to which Mr. Pherozeshah replied as follows.

Gentlemen,—I thank you most heartily for the high honour you have done me in giving me a public Dinner prior to my departure to Calcutta on a political mission. This is an honour greater than I deserve and I only wish, as Burns has said, that

I might see myself as others see me. Despite the services I may have rendered to my countrymen, I am conscious, unmistakeably conscious, of many a broken hope and many a failure for which I can only express my disappointment and regret. But, as the Chairman has just said, if the rising young men wish to follow in my footsteps, then it would be still better for them to take the noble and self-sacrificing example of my revered seniors, after whom I have shaped my public life, the late Mr. Nowrozjee Fardoonjee, the Tribune of the People, and the Grand Old Man of India, who is devoting his old age in England to obtain a seat in the mother of Parliaments. It is a rare spectacle, the activities of Dadabhai Naoroji, of that venerable and placid figure, who at his great age is now wooing the Finsbury Constituency with a perseverence, sacrifice and self-abnegation which are beyond all praise. And for whom is he undergoing all this trouble and worry and anxiety at such a time of his life when others of his age are prone to seek the bowers of retirement and seclude themselves away from the politics of the day? For whom? Not fortunately for Bombay alone but for all India irrespective of race or creed, caste or colour. It is the example of such unique personalities that the coming generation should strive to emulate and the Chairman might have done well to have referred the younger members of this Club to follow in their footsteps rather than in the footsteps of my humble self.

You will not, gentlemen, expect a long speech from me on this occasion. Those of you who are anxious to hear me on the questions of the day, might satisfy your desire by reading my Presidential Address which I will deliver shortly at Calcutta whither I am going to preside over the deliberations of the Congress. Nothing therefore now remains for me but to thank you warmly, gentlemen, once again, for the very kind manner in which you have referred to my services, not forgetting those connected with the Club itself of which I am one of the founders; and if, as you say, I have succeeded in doing some abiding good to the Country which has given me birth, I consider my services thoroughly and entirely compensated.

SEPARATION OF JUDICIAL AND EXECUTIVE FUNCTIONS.

THE HON. MR. PHEROZESHAH'S MEMORANDUM

The Hon. Mr. Pherozeshah Mehta submitted to the 6th Provincial Conference which met at Ahmedabad on the 1st, 2nd and 3rd November, 1893, a Memorandum regarding the separation of Judicial and Executive Functions. The Conference thereupon passed the following Resolution (VI), viz.,

"That this Conference puts on record its opinion that the separation of Executive and Judicial Functions should be effected as early as practicable: that it could be effected with economy and efficiency by transferring the judicial powers vested in the Assistant and Deputy Collectors and Mamlatdars, to the Subordinate Judges, and that a Committee consisting of the following gentlemen be appointed to work out a scheme for the various Districts in the Presidency on the lines indicated in the Hon. Mr. Mehta,'s Memorandum, with due regard to local circumstances and the said scheme when ready be submitted to Government for consideration:

The Hon. Mr. P.M. Mehta.	Mr. R.V. Putwari.
The Hon. Mr. C.H. Setalvad.	,, Motabhoy Motilal.
Mr. Varajray Sakerlal.	,, B.G. Tilak.
,, Moolay.	,, R.P. Karandikar.

The Hon. Mr. Pherozeshah's Memorandum runs as follows.

1. Since Lord Dufferin admitted it in his famous speech in 1886, on the Congress proposals, to be a counsel of perfection, the proposal to separate Judicial from Executive functions in the District Officers has been pronounced by the present[5] as well as past Secretaries of State for India to be a reform eminently desirable, and in his Budget speech for this year the present Under-Secretary of State[6] has again repeated the official approval of the measure, provided that the change did not involve increased expenditure.

2. It is needless, therefore, to say anything as to the reasons for advocating the separation—especially after the admirable manner in which Sir Richard Garth, late Chief Justice of Bengal, has discussed them in his letter on the subject in the columns of "India" particularly in connection with the Mymensing case.

3. The necessity for this reform, is, however, more urgent than is generally imagined—not for men of position and standing but for the masses of the people. Nobody, who is not intimately acquainted with the daily life in villages and small towns, can have an adequate conception of the intolerable hardship which the continuance of Magisterial powers in Revenue officers entails upon the people. The great bulk of the masses are rendered unhappy enough by the way in which life is made a burden not to the rogues but the honest folk by the practical working of the Salt, Opium, Abkari, Forest, Arms and Land Revenue Acts with their infinite rules and regulations hedging the people round in all directions; but, vexatious and harassing as these laws are, they would not be nearly so intolerable if all resistance to their unjust and oppressive enforcement and abuse were not practically rendered impossible by the ingenious device of combining the Prosecutor and the Magistrate in one and the same person. Under these acts, everything is guarded by prosecutions at every step; and these prosecutions, initiated and countenanced by Executive Officers, are tried by Mamlatdars and Magistrates who are all again Executive Officers. Those who have practical knowledge of the system are aware how naturally these prosecutions, however absurd and vexatious, end in convictions. Indeed, the general feeling about the matter is that no Mamlatdar or Magistrate, who valued his own interest and prospect, dare indulge, except rarely, in the luxury of an acquittal. Some of these cases sometimes reach the High Court where they are quashed or revised, occasioning a little mild surprise now and then that intelligent officers could be so wrong-headed. But these are not the hardest cases. The worst are those in which the people yield themselves up in sheer and sullen helplessness and of

which nothing is heard publicly, It is high time that a system under which irritation and discontent are engendered to no small extent should be reformed without loss of time.

4. The real obstacle in the way of so urgent a reform lies in the fact that executive officers are not willing to consent to a measure which would, they consider, materially diminish their importance and power. Unable to advance this reason openly, the plea is put forward that any alteration of the present system would entail a heavy increase of expenditure. But a little reflection is sufficient to show how hollow and unsustainable this plea is. The Magisterial adjunct is admittedly worked by Mamlatdars and Assistant Collectors in a most intermittent fashion. It is a common experience with legal practitioners to be told by these officers that they would not take up criminal cases till late in the' day, and then only for an hour or so, in consequence of the necessity of doing a certain amount of measuring and revenue work. A case is taken up for an hour or so at the end of the day and then adjourned; if the camp has to be removed to the next station, parties and witnesses have all to go on there. It can easily be conceived that a case, which, if heard out without interruption, would be finished in a day, would require several times the same period when heard intermittently in bits, the process involving a considerable amount of repetition. The waste of power and time thus caused is simply incalculable, and cannot but involve, in the very nature of things, increased cost. Any scheme which relegates magisterial functions from officers who can only work them intermittently to officers who can exercise them continually and regularly cannot but result in both economy and efficiency, and such a scheme is the one I sketched in outline on the occasion of the discussion of the last Provincial Budget in the Legislative Council.[7] It proposes to transfer these functions to Subordinate Judges as a part of their regular work, relieving Revenue Officers entirely of all Judicial work. I claim for this scheme the merits of simplicity and economy.

5. The scheme can be best explained by showing how it

would work in a particular District. Leaving Sind alone there are three divisions in the Bombay Presidency—the Northern, the Southern, and the Central. Each division is divided into a certain number of Districts or Collectorates. Each District has generally for its Executive Officers a Collector, who is also District Magistrate, two or more Assistant Collectors with Magisterial powers of the 1st or 2nd class, one Huzur and one District Deputy Collector and a number of Mamlatdars or Mahalkaries in charge of Talukas in which the district is subdivided. For its Judicial Officers, it has a Judge who is both a Civil and Sessions Judge, and a certain number of Subordinate Judges doing Civil work only with one or more S.C.C.[8] Judges. Taking the District of Poona, for example, my proposal would work thus. The Civil List of July 1893 shows for the District two First Assistant and one Assistant Collectors, one Treasury Deputy Collector, besides nine Mamlatdars of different grades under the Collector, and six Subordinate Judges under the District and Sessions Judge. Now, at the meeting of the Legislative Council above referred to, I had ventured timidly to say that the Assistant Collectors and Mamlatdars "certainly do not devote two full hours per day to criminal work," though in the Budget half their salaries were transferred from the head of Law and Administration to Law and Justice. As a matter of fact I knew the time devoted was much less, but I thought it discreet to take the case against my proposal as strongly as possible. The Hon. Mr. Nugent thought that he was irretrievably condemning my scheme when he assured the Council that the time devoted by Mamlatdars to judicial duties did not constitute one-eighth of their total work, and he was good enough further to inform me that in the case of Assistant Collectors it was still less. This fact, so authentically stated by an officer of such high knowledge and experience, blesses instead of cursing the scheme. Instead of demolishing it only strengthens my argument and shows the extreme feasibility of the transfer. For it establishes that the work in its totality is not more than one whole-time officer can perform, working at it not intermittently but regularly. All that is necessary to do under these circumstances is to do away with only one

Mamlatdar and in his place create one Subordinate Judge. The criminal work, of which the Executive Officers would be relieved, would be then distributed among the six old and one new Subordinate Judges. It must be carefully borne in mind that I do not propose to create the new Subordinate Judge for the purpose of entrusting him with the whole of the criminal work from which the Assistant Collectors and Mamlatdars are set free, but each Subordinate Judge of the District would be entrusted with the criminal work of his station. The number of Mamlatdars being only reduced by one could easily cope with the Talukas in the District, in some cases by a slight rearrangement and in others by assigning two of the smallest Talukas to one officer; all the rest of the Mamlatdars continuing in charge of one Taluka only.

6. Independently of achieving the great object of separating Judicial and Executive Functions, and thus removing the crying evils which the combination engenders, there are various subsidiary advantages secured by this scheme which I will now proceed to set forth briefly.

7. In the first place, there would be no increased expenditure, for the salary of a Mamlatdar saved would counterbalance the salary of the new Subordinate Judge created. But there would in many cases be economy. For the Assistant Collectors and Deputy Collectors being relieved of criminal work, it would be often possible to do without the supernumeraries who have often to be given to the Collector in many Districts.

8. In the next place, the work would be done by officers with special legal training instead of men whose legal education and training are at the best of a very superficial character. I do not mean to deny that several of the Mamlatdars are men of ability and intelligence; but without special training, we know that even able and intelligent men interpret law in a manner that is often little short of startling.

9. Both Civil and Criminal Justice would be brought nearer home both to parties and witnesses. A district divided into

the increased number of Subordinate Judges' stations would have smaller areas for their jurisdiction, thus reducing sensibly the present maximum distance of villages from the head-quarters which, being fixed and thus within easy distance, would obviate a great deal of the hardship which people have to suffer from the conditions attendant on shifting camps.

10. There hardly would be any need for any fresh legislation to carry out the change. It would be in the power of the Local Government according to existing law to invest the Civil Judges with Magisterial powers. The only difficulty would be in the case of jurisdiction vested in Mamlatdars under the Mamlatdars' Jurisdiction Act. But it may not be undesirable to leave to them the present summary jurisdiction in regard to possessory suits.

11. It would be very useful if the Conference deputed some of its members to work out this scheme with regard to each separate district in detail with the help of the knowledge of local circumstances and wants possessed by members conversant with each particular district.

The Times of India of 18th June 1894 has the following.

TO, THE EDITOR OF THE TIMES OF INDIA

Sir—You will perhaps remember that in noticing the Memorandum on the question of the separation of Judicial and Executive Functions, which I had placed before the last Provincial Conference held at Ahmedabad, you took exception to my remark on the inevitable tendency of the combination of both functions in one officer to cause injustice and oppression, and you were disposed to ascribe the mischief to the crudity of the law rather than to the unnatural position in which the officer was placed. I venture to ask you to publish the enclosed copy of the record of the proceedings and judgment in a case tried recently by the Superintendent of Matheran, which, I think, will help in elucidating our respective contentions. You will observe that the accused persons in the case are the muccadum of sweepers at Matheran and his wife, and that each of them is sentenced to one month's rigorous imprisonment for the offence of criminal trespass, inasmuch as they stayed on a piece of ground which they had occupied for years after being served with a notice of eviction. I have not the slightest doubt that Dr. Barry is honestly actuated by the desire to do all in his power for the improvement of the Hill. But this, as well as the fact that he is an officer of high intelligence and culture, only serves to point the moral which I ventured to draw in my Memorandum. You are aware that trespass, to be criminal, requires that the entry should be with intent to commit an offence, or to intimidate, insult, or annoy the person in possession. I am afraid the decisions of the Bombay and other High Courts on the interpretation to be put on the words "insult, annoyance and intimidation" were not present to the learned doctor's mind when he convicted the accused. But, however that may be, is it not refreshing to observe that he is perfectly unconscious of any glimmering idea that if the charge was of an offence which involved "the intimidation of the Superintendent," the Superintendent was scarcely the best person to try it? Then, again, does not the extraordinary sentence of one month's rigorous imprisonment, not only on the man, but his wife, make it a fit case to figure in Truth's Legal Pillory? Is it possible to imagine that any officer who was not using his judicial powers to carry out his executive purposes, could have passed such a monstrous sentence? And this is not an isolated case.

Yours etc.,
Pherozeshah M. Mehta

DADABHAI NAOROJI, M.P.

PRESENTATION OF ADDRESSES OF WELCOME

A mass meeting of the inhabitants of Bombay together with many up-country gentlemen who had come as deputations from all parts of the Presidency to present Addresses to Mr. Dadabhai Naoroji, M.P. on his first advent to this country after having entered the British House of Commons, was held on 16th December 1893 under the auspices of the Bombay Presidency Association. The Hon. Mr. Pherozeshah, who presided, explained the significance of the Meeting in the following speech.

Gentlemen,—You all know why we are all gathered together here today. We have met for the purpose of giving expression and putting on formal record our feelings of sympathy, affection and appreciation for one whom we have here in veritable flesh and body, Mr. Dadabhai Naoroji, Member of Parliament. Gentlement, no words of mine, in fact, no words from anybody can describe more eloquently those feelings of sympathy and appreciation in which we hold him than the demonstration with which he was greeted on his landing to this city. Gentlemen, I cannot describe that demonstration,—it required to be seen. It was not in the numbers of the people who turned out to greet him; it was not the rows of vehicles which followed the carriage in which Mr. Dadabhai rode; it was not the assembly of the rich and the wealthy, the educated and the enlightened, which gave to the demonstration its deep human interest. That interest lay in the fact that the artisans, the labourers and the workmen, they, their wives and their children, —all came out glad and rejoicing to see the face of the Apostle of India. I shall never forget the look of joy and sympathy to be seen on every face on the occasion of the advent of Mr. Dadabhai in our midst. The faces of the people were the truest and most genuine mark of their respect and affection for their fellow-townsman, who had brought such credit and distinction not only on this city, but on the whole of India, yes, on the whole of this country. It is impossible in a large assemblage like this to indulge in long speeches, and without any further remarks, I shall at once call upon the members of the different deputations who have come from all parts of the Presidency, to present the Addresses to Mr. Dadabhai Naoroji. It will be impossible to read all the Addresses and telegrams received from different parts of the Presidency, and one or two, or at the most three, can only be read out, the others being taken as read. We will begin therefore with the Address to be presented on behalf of the Bombay Presidency Association, the Address from the *Sarvajanik Sabha* of Poona, and then the Address from Ahmedabad. I will now call upon Mr. Wacha to read the first Address.

DADABHAI NAOROJI, M.P.

POONA'S WELCOME

A Public Meeting of the citizens of Poona was held at Hirabag, on 17th December 1893, to welcome Mr. Dadabhai Naoroji, M.P. on his advent into the ancient Mahratta Capital. At this gathering Mr. B.G. Tilak in expressing thanks to Mr. Dadabhai said—"We have been trying to receive our guest in as fitting a manner as we can. Our Bombay friends have come here to see how we perform our duty. I trust they can take favourable news to Bombay and we can only thank them for the kind visit they have paid us." After this there were loud calls for a speech from Mr. Pherozeshah to which he responded as follows.

Gentlemen,—Your friend Mr. Tilak has told you that I have come here as a spy. (Laughter.) I have come here in no such capacity. I have come here simply as one of yourselves, as an Indian, to join in co-operating with you at the national gratification at the election of one of our countrymen to the British House of Commons. I am delighted—I am more than delighted—I am moved at the sight I saw from one end of the great and ancient city of Poona to the other. I am moved and why? Because Poona has given one of the boldest answers to the challenge that has so often been thrown down to us, that we Indians have not a political genius in us and never will have. Let the people who say that come and see what I saw in Bombay yesterday and what you have seen today in Poona and they will have the answer to their challenge. Here is our answer to the accusation. When you find every man, woman and child, Hindu, Mohamedan and Parsi, of every variety of caste and creed, conscientiously co-operating together, feeling in the same way, their *hearts* and pulses throbbing in unison since the day of the landing of Mr. Dadabhai Naoroji,—with such manifestations before them, can they say that there is no germ of political genius in us? Are these manifestations not the dawning of a political regeneration the awakening of a political feeling? Gentlemen, I have not come here as a spy. I am moved at the deep human drama which will help us, God willing, to the amelioration of the country of which, whether we be Hindus or Mohamedans or Parsis, we are all proud to the children, the country of our birth and of our homes, and, I trust, the country of our exertions and self-sacrifices.

INCREASE IN THE BOMBAY POLICE FORCE

THE HON. MR. PHEROZESHAH'S MINUTE OF DISSENT

In consequence of the experience gained in the Hindu-Mohamedan riots in Bombay in 1893, the Commissioner of Police[9] submitted to Government proposals for an increase in the Police of the City. The Bombay Government thereupon appointed a Committee to report on the proposed increase and on the recommendation of the Corporation and to watch the interests of the Municipality, the Hon. Mr. Pherozeshah's name was included in it. The Committee submitted their Report to Government on 23rd December 1893 and the following is the Hon. Mr. Pherozeshah's statement forwarded to the President of the Corporation.

Junagadh, 2nd March 1894.

To
THOMAS BLANEY, Esq.,
President, Municipal Corporation, Bombay

Sir,

As it was at the instance of the Corporation that I was nominated a member of the Committee appointed to consider the proposals of the Commissioner of Police, Bombay, for a further increase in the city police force, I think it right to lay before them the circumstances under which I felt myself precluded from joining in the report of the Committee or recording a minute of dissent, and compelled to withdraw from it after presenting a letter of simple protest.

2. I cannot place these circumstances before the Corporation better than by giving a brief account of the proceedings of the Committee.

3. I was informed by Government of my appointment by a letter, dated 18th November 1893, and on the 29th November, when away from town, I received a letter from the Secretary of the Committee, dated 28th November, asking me to attend the first meeting of Committee on the 30th November 1893. It was impossible for me to do so, and I telegraphed to the Secretary to that effect. As I learnt afterwards the reason for this short notice was to enable one of the members, Mr. Cotton, to record a minute of the fullest approval of the proposals, for the joint consideration of which the Committee was appointed, before the Committee had even entered upon its deliberations. The opinion of a gentlemen of Mr. Cotton's position, ability and experience would at all times be most valuable; but he could hardly be said to have discharged the joint deliberative function, which rests upon the members of all Committees, by walking off after recording a minute. The incident is described in the minutes of the Committee, which were written, not by the Secretary, but by another member of the Committee, Mr. Campbell, and it is related therein as follows:

> "The orders of Government constituting the Committee are read. The Chairman states the chief reason for having so early a meeting is that one of the members, Mr. Cotton, leaves for England by mail of December 2nd. As the members had not the opportunity of reading the Police Commissioner's letter, the present must be considered a preliminary meeting. Mr. Cotton ask the Chairman to allow him to read a memorandum he has prepared after studying the Commissioner's letter. The Chairman agrees and Mr. Cotton's memorandum is read and put in. Mr. Cotton asks if any member has any remarks to make. As no member expresses any dissent the Chairman decides the memorandum should be considered when the report is being prepared and should be attached to it as a part of

the proceedings."

4. The next meeting was held on the 7th December 1893, and I went to it, prepared to do, to the best of my ability, my part in the enquiry and deliberation which it never occurred to me to doubt, would be at once undertaken by the Committee. My surprise may be imagined when I found that the Chairman got up and made a few short remarks which, he told us, were confidential, and then said (I prefer to to quote from the minutes), "As regards our procedure today, I would suggest that if any gentleman dissents from any of the proposals contained in the letter of the Commissioner of Police, he should state his reasons for dissent." After some time, during which we sat looking at each other's faces, I ventured to suggest that the proper procedure would be, in the first instance, to see if there were statements of facts in the Commissioner's letter which required enquiry or verification, and that if there were, such enquiry should be made. I had flattered myself that I had put forward my suggestion at once mildly but convincingly. I was not therefore a little surprised to find that my gentle suggestion was denounced by the Chairman and some of the members as simply impossible; and the Commissioner of Police looked at me in mute reproach at my presumption in requiring his facts to be investigated and verified. It was, I believe, Mr. Campbell who solemnly assured me that Government had set the Committee only an exercise in dialectics and the Chairman ruled that "the intention of Government in referring the papers to the Committee was that the Commissioner's report should be considered to establish the facts which it contains." I had nothing to do but to bow respectfully to the Chairman's ruling, and only begged that it should be recorded. A question was thereupon at once raised, whether it was all necessary to keep minutes, and it was ultimately decided that, though it was perfectly useless to do so, as members had ears to hear what was said in Committee, my wish might be gratified in that respect out of indulgence for my weakness. Nothing remained to do after this but to carry the Commissioner's proposals by acclamaticn, for not a single reason for

dissent was forthcoming. The prospect of so easy a victory did not, however, seem to be quite satisfactory and Mr. Douglas interposed with the suggestion that, though the Chairman's ruling was correct and that no enquiry could be made into the Commissioner's facts, still "he thought it would be suitable that any member should be allowed to ask the Commissioner any "question on any point in the Commissioner's letter regarding which the member might desire further information." The Chairman thereupon agreed that the "Commissioner of Police may be asked questions regarding the statements contained in his letter". This was scarcely a logical position in view of the Chairman's previous ruling, or a very satisfactory one in reference to my conception of the functions of the Committee. But as I hoped that a little cross-questioning of the Commissioner might succeed in showing to the Committee the necessity of an enquiry, I at once undertook to put some questions. But again, to my surprise, I was told that neither the questions nor answers were to be recorded. As it was imposible not to realise that my efforts to do what I honestly considered to be my duty were treated and resented as idle obstruction, and that my questioning were to be dedicated to empty air, I declined the fruitless task. What followed had best be quoted from the minutes prepared by Mr. Campbell:

> "On enquiry whether such questions and answers should form part of the minutes of the meeting, the Chairman holds that as members present will hear and can note any point, their entry in the minutes is not necessary. As Mr. Mehta declines to put any question to the Commissioner unless the questions and answers are recorded, the Chairman remarks that while personally he sees no necessity for it, 'if any member attaches importance to the point, the questions and answers may be recorded."

As I thought that one meeting would be devoted to settle the course of procedure to be adopted by the Committee, I was not, I confess, so fully prepared as I otherwise should have been, to carry on the interrogation. I tried, however, to do what I could. In the first place I thought it was necessary to ask the Commissioner to state more clearly and definitely than he had done in his letter, whether the object of the further increase was simply to enable the police to cope with the ordinary work of the city or to strengthen it for serious emergencies like the August riots. In the second place I wanted to sift the assertion about the men and officers being cruelly overworked, and the necessity of "reducing the hours of duty which the Commissioner "is compelled to exact from Europeans and natives." I put some questions on the first point without getting very satisfactory answers. When I came to the second, the Commissioner flatly declined to give answers. I asked him "wh ıt work was taken out of each policeman", with the view of enabling the committee to judge whether too many hours of work were or were not exacted from each policeman. The answer I received is recorded in the minutes as follows:—

> "The details of the police work are in my hand. I have given such details as "I think necessary in my report to Government. I do not think it necessary to give any details in addition to those shown in para 18 of my report."

The above answer does not fully record what the Commissioner said. What he really said was that the hours of work was purely an administrative matter and that he declined to give the details I asked for, as the Committee or any other person had no right to interfere with his arrangements in that respect. I tried in vain to explain to the Commissioner that nobody had the remotest conception of interfering with his administrative arrangements, but that my qnestion was asked for the purpose of eliciting the detailed extent of the alleged overwork. But all to no purpose; and I gave up the task of questioning in despair.

5. I still, however, attended the next meeting which was held on the 14th December 1893. I made another effort to explain to the Commissioner the object of my questions and to indicate to the Committee the several points on which it was desirable to obtain some further information and to make some

further investigation, if for no other purpose, at least for the purpose of being in a position to define what should be the extent of the further increase. But it was all of no use. The meeting was adjourned to next day, the 15th December, on which day, as I informed the Committee I could not attend as I had to leave town. At that meeting the proposals to be embodied in the report of the Committee appear to have been settled, and on the following Tuesday, the 21st December, the report was signed with minutes appended by Messrs. Cotton Douglas, Vijbhookandas and Campbell.

6. In due course I received a letter from the Secretary, dated the 22nd December 1893, enclosing a copy of the report, and enquiring if I would sign it, adding that "at the same time I am to state that the Committee has been dissolved, "but that if you will be good enough to forward your minute, it will be appended to "the report to be submitted to Government." I wrote back on the 27th asking for copies of the minutes of proceedings as well as of the minutes appended by members of the Committee. The minutes of proceedings were supplied, but I was told that "it was not necessary that copies of the minutes recorded by other members should "be supplied to you." On pointing out why the should be supplied, I was informed by a letter, dated 4th January 1894, "that as all the minutes made by the other members "of the Committee were neither read at the meeting of the Committee nor circulated "to the members, it is not necessary to send them to you for your perusal." I was further informed that "the report of the Committee has been already submitted to "Government", and was requested to forward my minute as early as possible for submission to Government. I wrote to the Secretary to enter a protest against the manner in which the entire proceedings of the Committee had been conducted and received the reply "that your letter of the 6th January 1894 has been recorded and "that your protest cannot form part of the proceedings of the Committee which has been already dissolved", and I was requested "to state whether you intend to forward your "minute of dissent." I replied to the

effect that "I am entirely unable to understand how "my protest cannot form part of the proceedings of the Committee on the ground that it "has been dissolved, while my letter containing it has been recorded in spite of the "very same dissolution. I equally fail to understand that, if the Committee is "dissolved and is thus functus officio, the Chairman can still ask me to send my "minute of dissent, while rejecting my minute containing my protest." I added "that "it seems to me that the only course now open to me is to ask you to send on this, as "well as my letter of the 6th January, to Government."

7. I should like to add that it is ture that the resolution of Government appointing the Committee requests it "to take into consideration the arguments "advanced by the Commissioner of Police in favour of an increase of the city police." But it never occurred to me that Government could intend to put the narrow interpretation upon the word 'arguments', that the Chairman of the Committee did. The word 'arguments', as it appears in the resolution, was not unnaturally understood by me in the general popular sense in which it is sometimes used to include statements of facts as well as the inferences drawn from them. There were two circumstances which justified the more comprehensive interpretation. It could be scarcely imagined that Government would delegate to a Committee the task of examining simply the correctness of the Commissioner's logic, on which it was bound after all to exercise its own judgment. Secondly if such was the intention, it would scarcely be worthwhile to ask the Corporation, as Government did, to recommend a nominee "leaving it to the Corporation to decide in what capacity their nominee should join the "Committee, whether merely as a member appointed to watch the interest of the "Corporation or as one duly qualified to represent the views of that body." I do not think the Corporation would have cared to recommend a nominee, if that nominee was only to watch the interesting, but not very useful, process of scrutinizing the dialectical capacity displayed by the Commissioner in his letter. As to how the nominee of the Corporation could have been in a position to represent the views of that body in such a

function, it is impossible to conceive.

I beg, etc.,
Pherozeshah M. Mehta

HIGH COURTS IN INDIA

SIR CHARLES SARGENT'S TERM OF OFFICE

A Public Meeting of the inhabitants of Bombay took place on 9th April 1895, Mr. L.R.W. Forrest presiding, to give expression to the high appreciation of the manner in which Sir Charles Sargent had discharged the responsible duties of a Judge and Chief Justic of the High Court of Bombay for the last twenty-nine years.[10]

The Hon. Mr. Pherozeshah Mehta spoke as follows:

Mr. Chairman and Gentlemen,—The next Proposition is entrusted to me and I am glad that I have thus an opportunity of actually joining in a movement of so excellent and so unexceptionable a character. No measure has contributed more to the consolidation of British rule in this country than the establishment of High Courts. In these days, however, a great deal of impatience is exhibited by a certain class of what we call strong-minded officials at the powers and jurisdiction of these courts; and only the other day it found the culminating expression in the Viceroy's Council, when, on the debate on the Police Bill, my honourable friend, Sir James Westland said in his humourous manner that in making an enquiry, one policeman on the spot was worth any day two Judges of the High Court. There is, no doubt, a certain amount of superficial plausibility in the remark, but the fallacy of the observation lies in this that the policeman on the spot gives very scant guarantee of honesty, impartiality, disinterestedness, freedom from bias and prejudice, trained capacity for observation and above all, of a knowledge of the judicial method, all of which go to constitute the qualifications of a Judge of a High Court. The High Courts, thus constituted, have been more potent factors in the promotion of loyalty and contentment among the masses of the people than is generally or fully imagined. And the Bombay High Court has been singularly fortunate in being able to show a roll of Judges and Chief Justices who have been distinguished for great and unusual culture, capacity and learning. In this illustrious roll, none has more worthily sustained the great traditions of the high and responsible position of Judge and Chief Justice as Sir Charles Sargent has done for the last thirty years. I will not enter into details as my friend Mr. Badruddin Tyabjee has dealt with them, but I have been more than once struck and surprised by finding people in the remotest corners of the Presidency, giving expression, in the most enthusiastic terms, to the esteem, confidence and admiration with which Sir Charles Sargent was regarded for his learning as well as for his singular freedom from bias and prejudices of every sort. Personally speaking, I do not know any greater intellectual treat than to sit at the Court presided over by Sir Charles Sargent, and to watch his severely clear and logical methods of argument and reasoning, interspersed with shrewd but by no means unkindly observations on life and conduct. In meeting today, we are giving expression to the unanimous feeling of all classes and communities, to do honour to one whom we have all learned to regard with the greatest esteem, confidence and admiration verging on veneration. I now propose "That a Committee be appointed to raise a fund for the purpose of establishing a memorial of the esteem and admiration in which Sir Charles Sargent is held by all classes and communities in this Presidency."

BOMBAY UNIVERSITY

WITHDRAWAL OF GOVERNMENT GRANT.

The Meeting of the Senate of the Bombay University held on 27th July 1895, considered a letter from Government saying "that the University of Bombay can safely be left as independent of financial support from Provincial Revenues as are the

Universities of Calcutta and Madras and that the University is informed that no provision is made in the Budget of 1896-97 for a grant to the University". The Hon. Mr. Pherozeshah, in moving the Notice of Motion that stood in his name in connection with the subject, spoke as follows.

Mr. VICE-CHANCELLOR AND GENTLEMEN OF THE SENATE,—

With regard to my Notice of Motion I suppose there are many members of the Senate present who perhaps think that we have met together on this occasion as if it were on a ceremony of condolence over the demise of one of the oldest institutions, namely, the Bombay University—the Government having withdrawn their grant which was as old as the University itself. But I hope that the majority of the Fellows will not consider this as a meeting of condolence, but would look at this meeting as doctors in consultation over a patient, who is in extremis but who is certainly not quite dead as yet. Taking this view of the matter I think I am justified in asking the Senate to adopt my proposal which is:

"That as recommended by the Syndicate, a representation be made to Government urging them to enconsider their decision to withdraw the University's annual grant."

As regards the letter of Government, I might say that it so happened that I came across a copy of the "Westminster Gazette" of a recent date, in which there is a cartoon descriptive of the attitutde of the present Government with regard to the question of the cost of the Indian Contingent to Suakim, and that cartoon is described in letters as "An Act of Melancholy Meanness." If it were permissible to members of the Senate to dismiss from their minds the respect and the reverence which they certainly owe to the Government of this Presidency, I might be tempted to say something analogous to that description. But, gentlemen, I am one of those who is given to pay great respect to constituted authorities and it is accordingly utterly impossible for me to hold any such comparison remembering the fact that the head of the Government is the Chancellor and that the Senior Member of Council was at one time the Vice-Chancellor of this University. Remembering these things I will for the present content myself by calling this act of Government as an act of untimely and impolitic parsimony. In using this expression and describing it in the manner I have done, I think I am justified by a reference to what has been laid down in the letter of Government itself, and I do not propose on this occasion to go any further than take the letter itself and point out to the Senate the inconclusive and illogical character of the arguments which have been advanced in it. I venture to say that if this letter had emanated from a private body, there could have been no difficulty in our describing it as somewhat confused in statement, misleading in argument and somewhat irrelevant in many of the subjects referred to in it. As for the third paragraph of the letter, if you go back to the time when the University was established, you will find that the policy of the Government then was the exact contrary to what they now enunciate. I contend that when the University was first established, care was taken to make it a State institution and not the department of Government, and to give effect to that view the Chancellor of the University was he who happened to be the head of the Government of the Presidency. That view of the matter prevailed year after year, and it is to be regretted that we have not at present one of those Vice-Chancellors like the late Sir Alexander Grant, who always stood up and supported the best interests of the University on an occasion of this character.

[The Hon. Mr. Pherozeshah then referred to other portions of the letter and in doing so he alluded to the remarks made by the Education Commission and the Finance Committee, and also to the Correspondence which had taken place between the Syndicate and the Government on the subject of the proposed reductions of the grant.] Continuing Mr. Pherozeshah said:

I contend that Government in a manner compel the University, by way of recouping its funds, to raise the fees levied on students who present themselves for the Matriculation Examination, though the number of students who go in for this examination in Bombay is comparatively smaller than those in Calcutta and Madras. The fees in Madras have been enhanced as the number of students had increased to 5,000 and more; but the University of Calcutta has not, as has been stated by Government, increased its fees, but they are the same as before. Again, when Government refer to the work done by the University as "admirable and successful", I am inclined to believe that they mean to be rather sarcastic and ironical, because when professors of colleges and officers of Government themselves have often proclaimed that the class of graduates turned out from the various colleges were far from being satisfactory, the Government now aver that the work done by the University is of an exceedingly satisfactory nature. Gentlemen, there appears to be a vein of sarcasm running in that paragraph. I would have attached great value to the apparently complimentary statement, if such a compliment had been paid at a time when the question of finances was not before us. With reference to the statement appearing in the letter that "the accounts for the year 1894-95 show that the receipts exceed the disbursement by more than Rs. 20,000",—no doubt there was a surplus of about Rs. 20,942 last year, including the Government grant of Rs. 5,000, but is it, I ask, sufficient for the numerous reforms which it is high time the University should take in hand for its legitimate growth and development? Let me point out that the first and foremost reform that may be introduced, is with regard to the accommodation of the ever increasing number of students for the Matriculation Examination, who are examined in mandups, which have such flimsy roofs provided that the burning rays of the mid-day sun peered through them and injured the health of the numerous students who have to sit for hours together under a temporary structure which after all afforded little protection to them.

The resolution passed at the instance of Mr. Justice Ranade at a recent meeting of the Senate would necessitate the holding of the examinations twice a year, and that would necessarily increase our expenditure, the several examiners being required to be paid their fees. As the work of the Registrar's office has of late greatly increased, and as the six-monthly examinations will entail a further burden on the staff, the Senate will soon have to consider the necessity of employing a full-time Registrar,—(Hear, hear")—and we must therefore be prepared to pay a higher remuneration than at present for that office. Again, the number of examiners appointed at present is not sufficient to cope with the increasing number of candidates, and if we wish that the examiners should do their work conscientiously and not in a perfunctory and mechanical manner, which they are, no doubt, obliged to do under the present circumstances, we must be prepared for additional expenses in that direction. There is again another reform which might be made, and it is that of appointing a supervising board of examiners, or chief examiners, who must be men of high culture and position and must be paid according to the work they are expected to perform. The University Library also, as it is, is quite useless and in order to make it more useful and attractive, we must spend some money over it. For these reasons the Senate should go up to Government and point out to them that taking into consideration the various circumstances which would entail a far larger expenditure than what is incurred at present, it is utterly premature and untimely to withdraw the small contribution made by them.

Some of the members of the Senate may ask,—Where is the necessity of appealing to Government now that they have already issued their Resolution? My reply to that question is that the English education I have received has taught me that the success of an Englishman lies in the fact that he never knows when he is defeated. Let the Senate never know when they are defeated. I know it is a very difficult thing to move

Government; particularly when matters of finance are concerned, I quite admit that they are a stone-wall, but that is no reason why we should not endeavour to prevail upon them to reconsider their Resolution. Whether the Senate is successful or unsuccessful it does not matter much, but I will impress upon the mind of the members that it is their bounden duty as guardians and trustees of the best interests of the University, to point out to Government that they are following a wrong policy and proceeding upon wrong premises and false inferences, and that they seem not to have taken into consideration the several circumstances affecting the financial interests of the University, and finally that they do not care to consult this body, which is appointed by themselves, before they passed such a Resolution.

The Hon. Mr. Justice M.G. Ranade seconded Mr. Pherozeshah's Motion. Dr. Pollen and Dr. Peterson having thereafter addressed the Senate—

Mr. Pherozeshah in reply said that Dr. Pollen was opposed to their approaching Government for what he called a "beggarly" amount of Rs. 5,000, but what could then be said of a Government who, notwithstanding that according to their latest budget statement, they had a balance of 40 lakhs of rupees at their disposal, had yet decided to withdraw that amount! It suggested an analogy to the description of the cartoon alluded to by him, but he would not indulge in such language towards the Government for whom he entertained such high respect. He agreed with Dr. Pollen that primary education should be supported, but what he contended was that Government should not rob Peter to pay Paul.

The Motion was then put to the vote and carried *nem. con.*

INDIANS IN SOUTH AFRICA

RIGHTS OF BRITISH CITIZENSHIP

Mr. M.K. Ghandhi, Bar-at-Law, delivered in Bombay an Address on the Political Disabilities of Her Majesty's Indian Subjects in South Africa, on 26th September 1896. The Hon. Mr. Pherozeshah Metha, who presided, in introducing the speaker to the assembly, spoke as follows.

Ladies and Gentlemen,—Very few words are necessary in introducing to you the learned lecturer who has so skilfully taken up the cause of the natives of India in South Africa. The present meeting is convened for the purpose of expressing our sympathy and recording a protest against the drawbacks, hardships and disabilities which our fellow-subjects are suffering in the land of the Boers. These difficulties will be described to you by my young friend Mr. Gandhi who is so nobly devoting his time and labour, on behalf of the natives of this land residing in that part of the world, with great skill, pluck, ability and perseverance. But I would like to remind you of one circumstance and it is this. We are told, on all possible occasions, to cheerfully bear the burdens cast upon us and not to grumble at them. We are told to accept, without any protest, the imposition of the excise duties, "which are levied to restore the financial equilibrium of the country", nor even to say a word against the heavy burden of providing the cost of military contingent in far Egypt with which this country has nothing to do. We are told to put up with and bear all this because we, forsooth, are enjoying the brilliant privileges—liberty and right of British citizenship—and also because we should bear our portion of the common and Imperial responsibilities of the British Empire. But, gentlemen, responsibility and privilege go together. It is therefore our duty now to ask for a share in the enjoyment of all those privileges which rightly belong to British subjects, namely, of representation. Whether we shall get it or not, is certainly a doubtful question, but that is no reason why we should not put forth our best energies and demand of our rulers the enjoyment of those rights and those liberties, which are the just heritage of every subject of the British Empire.

I now call upon Mr. Ghandi to deliver his Address which, I have no doubt, will prove both interesting and instructive.

CONGRATULATORY ADDRESS TO HER MAJESTY QUEEN VICTORIA

The following is the Address from the Municipal Corporation of Bombay forwarded to Her Majesty Queen Victoria on her Diamond Jubilee in June 1897. It was drafted by the Hon'ble Mr. Pherozeshah Mehta and is placed here amongst his speeches and writings as a specimen of his penmanship.

HER IMPERIAL MAJESTY VICTORIA,

Queen of Great Britain and Ireland,
Empress of India.

May it Please Your Imperial Majesty,

We, the President and Members of the Municipal Corporation of the City of Bombay, beg respectfully, on behalf of its citizens to lay at the foot of the Throne our earnest, sincere, and reverent congratulations on the consummation of sixty years of Your Majesty's glorious and beneficent reign. It has pleased Providence to afflict this City for several months past with the horrors and ravages of a severe epidemic of plague and with the dire consequences of a widespread famine in several parts of the Presidency. Heavy as our hearts have been from the sacrifices and bereavements thus inflicted upon this striken City, still we cannot allow this great occasion to pass without giving expression to our devout appreciation of the measureless beneficence of sixty years of the reign of a revered Sovereign whose womanly and motherly heart has always deeply and truly grieved for the sorrows of her subjects and participated in the anguish of their afflictions. We deeply and gratefully recognize that, were it not for the great and glorious achievements of a reign which has sought glory in the triumphs of peace, progress, and enlightenment more than in anything else, the evils that have wrought such havoc in this country in the present year would have been more widespread and dire than they ever have been. The glories and triumphs of Your Majesty's unprecedentedly long reign will be sung with heartfelt joy by Your Majesty's subjects spread over every quarter of the globe. But, though we may not participate in the outward rejoicing—owing to the afflictions which have brought death to so many homes—no portion of Your Majesty's subjects join more heartily or more earnestly than ourselves in praying that Heaven may continue to shower its choicest blessings on our beloved and revered Sovereign, than whom a greater and nobler has never reigned in the hearts and affections of her subjects of all races and creeds.

President,

Municipal Secretary,

Bombay, 26th April 1897.

THE BOER WAR

MEETING AT CALCUTTA

A Public Meeting was held at Calcutta on 27th January 1900 in aid of the Transvaal War Fund. The full text of the Hon. Mr. Pherozeshah's speech not being available, a part thereof is given below:

Well, gentlemen, it has always seemed to me that English strenghth and greatness has consisted in nothing so much as in the lofty conception of moral and political duty which has illustrated the lives and actions of her best and noblest sons, and has permeated and leavened the national life, thought and culture. Gentlemen, it is not a little that we have to be thankful for that, in spite of many drawbacks, many fallings off, many backslidings, in the midst of temptations and allurements' it is this lofty conception of duty which has largely succeded in moulding and directing the policy of the crown for the government of this country. It was in pursuance of that righteous policy, or, so to say, policy that maketh for righteousness that that inestimable and priceless boon, the boon of education, was conferred upon us. It has been said, and often said, by people whose historical bias has been apt to run away with their historical accuracy, that India was won by the sword and must be maintained by the sword. Well, gentlemen, this is true so far, that the soldier is abroad, maintaining peace and tranquility throughout the land. But it is equally true that the humble school master is also abroad, transforming the feelings of gratitude for the preservation of this peace and transquility into a sentiment of earnest, devoted and enlightened loyalty.

Gentlemen, look at the spectacle, the whole country, and the press that reflects its opinion, presents today. We have no reasons to be captivated by the glittering Imperial vision of a great South African Empire. We would rather that England kept to her old love, the Indian Empire, and that she did not divide her affections wilh another. But however that may be, what do we see but that her sons over all this vast land, unaffected by the differences that distinguish but do not divide us—men of different creeds—inheritors of varied traditions—descendants of distinct races yet sprung from the same soil—subjects of the same Sovereign and I will venture to add, soldiers in the same patriotic cause of their common country—are all acclaiming with united voice and heart their unswerving attachment to the throne and person of that noble and gracious lady who presides over the destinies of the great British Empire—and our deep and abiding loyalty to the British rule, in which we are firmly persuaded—in which we are convinced by the education we have received, lie implanted the germs and roots of the welfare, the prosperity, the regeneration and development of this country. Criticism there may be, and I hope always will be, sometimes wrong, ill-informed, and even prejudiced; endeavours there may be, and will be to expose supposed wrongs and grievances.

OVERCROWDING IN BOMBAY

Under the auspices of the Bombay Sanitary Association, a

Paper on the question of housing the poor of Bombay, was read by Sir Bhalchandra Krishna, Kt., on 30th April 1904. The Hon. Mr. Pherozeshah, who was voted to the Chair, in opening the proceedings, spoke as follows:

Gentlemen,—We have met here this evening to bear view supon one of the most important questions with affect the health and welfare of this city. That question is the overcrowding of Bombay. Though most of us disagree as to what is plague, how it came here, how it works and how it has increased the mortality of Bombay, I think as practical men we are all agreed upon one point and it is this that whatever might be the other causes, one cause which has largely enhanced the mortality of the city, has been overcrowding. It was not always so. I remember that after 1865 when Bombay passed through a very bad stage of mortality, its health continued to improve until we approached the nineties when it went down so low as 20 or 25 per thousand. It is since then that the mortality began to increase and it went up to such an extent that we would now almost welcome if it ranged from 40 to 50 per thousand. I am afraid that our prosperity during this period had been one of the causes of this overcrowding and the consequent increased mortality. We have been very proud of our mills and some of our best citizens are millowners who take a great interest in that industry. I am afraid that under the superstition that we must not touch anything that encourages and promotes plague, we have allowed to be built a large number of mills in the very midst of the city thereby not only causing overcrowding of the mills, but overcrowding of the people who are necessary for the working of the mills. Our very prosperity has contributed to the overcrowding. Then again the facilities which the Port Trust gave to the trade of the city must have also contributed very largely to the mortality. Here we are now, not knowing as to how we should proceed to diminish this overcrowding. I think that Sir Bhalchandra as a distinguished member of the Improvement Trust would tell us that that the Trust was trying and striving hard to improve this state of things. I am afraid I will not be able to agree with him if he tried to show that in his lecture. No doubt the Trust has now awakenad to see what should be done about the overcrowding. I think the Improvement Trust can be compared with a man in a hurry. It was created in a hurry, it took up large schemes in a hurry, and it has now suddenly discovered that working in a hurry it cannot provide for all the people who are unhoused. It might be said that the people who have been unhoused by the immediate operation of the Trust do not represent a very large number. Sir Bhalchandra might tell us that the Improvement Trust was trying all in its power to diminish overcrowding. But I venture to say that it has not realised either the importance or the complexity of the problem it has to solve. Some people in Bombay seem to imagine that if they succeeded in building a number of *chawls* in the city and provide a certain number of rooms to live in, overcrowding would cease. Experience, however, has told us that there could be no greater misconception than that. The same experiment was tried in some places in England, America and the Continent, and the result was that sometimes when sanitary houses were built, the overcrowding increased, for new people occupied new houses, and the people who had been unhoused went and lived in those parts which were already overcrowded. But this was not enough and judging from the reports that appeared in the papers, the Improvement Trust has up to the present no further conception of measures to be adopted than building more *chawls*. My friend the Hon. Mr. Vithaldas has taken an active part in formulating schemes as to how the various *chawls* and buildings might be built. I am afraid that unless we go to the very root of the matter, unless we consider the economic condition of the people for whom this accommodation is to be provided, and unless we find out where they would be properly housed, we will not be able to solve the problem satisfactorily. With such purpose in view, the Bombay Municipal Corporation tried to induce Government to appoint a representative Committee for the purpose of inquiring into and discussing this important question; but somehow or other, the Government have taken up a position of the fond Father of the Improvement Trust. With the affection which a parent bears to the youngest born, Government are fondling their newest baby and say that it does asmuch as it can and that if such a Committee as the Corporation suggested be appointed, it would be a reflection on the Improvement Trust. In their anxious desire to fondle their new baby, Government say that there is no necessity for such a Committee and that the Trust is able to solve the problem. I think Government will be awakened to the difficulty of the position which they have taken up when matters became very much worse than they are now. I am of opinion that no additional *chawls* would solve the problem and I hope and trust that it would be recognized that before the Trust proceeded with that scheme, a careful inquiry should be held by a Committee of the representative men of Bombay and a report received from it pointing out the direction in which those measures should be adopted.

With these few observations, I now call upon Sir Bhalchandra to read his Paper.

SIR PHEROZESHAH ENTERTAINED BY THE BOMBAY CORPORATION

The members of the Bombay Municipal Corporation entertained Sir Pherozeshah, the leader of the House, at a Banquet at the Masonic Hall on Ist August 1904, in celebration of the bestowal upon him of a K.C.I.E. by the King-Emperor, Mr. James Macdonald gave the toast of the evening to which.

Sir Pherozeshah said that he was extremely obliged to the company present for the kind feelings which had actuated them in getting up the entertainment in his honour. When he first came to know of the Municipal dinner he was a bit alarmed. All that he heard at the outset was from a friendly talk with the Chairman one afternoon after the Corporation Meeting was over, as to whether the speaker would dine with him. Innocently he at once replied in the affirmative that he would do so with the greatest pleasure. But a little later on he understood to his great alarm what he meant by that friendly dining. On such functions as those that he had lately to attend, a feeling crept over one that after all they were being overdone. However he was all the same thankful for the kindliness which prompted his colleagues both of the present and of the past Corporations to invite him to a sumptuous repast. Indeed that was the third instance of their kindness and generosity. At first, the President had greatly praised him in terms most flattering. Then his old and valued colleagues, one by one, spoke in warm and eulogistic terms, which he felt were more than his due; and now was the third function which spoke of their extreme kindness and goodwill. He would confess at once that he had done what little service he thought it was his duty to render to the city. But after all it was not over much to deserve such handsome treatment. He might however mention that the key to the success he had been able to achieve in the Corporation, remained to be revealed. Though the speakers at the Corporation had referred to many points, they seemed to have omitted one. It was the training and discipline, which by long years of contact with many an elder member of the Corporation, European as well as native, he had been able to acquire, and which is the true key of that success. They were stalwarts indeed, men of great culture, ability and experience who had made the public life of Bombay so admirable and so unique. They were Messrs. Forbes, Maclean, Geary, Martin Wood, Col. Hancock, Drs. Cook, Blanc, Hunter and Maconochie, Nowrozjee Fardoonjee Viswanath Mandlik, Sorabjee Bengali, and others,—stalwart men indeed, men whose memory deserved to be written in letters of gold in the Municipal history of Bombay. It was the training, Sir Pherozeshah observed, which he had received during the early days of his Municipal career, which enabled him later on to be so useful a member of the Corporation. He was glad also to emphasise another fact in the history of the Corporation, namely the non-sectarian spirit in which all worked together in harmony, with a singleness of purpose, viz., to do the city the greatest good. Whatever might be the political differences outside the Hall of the Corporation and however trenchantly they might be accentuated elsewhere, in the Corporation itself those differences were entirely forgotten. There was no conflict there. As an instance, he might mention Mr. Maclean. He belonged to a different school of politics from that of the many able Indians in the Corporation and even went once to the length of characterising natives generally as a "brood of vipers." But in the Corporation, the native gentlemen never remembered his hard sayings. Moreover, Mr. Maclean himself was a different man when he entered the Municipal Hall and all worked together as harmoniously and smoothly as possible. And Sir Pherozeshah was glad to say from his long experience that spirit had been maintained, and he hoped it would always be maintained if the great good and welfare of the city was alone to lead the aim and object of members entering the Corporation. Passing on to another theme, Sir Pherozeshah dilated at some length on what had been often said as to his leadership. He had been spoken of as leading the Corporation. In connection with that he would make another confession, and it was that instead of leading he rather followed the Corporation. The fact was this. He watched the trend of opinion of his colleagues on any given question; he tried to give out his own views with the object of evoking other views and by those means he found out on which side the correct opinion lay. That was his invariable practice for years and what he found from experience was that the Corporation in almost all cases took a sound common sense view of matters; indeed common sense has uniformly asserted itself, and it was because he was able to fall in with that common sense view that he was curiously said to be leading the Corporation. Lastly, apart from the Corporation, he could not refrain from giving his due meek of praise to the long line of Municipal Commissioners who have helped the cause of local self-government. In that respect he had nothing but the highest praise for the Government which had given them very best men from time to time. There had been Mr. Peddar, a most able and devoted officer, next there was Mr. Grant. Then came the long Commissionership of Sir Charles Ollivant to whom Bombay owed a great deal of the expansion of the city.

Not to speak of others, there was the present Commissioner Mr. Harvey, a most able, conscientious and far-sighted officer on whose services he would not dilate at length on that occasion, for every member knew his sterling worth. All these elements had combined to make local self-government in Bombay the success it was and he was glad to think he had his humble share in it. Sir Pherozeshah then once more thanked most cordially the company for the kind manner in which they had entertained him.

BOMBAY UNIVERSITY

MATRICULATION EXAMINATION, QUESTION OF AGE LIMIT

At the Meeting of the Senate of the Bombay University held on 9th February 1906. Principal F.G. Selby moved that the minimum limit of age far admission to the Matriculation Examination be raised from 15 years, as had been previously decided by the Senate, to 16 years, and that a corresponding change be made in the revised regulations. Mr. Selby said that in moving the proposition he, as well as Sir Pherozeshah Mehta, had not been influenced in any way by the letter of the Government which asked them to reconsider the advisability of raising the age limit but that long before that letter had been sent to them they had come to the conclusion that the age limit should be raised. Messrs, D.G. Padhye and N.M. Samarth opposed the above proposition.

The Hon. Sir Pherozeshah spoke as follows:

Mr. Vice-Chancellor And Gentlemen of the Senate,—

At the outset in reply to Mr. Padhye, I may say, that the reason why the Senate formerly ab indoned the limit of 16 years, was that at the time the limit of age fixed for the Civil Service Examination was lower than it now is, and hence many students found it difficult to appear at that Examination. As to the Medical Service Examination, I know that the limit of age has always been very high and the students are not required to take any medical degree in India to appear at that Examination. With regard to the age at which students in Bombay appear at the Matriculation Examination, I find from statistics that the average age is not 14 or 15, but 17 or 18. I consider that it is necessary to limit the age to 16, so that parents may not be tempted to push up their children to the University at an early age. My experienee is that not only the parents, but the students themselves—and particularly Brahmin students—are so ambitiuos to enter the University that they flock together in the towns and attend colleges at the sacrifice of their health. It is this indirect mischief that the proposition of Mr. Selby seeks to remove. I am afraid the real reason for opposing the proposition is that Messrs. Padhye and Samarth appear to think to that if they supported it, they would be carrying out a mandate of the Government. I ask you, gentlemen, to look at our constitution as it is. We have deliberately chosen to accept the new constitution, to work under it, and to enter upon the duties of Fellows. I, for one, think that we should not kick against that very constitution. I would remain in it,and if I find it perfectly useless to do so, I would resign. But while I remain in the Senate I can never lose sight of the fact that the constitution endbles the Government to impose upon us a regulation which, I should think, is neither irregular nor improper. It would be even constitutional for Government to say that the limit should be 16 years. But here the Government, instead of forcing upon us a regulation arbitrarily, asks us whether the limit should be raised from 15 to 16 and gives us an opportunity of expressing our opinion. I hope, therefore, gentlemen, that you will take this as a suggestion, and not as a mandate, from Government and if you consider it a desirable reform, I trust no Fellow will be led away by other considerations to oppose it.

The proposition was carried by a large majority.

INDIAN REPRESENTATIVES IN ENGLAND

INDIAN QUESTIONS BEFORE BRITISH PARLIAMENT

A Public Meeting, under the auspices of the Bombay Presidency Association, was held in Bombay on 3rd May 1905 to give effect to a Resolution passed by the Indian National Congress to send representatives from India to England, with a view to enlighten the British public on Indian questions.

The Hon. Sir Pherozeshah, who presided, in opening the proceedings, reminded those present of a similar meeting held in Bombay twenty years ago for sending delegates to England, and after referring to the views he had then expressed, he said that he still adhered to his opinion that the Indians could never hope for anything until Indian questions were thoroughly sifted and examined from every point of view before the British public and the British Parliament, and subjected to the clash of party warfare. Recenly they had received contrary advice, but so far as it proceeded from the Anglo-Indians and Anglo-Indian bureaucracy, they had no reason to complain. Such an advice from that quarter was natural; but he was sorry to say that there were certain people among them—for they had also their halt, their lame and their blind—who joined in that advice. With regard to them he would say that such advice could not come from them naturally. They expected but little from any party in England; but they could expect nothing if Indian questions were not made party questions.

Sir Pherozeshah then referred to the selection of the Hon. Mr. Gokhale, one of the Bombay representatives as the best they could make,—a representative than whom it would be difficult to find a better qualified man. Mr. Gokhale had proved himself a man of a great ability and possessed a thorough grasp of the various Indian questions. He had an eloquence which was really earnest, passionate and effective and his cordial manners and his praiseworthy character stamped him as a most high-minded gentleman.

BOMBAY UNIVERSITY

THE ARTS COURSE, GOVERNMENT INTERVENTION

Sir Alexander Grant, Bart the great educationist, in an Address delivered in Bombay in the early sixties, plainly told Sir Bartle Frere, the then Governor of Bombay that it was "unwise and impolitic that the Government should directly interfere with the work of the University Senate after it had been once formed." This golden advice was steadfastly adhered to by successive Viceroys and Governors until the advent of Lord Curzon whose imperialistic policy unfortunately led to his interference with the independence and integrity of Indian Universities by the appointment of the University Commission and the passing of the Indian Universites Act of 1904. Sir George Clark another autocrat a disciple of that Imperial Dictator landed in Bombay in the latter part of 1907, with administrative conceptions akin to the Curzonian schools of thought. Within a short time of his assuming the reins of Government, he caused a letter to be written, by the Secretary to Government, to the Registrar of the Bombay University, in which it was stated that the Governor-in Council was strongly of opinion that a revision of the then existing University curriculum was "imperatively demanded." "Viewed as a whole", the letter continued "the general results presents the appearance of patchwork, illogical in many respects and plainly inadequate to meet the demands of the present day". "Other changes", the letter proceeded, "of method and proceedure also appear to be needed in order that intellectual training, rather than the accumulation of illdigested knowledge, may become the primary aim of the University." The letter then submitted certain proposals for the consideration of the Senate, chief of which were :—

(1) That the Matriculation Examination "which was becoming unwieldy and was open to serious objections" should be abolished and the Colleges should conduct their own Matriculation Examinations;

(2) That the Previous Examination should be exchanged

for College Examinations to test progress during the first year;

(3) That for the College Entrance Examinations, the subjects of Chemistry and Astronomy should be eliminated;

(4) That Science should be excluded from the B.A. Curriculum;

(5) That no degree should be conferred on any student who does not possess a sound knowledge of the broad outlines of Indian History from the beginning of the Moghul period to the establishment of British Rule, and also of the general principles of British administration in the present day.

The letter also prescribed courses for the various University Examinations, with the different subjects which they should embrace, and concluded that "the Governor-in-Council was well aware of the difficulties which must attend so drastic a revision of the University curriculum as, in his opinion, was urgently required, and he fully recognised that the essential reforms must be carried out."

The University Senate, thereupon, at its Meeting on 3rd March 1909, appointed a Committee to consider and report on the proposals contained in the aforesaid letter. The Committee held 13 meetings and in its Report submitted—

(1) That the Matriculation Examination should be retained as part of the system of examinations conducted by the University;

(2) That the Previous Examination should be retained because it formed the point of bifurcation for the Arts, Professional and Scientific studies;

(3) That Chemistry and Astronomy should be retained in the Matriculation Examination;

(4) That the omission of Science from the B.A. course could not be justified;

(5) That History should be made a compulsory subject of study in the Examination for the degree of B.A.

The Committee partly agreed and partly disagreed with Government in the matter of the courses prescribed for the various University Examinations.

The Committee consisted of 19 members. The Report was signed by 6 members while a joint minute of dissent was also submitted to the Senate signed by 7 members,—a greater number than the signatories of the Report.

The reader may have easily perceived that the object of Sir George Clarke was to bring the University to surrender itself to the sweet will of the Government, and though his letter looked , at first sight, like the innocent flower, it had the serpent—a very venomous serpent—hidden under it. The Governor is, ex-officio, the Chancellor of the University, and had all the suggestions and demands, contained in the letter, come to the University from the Governor, in his capacity as the Chancellor, there would not have been any serious objection to it; but as it was, it was clearly a case of high-handedness on the part of Government who wanted to treat the University as a Department of the State. But thanks to the powerful debating and persuasive powers of Sir Pherozeshah Mehta, who fought hard against the interference of Government, day after day, that, in the end, the University came off victorious to a certain extent. The subject was particularly fitted for the display of all his powers of eloquence and never were they displayed with greater skill, force and vehemence. He had to overcome many prejudices and obstacles but he drew his strength from the principle for which he fought, for which he was many a times applauded by a listening Senate, and those who opposed him most, opposed him less than they admired him for his earnestness, his honesty and his independence.

It is regrettable that the newspapers of the day gave only a meagre report of Sir Pherozeshah's speeches on this important question, and what follows is all that is available on the subject.

A Meeting of the Senate of the Bombay University was held on 15th January 1910, the Hon. Sir N.G. Chandawarkar, the Vice-Chancellor, presiding. The following Proposition stood in the name of Sir Pherozeshah Mehta:

1. That the letter of Government and the Report of the Committee be recorded,

2. That the Senate agree with the conclusions of the Committee set forth in paragraph 5 of the Report regarding the abolition of the Matriculation Examination,

3. That the Senate approve of the recommendation of the Committee contained in the 8th paragraph of the Report for the improvement of the course for the Matriculation Examination and request the Syndicate to take early steps to obtain thereon opinions of High Schools and Colleges and the Faculties of Arts, Law, Medicine and Engineering and to place them before the Senate with their own recommendations,

4. That the Senate agree with the conclusions of the Committee contained in the 6th, 7th and 9th paragraphs of the Report that the Previous Examination should be retained and that it should be held in September,

5. That the Senate agree with the conclusions of the Committee contained in the 12th and 16th paragraphs of the Report as to the Intermediate Arts Course and the Intermediate Science Course,

6. That the Senate agree with the conclusion of the Committee contained in paragraph 17 of the Report,

7. That the Senate agree with the conclusions of the Committee contained in paragraphs 19 to 25 regarding the B.A. and B.Sc. courses,

8. That the Senate agree with the recommendation of the Committee in paragraph 24 for awarding Honours degrees in the B.A. and B.Sc. Examinations,

9. That the Senate agree with the recommendation of the Committee contained in paragraph 26 of the Report and in the institution of M.Sc. degree,

10. That the Senate agree with the opinion of the Committee that the age limit of 16 for the Matriculation Examination should not be increased,

11. That, in reference to paragraph 12 of the letter of Government, the Senate request the Syndicate to frame and submit to the Senate regulations for carrying out the changes in the Science courses proposed in the Report.

JUMBLE OF A REPORT

The Hon. Sir Pherozeshah said, in proceeding to lay before the Senate the Resolution of which he had given notice, he could not help feeling that he stood before his colleagues that day an object of some amusement, of some perplexity, and, he hoped, of a little commiseration; for in the whole history of the Senate, he believed, a Fellow had never had to stand in the position in which he stood that day and had never had the task of laying before the Senate a more extraordinary jumble of a report than was contained in the remarkable document that was before them. The main Report of the Committee was signed by six members, and there was a dissenting minute which had been ostensibly signed by seven members. Now, if the majority was substantially seven over six, then the signatories to the dissenting minute could have well claimed it to be the main Report. But that they should submit in spite of the numbers to call themselves dissenters was a mystery which, he thought, the Senate had a right to demand from all members of the Committee to unfold. He would unfold it to them as he proceeded in his remarks at some length. At present he would content himself by saying that Lars Porsena of Clusium —if his friend Dr. Harold Mann would allow him to speak of him under an Etruscan or Latin name—swore a big oath— "by the Nine Gods he swore"—that the minority of the Committee, though defeated on almost every conclusion which was arrived at by the Committee must masquerade before the public and the Senate as the majority. Like the Wandering Jew he wandered, walked to and fro, up and down, captured a member of the Committee here and captured a member of the Committee there; and his successful achievement was his capture of his gallant friend Major Street, whom he persuaded to sign the dissenting minute, but who being a man, as the speaker knew, of firm and sturdy convictions, would not sign the dissenting minute without attaching a dissenting minute to that dissenting minute. This was a phenomenon which he would have occasion to explain as he proceeded with his remarks.

COMPLETE MISUNDERSTANDING

But before he tackled this amazing conundrum which was set before them by the dissenters, there was one thing which he wanted to bring before the Senate for their preliminary consideration. It was of very great importance to point out that the letter of Government which they had met there to consider was a letter which had been addressed to them under a complete and palpable misunderstanding. In the eleventh paragraph of their letter Government said that they had made the proposals under consideration for the efficiency of higher education in this Presidency, in reply to the request made by the Senate in their letter of the 8th August last. If they turned to that letter it was perfectly clear that Government were under a complete misapprehension. The misapprehension was of an extremely vital character because the Senate did not invite any proposals from the Governor-in-Council; but they made it quite clear that the assistance they sought was his assistance as a Chancellor—or not even as a Chancellor—but as a gentleman whose attainments and qualifications were of a character which would enable the sub-committee of the Syndicate which was revising the Science course of the Intermediate Examination, to receive valuable help from him. This was a very serious misunderstanding on which the letter of Government was based. He called it very serious, because he considered that the direct interference of Government in the work of the Senate was unfortunate and undesirable, and was as unwise as it was impolitic. This kind of interference was considered undesirable when the Senate was composed of 200 members—officials and non-official who were all nominated by Government. He well remembered a public Address given in the Town Hall of Bombay by one of the most distinguished Vice-Chancellors they ever had—who was a Principal of the Elphinstone College, and who held for a time the post of Director of Public Instruction in this Presidency, and who retired only from that post on his getting an appointment in Edinburgh University—he meant Sir Alexander Grant. In that Address Sir Alexander directly and plainly told the then Governor of Bombay, Sir Bartle Frere, that it was unwise and impolitic that the Government should directly interfere with the work of the Senate after it had been once formed. It was an advice which was accepted by Sir Bartle Frere in the spirit in which it was given. But the advice was doubly weighty now when the Senate had been reorganised, as it had been, under Lord Curzon's Indian Universities Act of 1904. The Senate now consisted of one hundred ordinary members besides *ex-officio* members—of whom eighty were nominated by the Chancellor and twenty were elected in different ways. The eighty members nominated by Government were picked men—the best educational authorities available in the educational and other Government departments. Besides these there were *ex-officio* members including the Director of Public Instruction, who was *ex-officio* vice-chairman of the Syndicate. Again, the Syndicate was composed of a certain fixed element. Having got the Senate composed in this manner, Sir Pherozeshah put it to the Fellows of the Senate whether it was not right, wise and constitutional that they should be allowed without any direct interference from Government to work out the principles and details of the educational system in a manner that was considered to be the best by the deliberate and collective wisdom of that body? It should be remembered that there was a legal power placed in the hands of Government for the purpose of checking and restraining the action of the Senate, namely, the final sanction. They were aware that when the late Vice-Chancellor, who was also Director of Public Instruction, first got the letter of Government with regard to the proposed school of science, he was startled at what he thought might be a sort of dictation to the Senate, and said that Government had no right to interfere with the work of the University except in the way provided by law, namely, that they might either sanction or refuse to sanction a proposal of the Senate. Under these circumstances he for one deplored grievously that the Government should think it right to come before the Senate with proposals of the character embodied in their letter—proposals not only involving wide general principles, but also affecting absolutely the syllabus in the curricula which the University had to set down in different degrees and examinations. He could not help thinking that every Fellow of the Senate must to a certain extent feel that organised as that body was it would be for better for the integrity and independence of the University to allow educational men to bring forward proposals in their capacity as Fellows of the University in the first instance and then send them to the Governor-in-Council for his sanction.

DELIBERATION IN COMMITTEE

He now came to the contemplation of the extraordinary doucment which was before them. To his mind it was extraordinary and perplexing in the extreme. He did not want to make any reflection which might not be properly founded; but he did not know whether the position in which the Government placed the Fellows of the University, might not be the cause of the great embarrassment reflected in the doucment. He had told them how the doucment was signed, and he might now inform them that each and every conclusion embodied in the Report had been the conclusion arrived at by a majority of the Committee, and that too more than once. He spoke with feeling on this subject because the signatories to the minutes had not treated their colleagues on the Committee fairly. It was at his suggestion that the Vice-Chancellor, the Director of Public Instruction, the Rev. Dr. Mackichan and the Rev. Fr. Dreckmann were appointed a sub-committee to draft a Report on the conclusions of the Committee. As a matter of fact the Report before them was drafted by these gentlemen and he believed the Vice-Chancellor would bear him out when he said that the original draft which was afterwards altered in various ways was in the hands of the Vice-Chancellor himself. The first subject considered was the proposal of Government to abolish the Matriculation Examination and to make it over to the colleges. There was a great deal of discussion on the subject and the result was that the proposal was negatived by 11 votes to 4. He thought among those who were in favour of the retention of the Matriculation Examination were the Vice-Chancellor and the Hon. Mr. Sharp. In passing that Resolution it was recognised in the Committee that the course laid down for the Matriculation needed careful revision; and a proposition to that effect was also passed. The question was reconsidered a third time at a meeting when the speaker was not present and when it was again resolved that the Resolution passed in March last for the retention of the Matriculation should be adhered to. What was the dissenting minute now? It was that a Committee should be appointed for the purpose of considering three points: (1) recognition of other examinations, (2) introduction of alternative subjects and (3) transferring the conduct of the Matriculation Examination to a board composed of the Principals of the Arts colleges. It was with regard to this that the signatories to the main document had reason to complain that they had not been treated fairly. He asked, did they ever lay this suggestion for the consideration of the Committee? He was tempted to use another allegory and say that Dr. Mann acted like David when he ran into the cave of Adullam where "everyone that was in distress...and everyone that was discontented gathered themselves unto him." The cave of Adullam that he had formed was presented in this dissenting minute which was never laid before the Committee. He (the speaker) was laying the flattering unction to his soul that the worst of the matter had been over and that the fortunes of the Matriculation Examination were at least safe to a certain extent. But he could not describe to them his surprise when he found in the notices of amendments one from the Hon. Mr. Sharp asking to do away with the Matriculation Examination as a University Examination. He frankly said he did not believe his eyes when he read that amendment. After the various stages that Mr. Sharp had gone through in discussing the question, one would expect him not to waver or shuffle at every turn of the mind. He spoke with some amount of bitterness. He confessed it frankly, because he had better hopes from Mr. Sharp, who, he knew, had a level head, and who could bring to the deliberation of this question an amount of ability and experience which was possessed by few.

PREVIOUS EXAMINATION

Then he would come to the important question before the Committee with regard to the Previous Examination. There was a greater difference of opinion with regard to this subject than with regard to the Matriculation Examination. The first meeting which considered that question resolved by a majority of 9 to 4 that the P.E. being the point of bifurcation of the Arts and other professional and scientific studies should be retained. He charged Mr. Sharp with having misled them with regard to the P.E. It was resolved unanimously that to save students the strain of work and to give them the full benefit of the following vacation, the Previous Examination as well as the Intermediate Examination should be held at the end of the second term, i.e., in the last half of September instead of in November as at present and that the academic year should begin in November instead of in January following. He for one did not profess to be up in the technique of the University terms. But he voted in favour of that proposition as it was a recommendation from the Hon. Mr. Sharp. It was Mr. Sharp who led them into that, and then he turned upon them and wanted to throw up the P.E. along with the Matriculation. That matter was again considered and at one meeting it was negatived. It was reformed at another, and then an attempt was made to go through a second revision of the whole conclusions of the Committee, to which he strongly opposed and the majority decided that after having come to the conclusions after great consideration, it was not necessary to consider it over again. His principal complaint against Mr. Sharp was this that he not only concurred with the conclusion to retain the P. E., but he put it in a very earnest manner that it should be held in September and the academic year should commence from November.

Then with regard to the Intermediate Arts Course it was carried by 11 against 4. As regards the retention of Science in the B.A. Course, the decision of the Committee was arrived at very carefully. He knew that when the late Vice-Chancellor explained that matter properly to the Chancellor, the latter agreed that Science should be retained in the B.A. Course. There again the dissenters completely threw them over.

GREEK AND ROMAN HISTORY

Sir Pherozeshah next proceeded to say that the question of ancient Greek and Roman History was keenly discussed in the Committee. Some, though they voted for it, were against a compulsory study of it, recommending some Science subject instead. The Committee ultimately came to the conclusion to retain it in the Previous Course. Mr. Dastur[11] had in his minute of dissent vehemently asked where was the logic of sandwiching ancient history between the courses of English and Indian Histories at the Matriculation and the B.A. Examinations with a year's intermission of historical study at the Intermediate. But Mr. Dastur was not capable of taking a view from point of view of others. Mr. Dastur had asked why ancient Greek and Roman History should be retained in the Previous Course. It should be retained because all their studies in English, French or any other language required from them at least an elementary knowledge of ancient history. As to the question of ancient Indian History, the speaker said he was as strong a Swadeshi believer as Mr. Dastur himself; but as every scholar knew it was not possible to teach ancient Indian History in the same manner as Greek or Roman History—where were the books and materials available for a proper study of ancient Indian History? He would go in for ancient Indian History, but owing to the absence of materials for a proper study of it, he would prefer ancient Greek and Roman History. He would now leave the deliberations of the Committee and the extraordinary minute of the dissenters, who in the Committee voted in quite a different manner from what they had proposed in the minute. The Committee did not discuss any single question solely on its own merit, but in connection with the whole scheme.

GOVERNMENT LETTER

The Government proposals were of a detailed character, though the reasons given in the letter were by no means copious. The Government in their letter had stated that the basis of this curriculum had found acceptance half a century ago. It had subsequently received successive accretions as fresh demands arose, and revision as regards the B.A. degree took place about twenty years ago; but viewed as a whole, the general result presented the appearance of patchwork, illogical in many respects and plainly inadequate to meet the demands of the present day. The Governor-in-Council did not propose to offer detailed criticisms, which the most cursory study of the University syllabus would suggest. It sufficed to point out that there were too many examinations and too many subjects in certain cases, that there was no proper division into well ordered courses and no rational continuity of study, and that consequently there had been a marked want of thoroughness.

It naturally followed that the results of Higher Education in the Presidency had been disappointing. A high standard of excellence was rarely attained either on the Arts or on the Science side, and with too few exceptions, the University had not produced graduates who had evinced capacity for original work in the various branches of knowledge. The quest of marks as contrasted with the pursuit of knowledge was not peculiar to India; but a University curriculum should be so framed as to discourage the former. Then that history of the present curriculum was not fully given. It had been stated that the present course was settled half a century ago. That was not correct. Only a few years ago all India was stirred at the attempt at wholesale revision of the course. Had they forgotten the Universities Commission taking opinions from all parts of the country and embodying them in their Report? Did they not find in that Report every point considered in connection not only with Bombay but the whole of India? With many of the conclusions arrived at by the Commission, Sir Pherozeshah disagreed. But there was one recommendation made by the Commission to which he would draw the attention of the Senate. The Commission after a careful consideration of the whole question stated that the need of the Matriculation Examination as a University Examination was justified and added that the suggestion to abolish it was quite impracticable. He asked the Senate to ponder over that carefully considered opinion of the Universities Commission. Did any College in the Presidency give guarantee of that sort of education which, the Commission declared, must be demanded before doing away with this Examination? How many Professors were there who could give that sort of education? In Germany they came across Professors who could do so, but it was because in that country teaching had been made into a profession which carried with it dignities and emoluments. Learned men talked any amount of variations; and so the Senate as demanded by the Universities Commission, must also demand uniformity of examinations even before allowing the colleges to matriculate students. The Universities Act provided that each Senate should set itself to revising its curriculum and stated that if it did not do so, the Government would put its own curriculum instead. The Bombay Senate appointed a Committee which made a report. But nobody ever dreamt of recommending an abolition of the Matriculation Examination. This Committee, however, recommended an abolition of the Previous. Mr. Sharp agreed witn the recommendations of the Committee except where it was recommended to drop the Previous, and emphatically stood out for it. It was Mr. Sharp who ultimately brought the Senate to retain that examination. Again, the Government had the legal power to reject or modify the proposals of that Committee, but they did nothing of the sort.

THE AGE LIMIT

Coming to the question of an age limit for the Matriculation, Sir Pherozeshah stated that he was in favour of the limit being fixed at 16. The greneral public were in favour of the limit being fixed at 15; yet he never hesitated. The public feeling might be one way or the other, but when it was a question which was for the benefit of Higher Education, he did not hesitate to vote in favour of the limit being raised to 16. The Government in their letter had called the present curriculum a patchwork. But if the Government looked at it from the point of view of those who built up the present structure, they would find that the description did not fit the work.

At this stage as it about 7-30 p.m. the Meeting was adjourned till 4-30 p.m. on 22nd January 1910.

The adjourned Meeting of the Bombay University Senate was held on 22nd January 1910, the Hon. Sir N.G. Chandawarkar presiding.

NO PATCHWORK COURSE

The Hon. Sir Pherozeshah continuing his address said on the last occasion he was pointing out that the history and character of the lines and principles, or if he might say so, the conception of the higher education which was afterwards embodied in the Arts Course of that University, was incorrect and misleading, and he was trying to controvert the position that the Arts Course was a patchwork course. What was called Mr. Telang's Report was not a report in which Mr. Telang was the sole actor; but it was a report elaborately worked out by a Committee after consultation with great educational authorities, and all the questions now urged before the Senate were fully considered by that Committee.

Among others the question of reducing the number of examinations was also considered. Before going further he would impress upon the Fellows the desirability of not running away with the idea that too many examinations were a necessary evil. For his part, though not an educationist, but a person strongly and deeply interested in the educational progress of this Presidency, he was able to speak with some little authority as to what were the requirements of the Indian students. He hoped the Fellows would not be led away by the ideas which they might have carried from America, Germany or France, where the circumstances and conditions of student life were quite different. German higher education was essentially German. What was necessary for the habits and conditions of life of Indian students was that they should be employed in colleges so that they might not have any time for outdoor work. Their courses of study were so constructed that the whole time of the Indian students must be passed in academic studies or in the vaults of colleges. They should bear in mind that it was of the utmost importance in more ways than one that the attention of their students should be rivetted to their studies. He maintained that the P.E. was necessary for that purpose. They must also remember that the construction of their academic institutions was different from that of other countries. In their resolution upon the report of the Universities Commission the Government of India pointed this out and said that all their measures must be instituted in view of this exceptional fact of University education, namely, that the two years which in other countries were annexed to schools were annexed in India to colleges; that was to say, the first two years were a transition period here from the school to the college. In Prussia it was different. There the gymnasium courses extended to the greater po-tion of the Indian College courses. They must therefore take account of this fact that their students when coming from school into college required a stricter supervision and discipline then would be otherwise necessary if they came some years later.

"ENCYCLOPAEDIC GRAMOPHONES"

Coming back to the Report of Mr. Telang's Committee, he might say that the consideration of it took a year and a half before it was finally adopted. It was twise referred back to the Syndicate and in the debate which extended over days and days together some of the best authorities on education took part. He deplored that any one should forget for a moment the respect and gratitude which they owed to those gentlemen who bestowed their time and attention to the consideration of subjects of such great importance to the welfare of this Presidency. He deplored the tone and spirit in which his f-iend Mr. Dastur, for whom he had high respect, had criticised this conception so carefully considered. To him it was a matter of great pain that Mr. Dastur should have spoken of the men, who were parties to the measures which were taken in those days, as laying down vicious principles—principles which produced "noisy encylopaedic gramophones" rather than "a race of quiet modest thinkers", and which "turned out mere smatterers and crammers and pedants." He might be allowed to say that this sort of criticism would be more compatible with the noisy gramophones whom Mr. Dastur had very properly held up to their detestation, and was not compatible with that sober modesty and thoughtfulness which should be characteristic of the modest thinkers whom he held up to their admiration. He had another complaint to make against Mr. Dastur. They knew that he was a learned gentleman and could give them sound and valuable advice as an educationist. That had great hopes of his doing so when he was appointed a member of the Committee. If Mr. Dastur spoke at all, he spoke very little in the Committee,—perhaps he did not think it worthwhile to throw away his advice on people who were perfectly impervious to it and who would not take advantage of it. But he must say that Mr. Dastur had more than made up for his silence in the Committee by what he had done afterwards. He did not know if every Fellow had gone through the remarkable document which also formed the ultimate dissenting minute. He did not know how it had struck the Fellows who read it, but he confessed it had struck him as an eruption of Mount Etna or Vesuvius, throwing up hot subsance in the shape of undigested bits of Herbert Spencer, Frederic Harrison and Mathew Arnold, striking hard and emitting hot lava in which men like Mr. Wordsworth and Mr. Telang were held up as people who were not worth listening to with regard to any advice which they might have given as men experienced in education and educational training.

SPECIALISATION

The whole of Mr. Dastur's criticisms rested upon two misconceptions. The first was a complete misconception of the aim and object of University education. Nowadays, he knew it was a fashion to say that the aim and object of education was to train the intellectual faculties. Mr. Dastur himself had said it must be the development of the mind to its perfection in a natural and complete manner. In the Government letter there was also an indication of the same idea. This was neither an accurate nor complete description of the aim and object of education. He ventured to say that a more complete and more definite description would be (1) acquisition of knowledge, and (2) the training of the intellect so that knowledge might be properly and efficiently used. The two combined made up the aim and object of education, There was another fallacy in which, to his judgment, Mr. Dastur had fallen. It was partly the fallacy in which the dissenting minute of the seven dissenters also fell, but not so completely as Mr. Dastur. He said that special cultivation should be the basis of general cultivation. (Sir Pherozeshah) denied that special cultivation ought to be the basis of general cultivation. It was impossible to have special cultivation unless they had for its basis a general cultivation and reasons for this had been laid down time after time by authorities of the highest value. He thought it had been pointed out over and over again that at least in the first portion of their collegiate course, they must train not simply one faculty, but their education must be so constructed as to bring into cultivation all the different faculties and developed, before they could say that they had a proper reasoning faculty at all. Sir Pherozeshah then read extracts from an article in the "Edinburgh Review" written by Sir William Hamilton and also from Herbert Spencer in support of his contention. He added that the learned Vice-Chancellor himself had given expression to the same view in a lecture he addressed to law students that their specialised legal knowledge must be based upon a broad foundation of general culture.

He had already to a certain extent referred to the question of too many examinations. It had become a fashion to say—it was almost a parrot cry—that the examinations were a necessary evil and that they must not have too many examinations. This was not a proper way of looking at the examinations. They had a value of their own. An independent examination, if properly conducted, was a test which encouraged students to discipline their minds, to learn to concentrate their attention upon the analysis of a subject, and to acquire a training which was invaluable in their after life. Again, an examination was not only good for the students but it had a great value with regard to teachers and professors. They said in law that the rights of appeal were sometimes abused and that they must curtail those rights. But the great argument in favour of it was that appeals did a great deal in the way of making officers appealed against, very careful and industrious in the work which they performed. So also in the case of examinations. If they had independent examinations they would be the means of testing the work of teachers and professors in a regular and impartial manner and encouraging them to do it well.

Referring to the remarks of Government about the results of higher education in this Presidency, Sir Pherozeshah read an extract from a speech of the Hon. Mr. Sharp delivered by him at the Jubilee gathering of the Elphinstone College in praise of the Indian graduates and referred to the good work done by the Subordinate Judges. He also quoted the opinion of Mr. Giles, and drew special attention to the remark of Mr. Orange, Director of Education, to the effect that the reason why there was not a better output of their University than it was, was that at present their secondary schools were obliged to employ men who were not graduates as they were unable to pay sufficient salary to attract graduates.

ROOT OF THE EVIL

He must not be misunderstood. He did not say that he was entirely satisfied with the output of the University. There might be and should be a much better output. But they must adapt means to ends and find out what were the real reasons which prevented future improvements and what were the measures which were needed for the purpose of effecting those improvements. It was no use depending upon curricula. No. The mischief, he admitted, was much deeper, and he hoped the Senate and everybody connected and interested in education would bear in mind that the educational progress depended not upon the number of University examinations or the courses of study in colleges but upon the condition of their high schools. If they wanted to improve higher education in this Presidency or improve the output of the University, they must first improve their high schools, and man and equip them in a way in which they were equipped in other parts of the world. This was the opinion expressed by Sir Raymond West in a special minute. Without laying proper foundation of the education which their high schools gave, it would be futile to change the Arts courses.

He would not take up the time of the Senate by minutely going into the various proposals embodied in the Report and dissenting minute. They dealt with four questions : (1) Abolition or retention of the Matriculation Examination (2) retention of the P.E. as a University examination, (3) retention of History in the compulsory course, including the ancient history—Greek and Roman—and (4) retention of Science in the B.A. course. The abolition of the Matriculation was to his mind a measure fraught with the most mischievous consequences to the progress of education in this country. He did not know what was the result of the circular letter which the Director of Public Instruction sent to the headmasters of high schools inviting their opinions on the subject. It was not the best way of inviting the unbiassed and independent opinions of headmasters of Government schools and to a certain extent of aided schools, for they must take a colour from the department to which they belonged. But even then he believed that the opinions sent were not in favour of abolishing the Matriculation. But the Director of Public Instruction would tell them more definitely about that. He could not help thinking that after all the Indians possessed one Oriental faculty which they could not get rid of—he meant extreme courtesy. It was their habit when one came and asked their opinion about something, they tried to give an opinion which would please him. He did not know if the story was known of a gentleman in the mofussil going to an official superior and informing him of an addition that had taken place to his family. It was said that when the official congratulated him on the event, the Indian gentleman said: "By your favour." (Laughter.) But the question of retaining or abolishing the Matriculation Examination was a serious one. Nothing had been adduced against it except that it was of an unwieldy character. It was not regarded by the public simply as an examination for entering into colleges, but it was also looked upon as an independent examination for the purpose of putting a stamp as a result of the high school education which the students received. A large number of students who went up for the Matriculation went up for the P.E. and Intermediate and left off on their way. There were hundred circumstances in life which prevented a matriculate or undergraduate to complete his course. That was why the great wastage took place in the course of their University examinations. But it was simply undeniable, as pointed out by Mr. Orange, that the

Indian people put a value even upon the failure of an undergraduate or a student in passing a particular examination. So that the Matriculation enabled a large number of people to show to the public that they had received a certain amount of education tested and approved by the University. Moreover, itwould bear most hardly upon the lady students. The time had not come when all the lady students, who took their education in schools, could prosecute their studies in colleges; and they were most anxious that the education they had received in the high school should be tested by an independent examination and hall-marked by the University. In concluding his remarks Sir Pherozeshah called upon the members not to come to a hasty decision on the important questions before them. He said that ever since he left college, he had taken a keen interest in the education of the public and it was an irony of fate that he stood as an obstructionist, as people said, of the University Reform.

The Hon. Mr. Setalvad having seconded the Proposition, a short dicussion took place as to the procedure to be adopted in discussing the Motion. The Vice-Chancellor ruled that he would allow a general discussion on the first part of Sir Pherozeshah's Proposition and then other parts would be discussed separately. The first part of the Proposition merely asked the Senate to record the letter of Government and the Report of the Committee.

Several members having spoken, the debate was adjourned till 28th January 1910.

The adjourned Meeting of the Bombay University Senate was held on 28th January 1910 when the debate on Sir Pherozeshah's Proposition was resumed. Several Fellows having spoken for and against it.

Sir Pherozeshah replying said he fully joined in the well-deserved tribute which was paid to the attainments of the Chancellor of their University. ("Hear, hear.") What he maintained was that it was always wise and politic for a properly constituted body to take action in a matter in which it ought to do. A similar situation was created in 1891, when the Senate took up a similar attitude at the instance of Dr. Peterson whose views were then emphasised by the "Times of India."

Sir Pherozeshah's Motion to record the Government letter and the Report of the Committee was then put to the vote and carried.

MATRICULATION EXAMINATION

Sir Pherozeshah next moved

That the Senate agree with the conclusions of the Committee set forth in paragraph 5 of the Report regarding the abolition of the Matriculation Examination.

The Hon. Mr. D.A. Khare having seconded the Motion, Dr. A.G. Viegas moved an amendment which fell to the ground for want of a seconder and the Senate adjourned till 26th January 1910.

The adjourned Meeting of the Senate of the Bombay University was held on 29th January when debate was resumed regarding the Matriculation Examination several members speaking for and against it.

The Senate adjourned till 4th February 1910.

At the adjourned Meeting of the Senate on 4th February 1910 further debate took place on Sir Pherozeshah's Motion to retain the Matriculation Eaxamination and the Senate adjourned till 5th February 1910.

Several Fellows having spoken at the adjourned Meeting of the Senate on 5th February 1910.

Sir Pherozeshah in reply compared the debate with an imaginary debate on the abolition of the institution of matrimony and asked whether it would be right to abolish this institution because it let to various defects and disadvantages. The only d'rection, he said, in which Mr. Welinkar had suggested a change, was in regard to the introduction of variety in the subject of Science. But this did not necessitate abolition of the examination. As to the other subjects, they were taught not only in the Matriculation classes all over India, but also in Europe. Mr. Welinkar stood condemned on his own showing that he had failed in his attempt to conduct a high school on the system he advocated. He, therefore, thought that an argument of that sort coming as it did from a gentlemen who had failed to work a school on such lines, could carry little weight with the Senate. Dr. Reed and Dr. Robertson had pointed out that the Matriculation served a twofold purpose which it ought not to do and that as its more appropriate function was to examine those students only who intended to enter the University, it should be handed over to the colleges. The fallacy of the argument had not been perceived, for when they said the examination was serving two purposes, they were laying down a line which did not exist. Ninety per cent out of a hundred parents or guardians of the boys, who appeared for the examination, did not know what their boys would ultimately be fit for. They waited till they passed and then determined whether they should send them to college or not. Proceeding, Sir Pherozeshah said, to abolish the Matriculation Examination, was to disconnect the University from the colleges; but it must be remembered that the object of Lord Curzon's Universities Act was to bring the Universities and colleges closer together and to remove the separation of the University as a mere examining body from the colleges. Dr. Reed had argued that educationists in the Punjab and Bengal were against the retention of the Matriculation Examination, but Dr. Reed forgot that after a wholesale examination of the opinions of its experts, Lord Curzon's government appointed the Universities Commission in 1904, and the deliberate conclusion at which that Commission arrived, after gaining experience all over the country, was that the Matriculation Examination should be retained.

Sir Pherozeshah next referred to the constitution and the examiners for the Matriculation Examination and said that from the statistics he had collected for the past ten years he found that, barring only the vernacular and other languages which were not taught in the colleges, out of twenty examiners appointed by the Syndicate to hold the Matriculation Examination, seventeen were professors of colleges. He contended that practically it was the same kind of examination which Principal Covernton advocates. Sir Pherozeshah concluded by saying that he was convinced that the abolition of the Matriculation Examination would have a disastrous effect on the secondary and collegiate education of this Presidency.

On a vote being taken Sir Pherozeshah's Motion was carried by 47 votes against 17.

The Senate then adjourned till 12th February 1910.

At the adjourned Meeting of the Senate held on 12th February 1910, the Hon. Sir Pherozeshah moved his third Proposition:

> That the Senate approve of the recommendation of the Committee contained in the 8th paragraph of the Report, for the improvement of the course for the Matriculation Examination, and request the syndicate to take early steps to obtain thereon opinions of high schools and colleges and the Faculties of Arts, Law, Medicine and Engineering and to place them before the Senate with their own recommendations.

Sir Bhalchandra Krishna seconded the Proposition. There were three amendments standing in the names of three Fellows, two of which were ruled out of order and the last one was withdrawn. On the suggestion of the Rev. Father Dreckmann, the words "improvement of the course for the Matriculation Examination" in Sir Pherozeshah's Proposition were changed to "improvement of the Matriculation Examination" and the Proposition thus altered was carried.

THE PREVIOUS EXAMINATION

The Hon. Sir Pherozeshah's fourth Proposition was—

> That the Senate agree with the conclusions of the Committee contained in the 6th, 7th and 9th paragraph of the Report that the Previous Examination should be retained and that it should be held in September.

Sir Pherozeshah said he was prepared to drop the "7th paragraph" from the Proposition if the Senate allowed him to do so. The suggestion for changing the time for holding the Examination was due to the opinion of Government that owing to the present arrangements, educational officers had too long vacations. He did not know what view Principal Covernton held in the matter, but he gathered from the views of many members of the Senate that the proposal was impracticable. As to the question of retaining the Examination, Sir Pherozeshah said Government did not want to do away with the Examination altogether, but they proposed that it should be left to the colleges to hold it themselves and even to lay down the course of study for it. He really did not see what great difference that made, because after all, the Examination must take place. The change could not be justified on the ground that there were too many examinations and they bore heavily upon students. The Examination at the end of the first year would remain even according to the letter of Government. The question was whether it should be taken by the colleges or by the University. Lord Curzon's Universities Act emphasised the connection—the identity—between the colleges and the University and made the University the binding girdle over the colleges, and he submitted that this new connection required that the work should be done by the University itself. As to the argument that there ought not to be too many examinations, Sir Pherozeshah pointed out that the objection was groundless inasmuch as the authorities of the Elphinstone College themselves had now introduced the system of double terminal examinations instead of the single yearly examination. He thoroughly approved of the system, and asserted that the shibboleth that examinations were a necessary evil was a fallacy. He held that an examination, badly conducted, was an evil, but if properly conducted, it served as a useful test of the work of both the students and professors and encouraged them to do it efficiently. In view of the step taken by the authorities of the Elphinstone College there was no justification for abolishing the P.E., and he asserted that it would be a far more desirable thing to have the work of the students tested at the end of the first year by a somewhat independent, or rather he should say, a supervisory authority than leave it in the hands of the colleges themselves. After referring to the circumstances under which the P.E., was instituted in the time of Sir Richard Temple for the purpose of introducing the study of Science, to the attempts made by the late Mr. Justice Ranade to introduce a system of examination by compartments, and to his subsequent failure in getting the examination abolished, Sir Pherozeshah said the reasons which actuated them then to retain the Examination still held good and they were that it was dangerous to leave the students in the first year without their looking forward to some disciplinary examination.

After reiterating his argument about the necessity of keeping the Indian students busy with their studies in their academic homes during the first year of their college career, Sir Pherozeshah next urged that by allowing the colleges to take their own examinations, an equality of standard would not be secured, as all colleges were not alike in point of efficiency. The personnel of colleges changed from time to time and like all human beings educational officers were subject to idiosyncrasies, prejudices, prepossessions and predilections of various sorts. In view of these things it was not difficult to perceive that the making over of the P.E. from the University into the hands of the colleges would not be a change for the better.

Rao Bahadur G.N. Nadkarni seconded the Proposition. Mr. D.G. Padhye and Dr. Mackichan then moved amendments standing in their names, both of which were lost. The Senate then adjourned till 19th February 1910.

At the adjourned Meeting of the Senate held on 19th February 1910 further debate was resumed on the question of the retention of the Previous Examination. Several amendments were put to the vote and lost. Dr. N.F. Surveyor then moved his Amendment—"That the Previous Examination be adolished, and the first Arts and Science examinations be held at the end of two years, and that the standard for entrance to the professional colleges shall be decided after consulting the heads of these colleges."

The Amendment being seconded and opposed further debate on it was adjourned till 25th February 1910.

SIR PHEROZESHAH'S REPLY

At the adjourned Meeting of the Senate held on 25th February 1910, the debate was resumed on Dr. Surveyor's Amendment, Several Fellows having spoken.

The Hon. Sir Pherozeshah, replying on the discussion, said he had been astonished at the arguments that had been discovered in favour of the abolition of the Previous. Nothing had astonished him more than the way the Hon. Mr. Sharp had kept on the same strain, telling them that he and Dr. Scott did not realise the distinction between a college and a University examination. His consolation in this ignorance was that after experience as Professor and Principal of the Elphinstone College for 26 years, Mr. Sharp had never discovered this distinction, at least as late as 1904. He hoped that members would remember the time when the Report of their Committee was before them on that occasion and in that Report was a recommendation that the Previous Examination should be abolished. The Hon. Mr. Sharp wrote in a minute to that Report: "I am in favour of retaining the present arrangement for three examinations"—that was three University examinations. That was the deliberate opinion of the Hon. Mr. Sharp in 1904. That was not an opinion formed after only a few years' experience as Director of Public Instruction but was a view formed after years of experience as Professor and Principal of the Elphinstone College. To him it was a wonderful thing that the Hon. Mr. Sharp should now bring forward his arguments about the distinction between a University and a college examination. The Previous Examination was inaugurated in 1878 and in 1894 the Senate after carefully considering whether it should be abolished, came to the conclusion that in the interests of the University, the Previous Examination should be retained, even though the opposite view had been put forward by no less an authority than the late Mr. Justice Ranade. The Amendment was not fair and straightforward because it left the bifurcation point absolutely open. If they passed the Amendment, they would abolish the Previous Examination and having previously rejected Dr. Mackichan's Amendment, they would be prevented from definitely marking the bifurcation. He had listened with the greatest respect to the remarks of the Bishop as to what happened at his own college, but though the Bishop had had experience at Oxford, he was one of those who, as the Hon. Mr. Sharp had said, discounted the Bishop's remarks because he had not had experience of Indian colleges and universities and of the conditions under which Indian students were called upon to do their work. It was on these grounds that he thought that students should not be left to themselves for two years.

Dr. Surveyor's Amendment was then put to the vote and carried by 30 votes against 29. Sir Pherozeshah demanded division, the result of which was that the voting was equal, 32 for and 32 against the Amendment.

The Vice-Chancellor having given his casting vote against the Amendment it was declared to be defeated.

The Senate adjourned till 26th February 1910.

At the adjourned Meeting of the Senate held on 26th February 1910, Sir Pherozeshah Mehta's Resolution—part 4—

viz., "that the Previous Examination should be retained and that it should be held in September," was tost, 24 voting for and 25 against it. Sir Pherozeshah asked for a divisions, but said he did not care whether his motions were last or not because the Previous Examination must be retained in the absence of the passing of an amendment.

The result of the division was that Sir Pherozeshah's motion was defeated by 27 votes to 26.

Mr. Welinkar:—May I ask what is the position now?
Sir Pherozeshah:—The Previous remains.
Dr. Surveyor:—My Amendment should pass.
Sir Pherozeshah:—You are a little too late.

Mr. Padhye moved that the consideration of the whole resolution be referred back to the Syndicate. He said he thought that the result of the voting was that they were absolutely debarred from considering any of the subsequent portions of Sir Pherozeshah's Resolution because the other portions were to a certain extent based on the Previous.

Sir Pherozeshah:—How can you refer back to the Syndicate a matter that did not come from it?

The motion was ruled out of order.

Mr. Welinkar moved and Mr. Kadri seconded the motion for adjournment.

THE MEETING DISSOLVED

Sir Pherozeshah said the view he took was this. The Senate proceeded with the consideration of recommendations made by a Committee elected by itself. That Committee recommended that the Previous should be retained for reasons given. Amendments were put for abolishing the Previous, replacing it by another examination, and other objects. Every amendment was thrown out. Lastly the original Proposition was thrown out also. Surely they all knew what was the result of that. It meant that the Senate was not going to embark on any change or pass any opinions with regard to a change. Nothing in the debate had occurred which could possibly alter the existing state of things that the Previous was a University Examination held at the end of the first year. They might throw out the Resolution but nothing could possibly affect the fact that the Previous was retained except a formal decision of the Senate not to do so. No other amendment of that nature could now be brought forward. These was one way to obtain that object and that was the way that had been previously adopted when the question of the Matriculation was largely discussed. That was to dissolve the Meeting. To adjourn the Meeting was no good because every adjourned meeting was part of one meeting. If they dissolved the Meeting they could not proceed with the consideration of the Committee's recommendations but that did not necessarily mean shelving the matter; and it would be open to members to bring up motions on the subjects in another manner as they thought fit.

After further discussion the motion for the adjournment was defeated and a motion "That the meeting do new dissolve" was carried.

[Soon after the dissolution of this Meeting, Sir Pherozeshah left for Europe and did not return till at the beginning of the following year, and consequently he was unable to attend several important Senate Meetings held in his absence.]

At the Meeting of the Senate of the Bombay University held on 1st July 1911, the Hon. Sir N.G. Chandawarkar, the Vice-Chancellor, presiding, the Senate considered the Report of the Committee appointed by it on 3rd October 1910, to frame detailed regulations for the Arts courses in languages, history, philosophy and logic, and mathematics. The Rev. Dr. R. Scott moved that the Report of the Arts Committee be adopted by the Senate and in doing so submitted that it was not right that a work which had been entrusted to experts and for which the Senate held them responsible, should be handed over to a nondescript Faculty of Arts, in which there was a minority of professors, which did not meet regularly, and which proposed one method one day, another another day, and a third on the third day. The speaker then wished to refer to the new situation produced by the letter which had come from Government.

Sir Pherozeshah:—I should like to inquire whether Dr. Scott could refer to the letter which though it has been circulated among the Fellows does not form part of the agenda paper before us. In the ordinary course that letter should have gone to the Syndicate and sent up by that body to the Senate under proper notice, namely seventeen days. I submit therefore that the letter is not before the Senate as a part of the business to be transacted.

The Vice-Chancellor ruled that Dr. Scott was perfectly in order in referring to any letter which was officially or unofficially before them.

Dr. Scott having finished, the Rev. Dr. Mackichan moved as an amendment that the Report of the Committee be referred to the Faculty of Arts for its opinion.

Several Fellows having addressed the Senate, The Hon. Sir Pherozeshah said that the real reason why the labours of the Senate on the previous occasion referred to by Dr. Surveyor had abruptly come to an end owing to a motion for dissolving the meeting being carried was that an unfortunate method had then been adopted for the purpose of revolutionising the whole work of the University by a letter of Government which had told the Senate that they had been utterly wrong in the manner in which they had been proceeding, that Government alone had known how to proceed systematically and scientifically in building up the studies of the University and that everything that had been done in the past was wrong. The idea had been an impractical one as it had been thought that it would have been desirable to introduce the proposed changes in portions.

But nothing would satisfy the authorities, who wanted them to take up the whole thing at once, settle it the same day and come to an agreement according to the orders which had been laid down in that letter. Dr. Scott had advised them in a paternal way not to attribute motives to others. But it was a remarkable thing that people who asked them not to attribute motives to others were very often the people who were the readiest to attribute motives to those who disagreed with them.

Sir Pherozeshah then read a passage from Mr. Valentine Chirol's recent book on the Indian Unrest in which the latter had referred to Sir George Clarke's scheme for the revision of the University studies and remarked that though there was nothing in it to which any serious objection could be taken, "the politicians on the Senate effectively blocked the discussion." Sir Pherozeshah said he should have liked to have asked his honourable friend Mr. Sharp if he could have told them who the "politicians on the Senate" were? It was most remarkable that while they were asked not to attribute motives to those who differed from them, those who had agreed with Mr. Sharp on that occasion did not hesitate to say that it was the politicians on the Senate who had "effectively blocked the discussion." It was no use feigning false modesty but it was suggested that he (Sir Pherozeshah) as the ring-leader of the obstruction, and those who thought and worked with him were not actuated by any motives for the improvement and maintenance of the high standard of the Bombay University studies but that they had some political objects to gain by obstructing effectually those proceedings. They were the people who were now asked by Dr. Scott not to attribute motives to others.

Proceeding Sir Pherozeshah said he entirely agreed with Dr. Mackichan when he said that he thought Dr. Scott would have done well not to have spoken of the Faculty of Arts in the manner he had done. Was not Dr. Scott himself a member of that Faculty? He was; but Sir Pherozeshah took it that when Dr. Scott spoke of the members of the Faculty of Arts as "nondescripts" he modestly excluded himself. Dr. Scott now asked him to give a definition of the word "nondescripts." Well he would define it this way. Nondescripts were those people whose opinions were worth nothing and who did not work together for the purpose of giving effective results.

Referring to the amendment Sir Pherozeshah urged the Senate not to be carried away by the argument advanced by Mr. Natrajan and others that they were heartily sick of this controversy and that the matter should be expedited.

Dr. Mackichan's amendment was lost there being 32 votes for and 36 against it.

SIR PHEROZESHAH AND THE WHIPS

The adjourned Meeting of the Bombay University Senate was held on 17th July 1911 when the Senate resumed consideration of the Report of the Committee on the revision of the Arts Course. Mr. K. Natrajan moved the following Amendment to Dr. Scott's Proposition viz:—"That the subjects for the B.A. Examination should be English and a voluntary group and moreover that the History of England, Political and Constitutional should form part of the voluntary group "History and Economics,' etc." The Hon. Mr. G.K. Gokhale and the Hon. Mr. W.H. Sharp having addressed the Senate, the Hon. Sir Pherozeshah spoke as follows.

Mr. Vice-Chancellor and Gentlemen of the Senate,—

The Honourable the Director of Public Instruction asks me if I have not on some occasions at least issued a whip. I will give an answer which will surprise Mr. Sharp, and point out how misconceptions misimpressions and misreports are easily circulated and lightly believed with regard to the actions of people to whom one is opposed. Mr. Sharp will be surprised to hear that in the course of a public career which has extended over forty years, not only in this University, not only in the

Municipality, but also in the Legislative Councils of this Country, both Imperial and Provincial, there has never been a time when I have issued a whip. And why? Because I was brought up in the historical traditions of the great beings who have guided the educational history of this Presidency, whose antecedents and traditions have been respectfully watched by people like me and who have always taught us that in a body constituted like the Senate of the University, it was wrong, improper and objectionable to issue a whip. This I have learnt from the English masters, English professors and English Directors of Public Instruction, who were the predecessors in office of Mr. Sharp, and I have tried to act up to it in the whole course of my public life. But Mr. Sharp goes further. He light-heartedly justifies the issue of the whip. He says whips are necessary for various purposes besides that of stimulating the presence of members. I should like to ask whether whips are issued not only for the purpose of stimulating their presence, but also of stimulating their conscience and their judgment. Are not whips issued for the purpose of telling them that Government are anxious or want such and such a thing to be carried? Does Mr. Sharp justify whips of this character also? Surely Mr. Sharp was not speaking like a practical man when he said that there was no harm in doing that when Government wanted a certain thing to be done. Is it necessary to tell a gentleman of Mr. Sharp's experience that a whip of this character, if it does not consciously lead people to do what perhaps their judgment would tell them is not right, would unconsciously exert upon them an immense amount of influence in the matter in regard to which the whip was issued?

ATTEMPT ON THE LIVES OF LORD AND LADY HARDINGE

PUBLIC MEETING IN BOMBAY

A Public Meeting of the citizens of Bombay was held on 7th January 1913, H.E. Lord Sydenham, the Governor, presiding, to express its abhorrence of the recent attempt on the lives of the

Viceroy and Lady Hardinge on their State Entry into Delhi, the new capital of India. His Highness the Aga Khan proposed—"That this Public Meeting of the representatives of the City and Presidency of Bombay expresses its deep abhorrence of the dastardly attempt on the lives of Their Excellencies the Viceroy and Lady Hardinge; its profound thankfulness for Lord Hardinge's preservation and Lady Hardinge's escape; its admiration for Lady Hardinge's serene courage and its sympathy in her painful anxiety; and its earnest prayer that H.E. the Viceroy may soon be fully restored to health and enabled to complete the work which has already won for him the regard and gratitude of the whole country." The Hon. Sir Pherozeshah seconded His Highness as follows.

Your Excellency, Ladies and Gentlemen,—I have been asked to second the Resolution which has been moved by His Highness the Aga Khan with that ability and that effectiveness which have marked all his wise and statesmanlike utterances on Indian affairs. It almost seems a work of superarrogation to be called upon to second and support a Resolution such as that which His Highness has moved, for we can but only re-echo the deep sentiments which have been pronounced through the length and breadth of this land, from one end to the other, with the utmost abhorrence and detestation at the atrocious crime committed against our great Viceroy who is held in the highest esteem—I will not say by a majority but I will say—by the whole people of India.

Ladies and gentlemen, I think we may here sum up the outburst of sentiment which has been evoked on this occasion in a few words. In the first place, it evoked a cry of anguish and horror at the detestable crime which had been attempted. In the second place, there was a deep sob at the tragic pathos of the situation that arose. Then there was a sign of relief and gratitude and thankfulness to the High Providence that Their Excellencies had been saved in a providential and miraculous manner. Lastly, I think, as His Excellency the Governor has put it, came the note of admiration for the patience and fortitude with which Their Excellencies have borne the heavy and severe trial through which they have passed. Many of you are perhaps aware of the old familiar lines of Goldsmith in his description of the English people—

> Pride in their port, defiance in their eyes,
> I see the lords of human kind pass by.

Ladies and gentlemen, I have always maintained and I still maintain that the greatness of the English people does not lie so much in their physique, material strength and power as in the lofty conception of moral and political duty which has characterised the lives of so many great and wise English men and English statesman; and such a great and wise Englishman an statesman Lord Hardinge has proved himself at such a trying time. It was only the other day that in this very Hall when we held a Public Meeting for the purpose of expressing our profound gratitude at the Visit of Their Imperial Majesties the King-Emperor and the Queen-Empress, we recognised that Lord Hardinge was one of those statesmen of whom the Poet Laureate has sung:

> And statesmen at her Council met
> Who knew the seasons when to take
> Occasion by the hand and make
> The bounds of freedom wider yet.

And under the benign leadership of our gracious Sovereign, Lord Hardinge has again proved himself such a statesman on this occasion.

BRITISH INDIANS IN SOUTH AFRICA

Public Meeting in Bombay, 1913

A Public Meeting was held at the Town Hall, Bombay, on 10th December 1913 to pass resolutions in reference to the treatment of Indians in South Africa pressing for an inquiry into the allegations of ill-treatment of strikers in Natal and expressing gratitude to the Viceroy, Lord Hardinge and Lord

Ampthill for the way in which they had championed the cause of the Indian Community in South Africa. H.H. Aga Sir Sultan Mohammed Shah, the Aga Khan, presided. Sir Pherozeshah who, on rising to address the assembly, was received with loud and continued cheering which lasted for several minutes, spoke as follows.

Your Highness, Ladies and Gentlemen,—I am entrusted with the task of moving the first Resolution before this Meeting Let me assure you, ladies and gentlemen, that in proceeding to move that Resolution I do not propose to make a long speech for in the longest speech which I might make, what could I tell you but the thrice told tale of woe and suffering, of patience and resignation, and above all that blessed word—moderation of our country men and women in South Africa, which has stirred the heart of this country to its very depths? In this state of things I was surprised, and I may be allowed to add, I was grievously disappointed in reading in one of the papers, where after referring to the project of a public meeting, the writer on goes to say "this agitation has done one thing and that is to show that there are political agitators who, whilst being far removed from the Extremists, are perfectly prepared to use all the means in their power to embarrass the Government." I ask, could there be a more unjustifiable aspersion on those who are toiling to keep this agitation within limits and moderate limits in this country? Does the writer refer to my friend the Hon. Mr. Gokhale (Cheers) who has devoted his whole heart and soul to this question, or to a mild Parsee like me who, if anything, has been reproached with not being violent on occasions which would have justified wild language? But, gentlemen, the comment which I make on that observation is that the writer has utterly and entirely failed to realise the depth and intensity of the feeling which on this occasion pervades everybody in this country, high and low, rich and poor, young and old, however divided from each other by caste or creed, race or religion. He has utterly failed to measure the extent of the emotion which is agitating the whole country in consequence of the sufferings of our countrymen and above all of our country—women in South

Africa.

Ladies and gentlemen, what is it in the first place the Indians in South Africa have been fighting for, pleading for praying for, with all the persuasion at their command? His Highness the Aga Khan has told you that there were some restrictions placed upon the Indians in South Africa during the Boer regime, but even the Boers by no means rigorously enforced the legal restrictions that were on the Statute Book. But when they treated the Indians in this mild manner, what did one of England's great statesmen say on that occasion? Lord Lansdowne, then a responsible Minister of the Crown, said in the House of Lords in grave and forcible and emphatic terms that even that mild manner of treating the subjects of the British Empire could not be endured and that such treatment was an adequate casus telli against the Boers. Now the Transvaal has passed into the British Dominions, and with what result? Have those restrictions been abandoned or repealed? Alas for the loyal subject of the British Crown!—it is depressing, grievously depressing to find that far from being removed, they are being more rigorously enforced than before. The argument has been brought forward that the mighty British Nation which could make a casus belli of that treatment against the Boers, then a foreign State, could not interfere to prevent worse treatment in the dominions over which the King-Emperor presides! What a deplorable admission to make that the British Government cannot repress the sort of treatment in their own dominions which they did not tolerate in a foreign State! I deplore such a statement, such an argument, for this reason—for the reason of the effect which it would produce on the minds of the loyal people of India—an effect which we can scarcely contemplate with equanimity in our full sense of the full sense, I will not say loyal, of the benefits of English Rule. These further repressive measures were undertaken in the time of the British occupation of that province. And what did Mr. Gandhi and his associates do under these circumstances? They argued, they reasoned, they implored; they said: Do whatever you will even in your might but do not deny to those already settled in the country the simplest and the barest rights of ordinary citizenship of the Empire—the bare dignity of humanity. They begged and they prayed for this. The poor Indian had never commenced by taking up a defiant and aggressive attitude. He pointed out that he and his fellow countrymen had been ready to help the British during the Boer War and begged and prayed for nothing more than that those already settled there should be allowed the simplest rights of citizenship. No ear was given to what he urged until utterly baffled he resorted to one of the only remedies that remains open to a loyal subject of the Crown. For four years did that Passive Resistance last, from 1906 to 1910, and then people began to realise that the cause for which sufferings could be endured by men like these, must be just and righteous. This was acknowledged and a promise given that the simple rights demanded would be incorporated in the next legislative enactment. What were these claims? I ask you to remember this, I have all along held that a subject of the British Crown has a right of free entry and access to every part of the Empire. I have always disagreed with some of my friends and have always said and maintained that Indians can never give up this great and vital principle of Imperial Citizenship. What did Mr. Gandhi do? Did he ask for that? Never He bowed to fate and said: "Very well, let immigration go. I only ask for a recognition of the legal rights of those settled there, of their social customs and domestic economy." All these were promised him, but when the legislation came, what was the result? It was an absolute negation of those promises. And still we are told that it is the Indians who should practise moderation and that the Boers should be satisfied that the demands are of a moderate character. Finding that Mr. Gandhi was again at his own game of persuasion and reason and argument, I call this unpractical, and I disagree with this saintly character only here. I say it was a mistake that they asked for too little, and they failed because they did so. If he had asked for more, and if he had struck out for that full demand, he would have got something. He would not have been told that because he had asked for so little, therefore he would get still less. That, I think according to my poor judgment, was a great blunder, but it illustrates the reasonable and moderate character of the campaign carried on by Mr. Gandhi. Surely, the South Africans ought to have recognised the extreme docility and moderation of these demands toned down to the lowest depths. I ask your attention to this because it is the Indians who have been charged with not exercising patience and moderation, and Mr. Gandhi was still at his old game of reasoning and persuading—but with what result? Nobody listened and upto the present nothing has been done and still we are asked, and the Indians in South Africa are asked, to practise moderation. Now the situation has developed in a way which has caused intense pain and agony to people in this country. Look at the way in which this aggressive Union Government of South Africa treats the Marriage Laws of the Indians settled there in their high superiority.

Sir Pherozeshah continuing said:

As the Chairman has said there was a time when Indians were highly civilised when Boers and Britons were unknown. And denying that everything must be recognised by religious custom, they say that Indians married according to their own rites and customs are not to be considered as married at all.

I tell you, ladies and gentlemen, what I feel sincerely, that there has been no more touching episode in the whole history of this campaign than the conversation which Mrs. Gandhi had with her husband before she cast in her lot with him in the Passive Resistance Movement. After the decision of the Supreme Court there, denying the legitimacy of Hindu and Mohammedan marriages, she asked him:—"Am I your wife or not? I am not your wife if this decision stands, and if I am not your wife, I am not a woman of any ture womanhood in the estimation of my own sex, and my children are illegitimate." Mr. Gandhi must have known what it was to expose tender women to the hardships of the campaign but in spite of his pleadings, that brave lady decided to cast in her lot with those men who were fighting for the cause. History records the deeds of many heroines, and I feel that Mrs. Gandhi will stand as one of the foremost heroines in the whole of the world.

But we are told, ladies and gentlemen, what can His Majesty's Ministers do in a matter of this character, which concerns the internal economy and discipline of a self-governing colony? I entirely and absolutely agree with His Highness the Aga Khan that we are bound to speak with due respect for the Ministers of the Crown. But with all that it is impossible not to tell that the people of this country cannot but consider that they have not extended that protection to the Indian subjects of His Majesty the King-Emperor which as Ministers of the Crown they were bound to accord to millions of his subjects in the Colony.

It is a piece of singularly good fortune that we have at the head of the Indian administration a man who has proved himself one of the greatest and noblest of Viceroys[12] a man cast in a large mould in every way—a high-minded, high-souled, and high-hearted statesman who fully realises that no statesmanship can be high which is not based on justice, righteousness and sympathy. His Excellency the Viceroy has won the hearts of the people of this country, and done a great service to the Empire by his magnificent speech at Madras. People in England do not realise the great service he has rendered by his words. Whilst we feel dissatisfied with the way in which great Ministers of the Empire have treated this subject, we are consoled with the thought that the Viceroy of this country, His Majesty's representative, is suffering in sufferings and pained by the pains borne by our countrymen in South Africa.

Ladies and gentlemen, I am afraid that I belie the promise that I made at the beginning of this speech. I told you I was not going to make a long speech, but it is difficult to contain oneself under the circumstances, and long as I have been already,—I haven't kept my watch in my hand as we do in the Legislative Council—I cannot help making a further observation that I think it is a wrong and a narrow-sighted policy which has allowed the larger question to be brought out, the question of the rights of Indians as citizens of the British Empire As I said once before on a similar occassion in this Town Hall it is not a good thing to set Asiatics and Indians to ponder too much on the question of open door and closed door. I think it is a blunder of a most serious character that we should be led to think that while white races can claim by force and might to go everywhere and to enter the fairest places on the world's surface, and that at the same time they should lay down a principle that other races must not enter the places occupied by them. And though you may talk of Yellow Peril and Black Peril, but by this conduct you bring out more and more the gravity and seriousness of the Yellow Peril and Black Peril, —hence we cannot say what will happen in the future. But, I think, English and European statesmen had better take warning that while they claim the right of going over the whole world, and of invading the North of Africa, it is a grave mistake to set down too definitely and too formally that they will prevent other races going to parts occupied by the white races I said that it was a piece of singular good fortune that we possess a statesman of the calibre of Lord Hardinge, who has fully realised the volume of the feeling in this country on the matter. Let us again go to him and implore him to approach —even if necessary—the foot of the Throne and implore the Crown that under the circumstances which existed and have since developed, it would not only be a righteous but also a wise policy that, if nothing else prevails, the Veto of the Crown be exercised. Was the Veto given for nothing? Was it not given to preserve and maintain Imperial interests? For with all the talk of the discipline and internal economy of self-governing colonies, are they not as much part of the Empire as any other part, and the Veto can only mean that if the colonies will not take care to preserve and maintain the Imperial interests involved, the Crown will step in and prevent them from doing irreparable injury and mischief to the Empire. We therefore appeal to the Crown that if nothing else prevails its Veto must be exercised. I mean to tell you one reason why we are feeling so intensely on the present situation. While we are speaking and speechifying, those mild and gentle women who have enrolled themselves with husbands and brothers, under the banner of Passive Resistance, are lying in jails herded with common criminals. And surely with all the advice about moderation dinned into our ears, does not our blood boil at the thought that while arguments are being set forth and negotiations carried on, these women in South Africa are suffering the lot of ordinary criminals? And if a way is not found to end these sufferings, I will not say what the consequences might be. But gentlemen, the Pagan and Greek theory of the Nemesis, is founded on absolute truth, and acts like these must rebound on their authors, and therefore it is that we implore our rulers in the interests both of England and India, to bring about a reasonable and speedy solution of the question. With these words I move the first Resolution.

References

1. See his Speeches.
2. *Ibid.*
3. The Marquess of Dufferin and Ava.
4. Reference to Lord Tennyson.
5. The Earl of Kimberley.
6. George William Erskine Russel.
7. C. Y. Chintamani, (ed.), *Speeches and Writings of Sir Pherozeshah M. Mehta*, pp. 363-76.
8. Small Causes Court.
9. R. H. Vincent.
10. He was a Judge, Bombay High Court from 1866-82, and Chief Justice 1882-95. He died in 1900.
11. Prof. Fardunjee M. Dastur, Registrar of the University.
12. Lord Hardinge.

3

Congress President

As it is evident, Pherozeshah Mehta's career was ardently devoted to the cause of the Indian Nationalism, he did not miss any session of the Indian National Congress.[1] Within a few years he was honoured by this organisation when he was asked to present a welcome address to the delegates at the Bombay session in December 1889. Indeed the Congress was fairly going at that point of time and it was putting forwards its constitutional programme with no bearing on any kind of agitational approach.

Next year, in 1890, he was honoured to chair its session held at Calcutta. He enlogised the services rendered by Dadabhai Naoroji and Syed Ahmed Khan. He explained what Indians really want and discussed several themes, viz., Muslims and the Indian National Congress, the era of Congress achievement, services rendered for India by Charles Bradlaugh, Lord Cross's Indian Councils Bill, attitude of Lord Salisbury towards the Indian Council's Bill, opinion of the Viceroy on the Indian Council's Bill, Lansdowne and Macaulay's prophetic words, opinion of Gladstone on the Indian Council's Bill, work of Indian delegates in England, Indian budget in the House of Commons, voice of the Congress, and faith in England.

In 1904 he was honoured once again to present as a welcome address at the Congress session held in Bombay. At this point of time, the Congress was about twenty years old. He explained in an exhaustive note about the achievements of this organisation in the last two decades under the successive Viceroys.

ADDRESS BY PHEROZESHAH METHA

Ladies and Gentlemen,—On behalf of the Reception Committee, I beg to tender to you all, delegates of the Fifth Indian National Congress, a cordial, sincere, and earnest welcome. It would be at all times a high pleasure and privilege to receive and welcome so many and such distinguished guests from all parts of the country. But when I remember that, though you may not be the chosen of the people by any scientific mode of election, you virtually and substantially represent them, their wants, wishes, sentiments and aspirations, in all the various ways in which representation mainifests and works itself out in the early stages of its progressive development, that pleasure and that privilege are infinitely enhanced. There is, besides, a peculiar zest in our welcome of you; for in welcoming the Congress to Bombay we welcome it back to "its own native land". I well remember the day, this time four year ago, when, anxiously but hopefully, we launched the Congress on its enterprise, not of supplanting the existing rulers of the country, but of supplementing the endeavours of the best and most sagacious among them by proposing modifications and developments based on our peculiar and native knowledge and information, and suggested, gratefully, by that enlightenment and education, which is one of the most precious gifts bestowed upon us by British rule. The young enthusiast, whom we thus started, has now come back to us, robust and manly, broadened and strengthened, with a record of achievements of which we may be justly pround.[2]

Even the indirect political gains of the Congress have not been inconsiderable. It has brought vividly into clear and emphatic recognition that most important fact of the growth of the national idea amongst us. Despite social and religious differences, we have all begun earnestly to realize that we are fairly on the way to a common national existence, united and bound together by the common political ties of an equal impartial, and enlightened rule, just as the United States have raised up the American nation on the basis of an infinite diversity of races and creeds. When we call the Congress national, we give expression to this nationalizing tendency which is now so powerfully leavening New India. Instead of being jealously resented and angrily denounced, this free and frank acknowledgment of the grandest outcome of British rule ought to be welcome as a sure token of our rational and discerning loyalty at least by those who are always so mightily distressed that we do not set up a perpetual hallelujah in praise of it, in season and out of season. Then, gentlemen, the labours of the Congress have contributed to do that which is a necessary prelude to all reform a thorough shifting and searching of some of the most vital of Indian political problems. Nothing that passion or prejudice, or malice could urge has been left unsaid.

And now that the proposals of the Congress have bravely stood the test, our opponents have recourse to the familiar device, which is so often employed to cover retreat, and they are lost in wonder that we are making so much fuss about things which have nothing new in them, and which have been long contemplated by many an Anglo-Indian statesman at the head of affairs. Now, gentlemen, we are quite ready at once to plead guilty to this not very dreadful impeachment. But though it may not be said of these statesmen what was once said of the Anti-Reform party in England, and can certainly be said of some Anglo-Indians, that they never have anything kind or generous to say of the Indian people, this may surely be said of them, that though they do sometime have something generous to say of the Indians, they have never shown the slightest disposition to confer upon them any portion of political rights. If the Congress has done nothing more than quicken into action these political yogis, so that lost in contemplation, it will not have laboured in vain.

Laden with these and other gains, the Congress has now

come back to us, but not without undergoing trials and ordeals, two of which have been of exceptional severity. The first device employed by our opponents was to create disunion and dissension among ouselves. Well, gentlemen, in a country so vast and varied as India, it would be impossible, it would be unnatural, to expect perfect and absolute unanimity. It is no wonder that we have our halt, our lame, and our blind, and that they should hobble off to what I may call the Indian Political cave of Adullam at the call of Sir Syed Ahmed and Rajah Shiva Prasad. But when two gentlemen, so amiable, so patriotic, so anxious to display their loyalty, were united together in one party, and formed the Anti-Congress United Patriotic Association, the same difficulty arose that was described by Mr. Bright, from whom I have borrowed my illustration, as having arisen in the case of the Anti-Reform Adullamites. They were too like the traditional Scotch terrier, which was so covered with hair, that you could not tell which was the head or which was the tail of it. Sir Syed Ahmed pulled vigorously one way, Rajah Shiva Prasad as vigorously the other; and they so pulled between them the poor popinjay they had set up—that it burst, and poured out—to the amazement of a few and the amusement of us all—not the real patriotic stuff with which it had been announced to be filled, but the whitest and the purest sawdust. The utter collapse of this vaunted Patriotic Association has taught our opponents significant lesson. Every blandishment had been employed to lure prince and peasant; but prince and peasant alike would have none of it. It would be difficult to find a more convincing, if passive and indirect, proof that the heart of the country is with us, and that it understands and appreciates the honesty, the loyalty, and the propriety of the movement. I should like to say here one word to the delegates from Bengal and the North-West Provinces, lest they should imagine that I have referred to these events which pertain more particularly to their Provinces, with the object of indirectly boasting of our own immunity from human frailty.

Let me at once proceed to assure them that we in this Presidency, have also our halt, our lame, and our blind. We also have had our little cave of Adullam. But I am glad to be able to inform you that we have taken the infection very mildly, and that there is every hope of a speedy and complete recovery. Baffled in the attempt to disunite us, our opponents had recourse to a measure of extraordinary virulence. They raised against us a cry as terrible as the cry of heresay which was sometimes raised in the old days of the Inquisition to crush an obnoxious personage, otherwise unimpeachable and invulnerable. They raised against us the cry of sedition and disloyalty. It was a cry well calculated to create alarm and uneasiness even among persons otherwise well disposed towards us. The Congress has, however, met the charge firmly and boldly—by a stadfast appeal to the authoritative record of our words, thoughts and deeds, and to the personalities of the members composing it year after year. It was conclusively shown that the charge was founded on calumnies, lies, and misrepresentations. Then gentlemen, something like the old story of the wolf and the lamb enacted itself. True, you may not be disloyal yourselves; said the wolf, that does not matter at all; it is quite enough that your great-grandfathers were, and your great-grand-children might be.

The Congress has, however, emerged unscathed even from this trial. Never was a greater truth uttered than that to which our esteemed friend Mr. Caine gave utterance, that we of the Congress are more loyal than Anglo-Indians themselves. If by loyalty is meant a keen solicitude for the safety and permanancy of the Empire, in which, we are firmly persuaded lie implanted the roots of the welfare, the prosperity, and the good government of the country, then we are certainly more loyal than Anglo-Indians, who do not hesitate frequently to subordinate the interests of that safety and that permanence to the seductions of conquest and vain glory, or to the immediate gains and temptations of commercial enterprise. Therefore, it is that all our greetings of welcome go forth to you, and with a full heart we wish you God-speed in your labours. Those labours have for their aim and object measures of which the central idea has been recently admirably summarised by one of the most sober and sagacious of modern politicians, Sir Charles Dilke, when he said that the time had now arrived when it was neither safe nor expendient to continue the administration of the country by the hands of a secret and irresponsible bureacracy, and that working on lines already laid down, a distinct step in advance should now be made. The policy of the Congress is thus a policy, not seditious or revolutionary, but "conservative of the public welfare, strengthening the just authority of the British Government, and adding day by day fresh lustre and dignity to the Imperial Crown." I do not know whether we are doomed to failure or destined to succeed; but the blessing which rests upon all high and honest endeavour will surely rest upon a mission imposed by duty, sanctified by patriotism, and guided by loyalty. And now, gentlemen, I know you will not allow me to conclude without giving utterance to the deep thankfulness which we feel at the presence among us today one whom we have learned to hail as the Member for India in the British House of Commons. The strength and greatness of the English character has been proudly sung by one of their most charming poets in lines with which we are familiar:

"Pride in their port, defiance in their eye,
I see the lords of humankind pass by."

But it has always seemed to me that English strength and greatness consist in nothing so much as in the lofty conception of moral and political duty which illumines the life and career of many an illustrious Englishman. We still mourn the loss of that great and good man whose heart was always with us, and whose voice was always raised for us during many a long and eventful year. The memory of John Bright is reverently enshrined in our hearts. His place was filled by one whose life has a singular charm for all who prize sober simplicity and nobility of character above rank and riches. I mean Professor Faweett. The mantle has now descended upon Mr. Bradlaugh. We sincerely and unaffectedly joined in general grief at his recent illness, not simply out of selfish fears of losing our chosen champion, but out of that single-hearted feeling of sorrow which all men feel, when peril threatens a life devoted to high and unselfish ends. I know I am not employing the language of exaggeration when I say that our hearts are unutterably stirred within us at his presence among us today, restored to health and usefulness. With no particular thoughts of the Congress in our minds, let us wish him that simple welcome which is in all our hearts and the hearts of people all over the country. Having now delivered to you my message of welcome, I invite you to proceed to elect your president.

After the Welcome Address was over, Mr. W.C. Bonnerjee rose and proposed the name of Sir William Wedderburn to be elected as President which was seconded by Pt. Ajoodianath. As no other name was proposed Sir Wedderburn was declared elected. Sir Wedderburn then delivered his Address.[3]

PRESIDENTIAL ADDRESS BY PHEROZESHAH MEHTA

Ladies and Gentlemen,—I beg to tender to you my most sincere thanks for the honour you have done me in calling me to preside over your deliberations this year. I cannot imagine a greater honour for a native of this country than to be elected, by your free and spontaneous suffrages, President of an assembly which in now one of the recognised institutions of the country. An unconventional Convention of the Empire which, we may say without undue ostentation, has already earned a place in history—not less surely, let us trust, than the famous St. Andrews Dinners of the city,—as making an epoch in the march of events moulding the lofty destinies of this magnificent land. In speaking of myself as a native of this country, I am not unaware that, incredible as it may seem, Parsis have been both called and invited and allured to call themselves foreigners. If twelve centuries, however, entitle Angles and Saxons, and Normans and Danes, to call themselves natives of England, if a lesser period entitles the Indian Mohammedans to call themselves natives of India, surely we are born children of the soil, in which our lot has been cast for a period of thirteen centuries, and where, ever since the advent of the over

British power, we have lived and worked, with our Hindu and Mohammedan neighbours, for common aims, common aspirations and common interests. To my mind, a Parsi is a better and a truer Parsi as a Mohammedan or a Hindu is a better and truer Mohammedan or Hindu, the more he is attached to the land which gave him birth, the more he is bound in brotherly relations and affection to all the children of the soil, the more he recognizes the fraternity of all the native communities of country, and the immutable bond which binds them together in the pursuit of common aims and objects under a common Government.

Is it possible to imagine that Dadabhai Naoroji, for instance, true Parsi that he is, is anything but an Indian, living and working all his life for all India, with the true and tender loyalty of a son? Can anyone doubt, if I may be allowed to take another illustration, that Sir Syed Ahmed Khan was greater and noble when he was devoting the great energies and talents with which he is endowed, if, for the benefit of Mohammedans in particular for the benefit of all Indians in general—than when, as of late, he was preaching, a gospel of selfishness and isolation? The birthright, therefore, gentlemen, which the Parsis thus possess of so indefeasible and glorious a character, they have refused and will always refuse to sell for any mess of pottage, however fragrant and tempting. More especially, therefore, as an Indian, it is that I return to you my grateful thanks for the honour you have done me.[4]

I have ventured, gentlemen, to ascribe to the Congress the credit of making an epoch in Indian political progress. A very brief survey of the incidents of the twelve months that have elapsed since we last met will amply justify our title to that distinction. In the admirable address which was delivered by my predecessor in this chair at Allahabad, Mr. Yule pointed out that all movements of the kind in which we are concerned pass through several phases as they run their course. The first is one of ridicule. That is followed, as the movement progresses, by one of abuse, which is usually succeeded by partial concession and misapprehension of aim, accompanied by warnings against taking "big jumps into the unknown". The final stage of all is a substantial adoption of the object of the movement, with some expression of surprise that it was not adopted before. Well, gentlemen, we have pretty well passed the first two stages. We have survived the ridicule, the abuse, and the misrepresentation. We have survived the charge of sedition and disloyalty. We have survived the charge of being a microscopic minority. We have also survived the charge of being guilty of the atrocious crime of being educated, and we have even managed to survive the grievous change of being all Babus in disguise.

What Indians Really Want

The question of our loyalty is set at rest for ever. In the debate on Lord Cross's India Reform Bill in the House of Lords, ex-Viceroy after ex-Viceroy bore emphatic testimony to the loyal and peaceful character of our aims and efforts. Within the last few days the voice of no less a personage than one of our former Secretaries of State has confirmed this testimony. Lord R. Churchill—it is to no less distinguished a public man that I refer—has publicly declared that:

> "He could sincerely remark that no one will rejoice more than himself if the deliberations of the Indian National Congress shortly to be resumed were to contribute effectually to the progress and the welfare of the Indian people."

Then, gentlemen, it is made clear that we have not learnt the lessons of history so badly as to demand the introduction of the full-blown representative institutions which, in England, have been the growth of centuries. It is made clear that we have not asked for even such a modicum as was enjoyed by the English people even before the time of Simon de Montfort, more than five centuries ago, nay, that we have not asked even for representative institutions of a governing or ruling character at all. Indeed, so far as this historical argument is concerned, we have not alone proved that we have not been guilty of disregarding it, but we have been successful in turning the tables upon our adversaries. We have shown that it is they who defy the lessons of history and experince, when they talk of waiting to make a beginning till the masses of the people are fully equipped with all the virtues and all the qualifications which adorn the citizens of Utopia, in fact, till a millennium has set in, when we should hardly require such institutions at all, we have shown that people who indulge in such vain talk have never understood the laws of human progress, which, after all, is a series of experiments, in which men and institutions react upon each other for their mutual improvement and perfection.[5]

Anglo-Indian Knowledge of Indian Affairs

We have also proved that, in spite of our education, and even with our racial and religious differences, the "microscopic minority" can far better and far more intuitively represent the needs and aspirations of their own countrymen, than the still more "microscopic minority" of the omniscient district officers, whose colloquial knowledge of the Indian languages seldom rises above the knowledge of English possessed, for instance, by French waiters at Paris Hotels which proudly blazon forth the legend; Ici on Parle Anglais; and whose knowledge of native domestic and social life and ways and habits of thought seldom extends beyond a familiarity with flattering expressions of the Saheb's greatness and paternal care, sometimes inspired by courtesy and sometimes by interest. An amusing story was related to me of a little incident that occurred only the other day which is not without instructions as illustrating the amount of knowledge possessed by Anglo-Indians of the people among whom they have moved for years. The wife of a member of Parliament, who has come out on a visit to India this year—herself as distinguished as her husband for her kindly sympathy in Indian welfare—was sitting at dinner next to a learned member of my profession, who in the course of conversation, grew humorous and sarcastic by turns, in the fashion of Mr. Rudyard Kipling on the ridiculous and outrageous pretensions of globe-trotters to know the country and its people better than Anglo-Indians who had lived in it for years.

He was rattling away, well satisfied with himself and the impression he thought he was producing on the lady, when, with the sweetest of smiles, she gently asked him how long he had been himself in India. "Fifteen years—more or less" was the answer. "I suppose you know well Mr.—" naming a gentleman whose recent elevation to the Bench of one of our High Courts was received everywhere with pleasure and approbation. "Of course, I do", said his brother in the same profession. "Can you tell me if he has only one wife or more than one"? Slowly came the answer, "No; I fear I can't." "Well, I can tell you. You see I have been only a few days in the country," said the lady quietly, "and yet I think I know a thing or two which you don't." I trust my learned friend, who is the hero of this story, was properly grateful to the lady for giving him some serious food for reflection.

Mohammedans and the Congress

Then, gentlemen, our right to the designation of a national body has been vindicated. It is so admirably set forth in an article which appeared in a Conservative Review—The National—from the pen of a Conservative who, however, speaks from the fulness of intimate knowledge, that I cannot resist the temptation of borrowing from it:

> "The supposed rivalry," says the writer, "between Musalmans and Hindus is a convenient decoy to distract attention and to defer the day of reform. I do not wish to affirm that there is no antagonism between the adherents of the two faiths; but I do most positively assert that the antagonism has been grossly exaggerated. Every municipal improvement and charitable work finds members of the two faiths working together and subscribing funds to carry it out. Every political paper in the country finds supporters from believers in both creeds. Just the same is witnessed in the proceedings of the Congress. The members of the

Congress met together as men, on the common basis of nationality, being citizens of one country, subjects of one power, amenable to one code of laws, taxed by one authority, influenced for weal or woe by one system of administration, urged by like impulses to secure like rights and to be relieved of like burdens. If these are not sufficient causes to weld a people together into one common alliance of nationality, it is difficult to conceive what would be sufficient. It is for the reason the organisation has been called the Indian National Congress; not because, as many besides Mr. Keane have assumed that it claims a non-existent unity of race, but because it deals with rights and interests which are national in character, and matters in which all the inhabitants of the Indian peninsula are equally concerned."

I think we may take it, gentlemen, that we have passed through the first two stages, and that the loyalty, the moderation, the propriety, and the constitutional and national character of our mission, are now established beyond a doubt. But, however arduous and however provoking some of the experiences of the trial through which we have passed, they should not leave any trace of bitterness behind. For let us not imagine that they were devoid of chastening and beneficial effects upon ourselves. Let us frankly acknowledge that they also must have had their share in contributing to add clearness to our thoughts, sobriety to our methods, and moderation to our proposals. If I might use a prescribed, but not unscriptural, phrase, we must give even the devil his due.[6]

The Era of Congress Achievement

It is on the third stage—the era of achievement—that we have now entered. It is true that a majority of the Congress proposals do not still seem to have made much headway. Even as regards the proposal to separate the executive and the judicial functions, lauded by Lord Dufferin "as a counsel of perfection to which the Government were ready to subscribe."

Government are yet so absorbed in admiration of it that they have not recovered themselves sufficiently to take action. There is, however, no reason to despair. It was once proved upon sworn testimony in the Bombay High Court, before the late Chief Justice Sir M. Westropp, that a woman required 22 months for parturition in the air of the province of Kattyawar. It is not impossible, gentlemen, that the air of Simla may similarly necessitate a more than ordinarily long period of gestation to perfect even counsels of perfection; and therefore, we must possess our souls in more than ordinary patience, lest any precipitate pressure might occasion a miscarriage. In one little matter, complete success has attended our efforts, viz., as regards the duty on silver-plate. The Abkari cause is also safe in the custody of that redoubtable champion, of whose formidable prowess you can form some idea, when you remember that it was he who so completely put to rout Mr. Goschen's Compensation Clauses. It is a matter of no small congratulation to us to welcome Mr. Caine as one of our own delegates.

He first came out to this country with a free and open mind on the Congress question. With that fearless independence which characterizes him, and which always, when I see him, recalls to my mind those famous lines of Burns, "The man of independent mind is king of men for that", he went for his education to Aligarh. Thanks to Mr. T.H. Beck and Sir Syed Ahmed, he has come to us, not only a staunch Congressman in principles, but, as a member of the British Committee, he has thrown his indomitable energy and his high-souled advocacy into active support of the movement. Mr. Caine can truly boast that, if he has not succeeded in extorting from Mr. Pritchard and all the most zealous Abkari officers the confession that they are Bacchus and his crew in disguise, they dare not, at least, throw off their masks while his watchful eye is upon them, but must continue to do penance in the assumed garb of uncomfortable and uncongenial principles. Leaving Christian to continue his combat with Apollyon, it is when we come to the central proposal of the Congress regarding the

Legislative Councils, for the purpose of expanding and putting life in them, that we can congratulate ourselves on being on the verge of an important step. Many have been the circumstances, and many the forces and influences, that have contributed to this result. First and foremost among them is the circumstance that, without legal votes and legal qualifications, we have had the good fortune to become possessed of a member of our own in Parliament. Do not imagine, gentlemen, that Dadabhai Naoroji or Lalmohan Ghose has at length been returned.

Charles Bradlaugh's Services to India

But what member, even if we had the direct franchise, could have served us as Mr. Bradlaugh has done during the last twelve months? To say that the whole country is grateful to him for the untiring energy, the indefatigable care, the remarkable ability with which he has watched and worked for its best interests in that House, where he has achieved so honourable a position for himself, can only most imperfectly express the depth and extent of the sentiments that are felt for him throughout the length and breadth of the land. His name has literally become a household word. He is raising up to himself a memorial in the hearts of the people of India, which will reflect more lustre on his name than titles and orders, and endure longer than monuments of brass or marble.

We have been fortunate indeed in securing the sympathies of such a champion. No sooner did he return to England than he at once proceeded to redeem the promise he had made on that behalf, by introducing in the House of Commons his India Councils Reform Bill, drawn on the lines which were sketched and formulated at the last Congress, and with which you are all familiar under its justly deserved brief designation of the Madras Scheme. Two important results were the immediate outcome of this step. The scheme which was thus propounded was in its nature a tentative measure, so far as its details were concerned; and it at once drew forth useful and guiding criticism. In several respects its scope was misunderstood, especially as regards its supposed sweeping character which might have been avoided had we specified in the Congress skeleton sketch the restrictive limitations hedging the qualifications of the electorate. The criticisms of men like Sir W. Hunter and Sir R. Garth, for whose thoughtful, sympathetic and friendly attitude towards Indian progress, we are always so deeply grateful, exposed, however, one defect demanding serious consideration, viz., that the scheme was laid on new lines, and had a somewhat theoretical air, which Englishmen rather fight shy of in practical politics. In justice to the scheme, however, it should be said that Sir Richard Garth put his finger on a possible, rather than a probable, result when he thought that it would enable the Hindus to submerge the other Indian communities. Experience has shown that even in a preponderating Hindu electorate, it does not happen that Hindus only are elected, as so many other, besides racial, forces and interests concur in influencing the selection. If we may apply the lessons learnt from experience in municipal elections, I may mention the remarkable fact that in the Town Council, or what is now called the Standing Committee of the Bombay Corporation, composed of 12 members, there have been frequently 5 Parsis, 3 Europeans, 2 Hindus, and 2 Mohammedans. Sir R. Garth's criticism on this point, however, throws out a warning which should not be hastily disregarded.

Lord Cross's Indian Councils Bill

But the next result, which the introduction of Mr. Bradlaugh's Bill achieved, was gratifying in the highest degree. It at once dispelled the fit of profound cogitation, in which men at the head of Indian affairs are so apt to be lost that they can never spontaneously recover from it. Lord Cross's Indian Counc'ls Bill promptly saw the light of day in the House of Lords. It was at once the official recognition of the raison-d-etra of the Congress, and the first fruits of its labours. In itself, however, it was a most halting and unsatisfactory measure. In framing it, the Prime Minister and the Indian Secretary of State seem to have been pervaded with a conception of the Indian people as a sort of Oliver Twist, always asking for more, to whom it would be therefore a piece of purdent policy to begin with offering as little as possible. The Government Bill may be aptly described as a most superb steam-enging, in which the necessary material to generate steam was carefully excluded, substituting in its place coloured shams to look like it. The rights of interpallation and of the discussion of the Budget were granted, but the living forces of the elective principle, which alone could properly work them, were not breathed into the organisation of the enlarged councils. The omission of the elective principle from the bill was boldly justified by Lord Salisbury on the ground that:

> "The principle of election or government by representation was not an Eastern idea, and that it did not fit Eastern traditions or Eastern minds."

I wish to speak of his Lordship with all the respect to which his high talents and great intellectual attainments justly entitle him; but it is not a little surprising as well as disappointing to find the Prime Minister of England, a statesman who, as Lord Cranborne, was once Secretary of State for India, displaying such profound ignorance of the history of the Indian people and the genius of the Indian mind. The late Mr. Chisholm Anstey, a man of immense erudition, once pointed out at a meeting of the East India Association in London, that:

> "We are apt to forget in this country when we talk of preparing people in the East by education, and all that sort of thing, for Municipal Government and Parliamentary Government, that the East is the parent of Municipalities. Local Self-Government in the widest acceptation of the term, is as old as the East itself. No matter what may be the religion of the people who inhabit what we call the East, there is not a portion of the country from west to east, from north to south, which is not swarming with municipalities, and not only so, but like to our municipalities of old, they are all bound together as in a species of network so that you have ready-made to your hand the framework of

a great system of representation."

Sir H. Maine has shown that the Teutonic Mark was hardly so well organized or so essentially representative as an Indian village community, until the precise technical Roman form was engrafted upon it.[7]

Lord Salisbury's Attitude on Indian Council's Bill

But leaving village communities alone, what do we find at the present day over the whole country but all sorts and conditions of people, from the highest to the lowest, meeting together and transacting the business of their numberless castes, in assemblies which, in their constitution and in their mode of working, are the exact prototype of the Saxon Witans, from which the English Parliamentary institutions have sprung. It is true that circumstances never allowed the representative genius of the people to develop forms and organisations for higher political functions. But it is no less true, that the seed and the soil are therc, waiting only for the skilful hand, and the watchful mind, which we of the Congress firmly believe we have secured in the presence of Englishmen in this country. The disdainful attitude of Lord Salisbury as to our aptitude for representative institutions need, however, bring no dispair to our minds. His late chief, Lord Beaconsfield, once said of him on a memorable occasion that he was a man who never measured his phrases or his sweeping assertions. On the contrary, I draw an augury of good hope from his pronouncement and that made by his son Lord Hugh Cecil that:

> "The Indian was not only a good Government, but it was probably the best conceivable Government, that the population could possible live under."

On the eve of the passing of the great English Reform Bill, the Duke of Wellington, then the Tory Prime Minister, proclaimed in the same House of Lords that the existing constitution of the House of Commons was perfect, and that the wit of man could not a priori have devised anything so perfect. The declaration was received by the Liberals as a sure portent of victory; and the Reform Bill was passed within little more than a year after. I trust that the Salisbury pronouncement may prove prophetic in the same way.

Charles Bradlaugh's Indian Council's Bill

It is needless to discuss Lord Cross's perfunctory measure any further; even with the amendment which Lord Northbrook succeeded in getting accepted, it left the House of Lords in the same lifeless condition in which it entered. As soon as it reached the House of Commons, Mr. Bradlaugh fastened on it at once. It was true that he had got there his own Bill, but Mr. Bradlaugh is a master of Parliamentary tactics, inferior, if to any, only to Mr. Gladstone. He at once perceived that the supreme struggle was to be no more between one scheme and another, between territorial electorates or local Boards, but that every nerve would have to be strained and every resource husbanded, to obtain in the first place recognition of the elective principle. That secured, everything else would follow in its own good time.

With a masterly comprehensive of the situation, he placed before the House amendments to the Bill, directed to substitute the process of election for that of nomination. The Bill and the amendments have, however, all gone the way of the majority, and the session closed without the opportunity of discussing them. Profiting, however, by the lessons in which the experience of the last twelve months was prolific, both without and within the walls of Parliament, Mr. Bradlaugh has hit upon the notable expedient of ploughing with Lord Cross's heifer. He has already introduced a new Bill, based on the same lines as Lord Cross's Bill, but vivifying it by the affirmation of the principle for which we are fighting. That Bill will be laid before you for your consideration. It will be for you to deal with it in your wisdom. However you may decide, of one thing I am certain, that you will maintain your character for moderation, sagacity and practical good sense which you have so arduously acquired by your self-sacrificing and noble labours during the five years of the existence of the Congress. It is not for me to anticipate your verdict. But I am sure you will allow me, out of my anxious solicitude for the triumph of the cause we have all so earnestly at heart, to state the reasons which to my mind, make so imperatively for the acceptance of the new draft, in which I cannot but recognize the statesmanlike craft and thorough knowledge of the shifting phases of English politics which Mr. Bradlaugh so eminently possesses, and which, as we all earnestly pray, promises to place him at no distant date in the front ranks of politicians in office, as he already is in the front rank of those not in office.

Viceregal Opinions on the Indian Councils Bill

The old draft, admirably devised in some respects with many virtues and a few faults, has not proved congenial to the English political mind, averse to new departures, and looking askance at theoretical airs of perfection. The new Bill has, on the other hand, all the elements of success in its favour. Its most striking merit is that it gathers round it the cautious, the carefully weighed, and responsible opinions of some of the best Viceroys we have ever had. Lord Northbrook has pronouced in favour of a properly safe-guarded application of some mode of election. The righteous sympathies of the Marquis of Ripon are as warmly with us as ever, and his great authority weighs on the same side. Still more valuable, as coming from a Viceroy who left only the other day, is the measured and calculated approval which Lord Dufferin has recorded in a despatch, in referring to which I hope I am not making myself liable to the terrors of the Official Secrets Act. In mentioning Lord Dufferin, I will frankly say that we have not sufficiently recognised the great debt of gratitude which we owe to him in this respect, partly, I believe, through ignorance, and partly through misappreciation of the course he adopted to neutralize opposition against the measures he recommended. An unrivalled diplomist, his wary statesmanship was apt to assume the hues of the craft of which he is so accomplished a master. He sought an occasion when he could launch his proposals without provoking disagreement, endeavouring rather to conciliate it. The epoch-making St. Andrew's Dinner of 1888 offered him the needful opportunity. He knew Scotchmen and their matter-of-fact character, so inimitably delineated by Charles Lamb. He knew, as that charming essayist tells us, that:

> "surmises, guesses, misgivings, half institutions, partial illuminations, dim instincts, embryo conceptions had no place in their brain or vocabulary."

He drew before his hosts a vivid and alarming picture of imaginary Congress proposals—of "an ideal authoritatively suggested of the creation of a representative body or bodies, in which the official element shall be in a minority, who shall have what is called the power of the purse, and who, through this instrumentality, shall be able to bring the British executive into subjection to their will."

But, while his excited and valiant hosts rushed off, crying "Scotchmen to the rescue," to tilt at windmills, he quietly threw in a sympathetic recognition of our just and legitimate aspirations, and proceeded to record a minute in which he substantially backed up the veritable Congress proposals. In this despatch Lord Dufferin has briefly described his scheme as a plan for the enlargement of the Provincial Councils, for the enhancement of their status, the multiplication of their functions, the partial introduction into them of the elective principle, and the liberalization of their general character as political institutions. At this year's St. Andrew's dinner, Sir Charles Elliott eulogized Lord Dufferin's speech as epoch-making and fixing the bounds and limits of our demands 'so far and no further'. We are quite content to go as far; we have never asked to go very much further. We may, therefore, fairly infer from Sir Charles Elliott's speech that he is in accord and in sympathy with the main underlying principles of Lord Dufferin's scheme, and we can therefore congratulate the people of Bengal on their good fortune in possessing a ruler whom we can justly claim to be a true Congresswalla at heart.[8]

Lord Lansdowne and Macaulay's Prophetic Words

I will not speculate, without official sanction, on the views of the present Viceroy. But I may permit myself to remind you that it was to Henry, Marquis of Lansdowne that Macaulay dedicated those speeches, in one of which, dipping far into the future, he spoke about the future Government of India in that noble passage with which we are all familiar.

"The destinies of our Indian Empire are covered with thick darkness. It is difficult to form any conjecture as to the fate reserved for a State which resembles no other in history, and which forms by itself a separate class of political phenomena. The laws which regulate its growth and decay are still unknown to us. It may be that the public mind of India may expand under our system till it has outgrown that system; that by good government we may educate our subjects into a capacity for better government; that having become instructed in European knowledge they may in some future age demand European institutions. Whether such a day will ever come I know not. But never will I attempt to avert or retard it. Whenever it comes it will be the proudest day in English history. To have found a great people sunk in the lowest depths of slavery and superstition, to have so ruled them as to have made them desirous and capable of all the privileges of citizens, would indeed be a title to glory all our own."

The dawn of that day which Macaulay foresaw, in dim but prophetic vision, is now breaking on the horizon; the curtain is rising on the drama which unfolds the vista to that title to glory. Let us earnestly hope that the present illustrious bearer of the great historic name of Lansdowne, who, by a wonderful ordering of events, has now come to rule over us, may watch the glowing streaks of light with generous sympathy, and may preside over the march of events with timely and provident statesmanship.[9]

Gladstone's Opinion on the Indian Councils Bill

This weighty concensus of the best Viceregal opinion which I have placed before you, in favour of the principle of the new draft, we may expect to be backed up by the potent voice of that Grand Old Man, whom we reverence, not only as the greatest Parliamentary leader of modern times, but as the individual embodiment of the highest conception of moral and political duty which English statesmanship has reached in the 19th century. You are aware that Mr. Bradlaugh has recently declared that he was authorized to say that the course pursued by him in reference to the Government Bill, in endeavouring to obtain a recognition of the elective principle, was approved by Mr. Gladstone, who intended to have supported him by speech. It would require considerations of overpowering force, indeed, to persuade us to any course by which we might run the risk of losing such an almost certain pledge of ultimate victory.

Work of Indian Delegates in England

Another potent factor has come into existence within this year, which is calculated to help us materially—if we confine our efforts to the simple issue of election versus nomination—in the force of English public opinion which, without undertaking to pronounce on questions of detail, has now declared itself to a very considerable extent emphatically in favour of vital principle of election. The credit of informing the English mind and stirring the English conscience on this momentous question belongs to that small band of noble workers who were appointed at the last Congress to plead the cause of India before the great English people in their own country, and who cheerfully crossed the seas in obedience to such a call of duty, without counting the inevitable cost and sacrifice. The task which they undertook was a formidable one; they have discharged it in a manner of which it is difficult to speak too highly. Of the leader of that band I cannot trust myself to speak with sober moderation, when I remember that it is to his genius we owe that flash of light which pointed out the creation of a body like the Congress as fraught with the promotion of the best interests of English rule in India. I know there are numerous claimants for the credit of the idea, but if I may be pardoned for employing the rudely forcible language of Carlyle:

> "The firepan, the kindling, the bitumen were his own; but the lumber of rags, old wood, and nameless combustible rubbish (for all is fuel to him) was gathered from hucksters and of every description under heaven. Whereby indeed hucksters enough have been heard to exclaim: 'Out upon it, the fire is mine."

He brought to bear upon his new enterprise the same zeal and fervour, combined with thoughtful judgment, that he has unsparingly bestowed for so many years upon the cause to which he has devoted his life. His presence on the Congress Deputation entailed a further sacrifice and affliction, for which we can offer no consolation or reparation except our deepest and most respectful sympathy. In his great and noble mission, Mr. Hume had the entire co-operation of a man of no ordinary powers and capacity. The rare and unrivalled powers of oratory which we have learned to admire in Mr. Surendranath Bannerjee—for it is of him I speak—never shone with more brilliant effect than when he was pleading the cause of his countrymen at the bar of the English people, with a fire and energy that extorted universal respect and admiration. They had a powerful co-adjutor in my friend Mr. Eardley Norton, who has known so well how to make splendid use of the heritage of great thoughts and noble deeds which he received from his distinguished father Mr. Mudholkar from the Central Provinces did yeoman's service in the same cause, and his sober and thoughtful eloquence did not carry less weight than that of his brilliant colleagues. There is no need for me to say anything of the services of Sir William Wedderburn, Mr. Dadabhai Naoroji, and our other friends in England. But I cannot allow this opportunity to pass without grateful acknowledgement of the unceasing toil, the prodigious energy, and the organizing capacity contributed by Mr. William Digby. The delegates assembled here might render no inconsiderable service to our cause if they exerted themselves to stimulate by thousands and tens of thousands the circulation of the Congress paper entitled 'India', started under the auspices of our British Committee, and conducted with such marked ability by him; and which has done, and promises to do more and more, such incalculable benefit to the object we have at heart. The result of the English campaign clearly shows the wisdom of the new plan of operations suggested by Mr. Bradlaugh. It seems to me that success is well within our reach if we resolutely apply ourselves to obtain, in the first instance at least, the recognition and application of the principle of election in the organization of our Legislative Councils. Let us then strive for it with the sagacity of practical men, who have not learnt in vain the lessons taught by English political history, and who know the value of moderate, gradual, and substantial gain.

Indian Budget in the House of Commons

To the many reasons which have been set forth in Congress after Congress, proving the imperative need of reformed Councils, another has been now added. The discussion of the Indian. Budget in the House of Commons was always more or less of a sham, but it was a sham for which the officials of the Indian Office thought it at least a matter of decency to shed a tear of remorse. But now Sir John Gorst has boldly and candidly declared in his place in the House that there need be no sham regret at all; that, if anything, it was rather to be hoped and wished for, that the House of Commons should not waste its time over the weary farce. It is now officially declared that it is right and proper that Parliament should—to use Mr. Yule's happy way of putting it,—throw "the great and solemn trust of an inscrutable Providence" back into the hands of Providence, to be looked after as Providence itself thinks best, with such grace as Providence may choose to pour on the heads of Sir John Gorst, his heirs, successors, and assigns. I think you will agree with me that, when the responsible advisers of the Crown on Indian matters propound doctrines of such a character, it is high time that we should raise our united voice to demand Local Councils possessing some guarantees for energy and efficiency.

Congress Voice: A Cry in the Wilderness

It has been said that our united voice is the voice only of a certain portion of the people and not of the masses; and that it is even then the voice of indifference, and not of urgency of excitement. These remarks are intended to be cast as matters of reproach against the Congress; properly understood they constitute its chief glory. If the masses were capable of giving articulate expression to definite political demands, then the time would have arrived, not for consultative Councils but for representative institutions. It is because they are still unable to do so that the function and the duty devalue upon their educated and enlightened compatriots to feel, to understand, and to interpret their grievances and requirements, and to suggest and indicate how these can best be redressed and met. History teaches us that such has been the law of widening progress in all ages and all countries, notably in England itself. That function and that duty, which thus devolve upon us, is best discharged, not in times of alarm and uneasiness, of anger and excitement but when the heart is loyal and clear and reason unclouded. It is, I repeat, the glory of the Congress that the educated and enlightened people of the country seek to repay the debt of gratitude, which they owe for the priceless boon of education, by pleading and pleading temperately for timely and provident statesmanship.

Faith in England

I have no fears but that English statesmanship will ultimately respond to the call. I have unbounded faith in the living and fertilizing principles of English culture and English civilization. It may be that, at times, the prospect may look dark and gloomy. Anglo-Indian opposition may look fierce and uncompromising. But my faith is large, even in Anglo-Indians. As in the whole universe, so in individuals, in communities, there is a perpetual conflict going on between the higher and lower passions and impulses of our nature. Perhaps some of you have read a little novel, called. Dr. Jekyll and Mr. Hyde, the plot of which hinges on the conflict between the two sides of a man's nature, the higher and the lower, embodied each, for the time being, in a separate and distinct individuality. If the lower tendencies are sometimes paramount in the Hydes of Anglo-Indian society, if, as our last President, Sir W. Wedderburn said, the interests of the services are antagonistic to and prevail over the interests of the Indian people, it is still the oscillation of the struggle; it is still only one side of the shield. They cannot permanently divest themselves of the higher and nobler nature, which, in the end, must prevail, and which has prevailed in so many honourable, distinguished and illustrious instances. They are after all a part and parcel of the great English nation, bone of their bone, and flesh of their flesh, and they must even work along the main lines of that noble policy which Great Britain has deliberalely adopted for the government of this country. When, in scrutable dispensation of Providence, India was assigned to the care of England, one can almost imagine that the choice was offered to her as to Israel of old:

> "Behold, I have placed before you a blessing and a curse; a blessing, if ye will obey the commandments of the Lord your God; a curse, if ye will not obey the commandments of the Lord your God, but go after other gods whom ye have not known."

All the great forces of English life and society, moral, social, intellectual, political, are if slowly, yet steadily and irresistibly declaring themselves for the choice which will make the connection of England and India a blessing to themselves and to the whole would, for countless generations. Our Congress asks but to serve as a modest handmaiden to that movement, asks but to be allowed to show the pits and the falls, asks but to be allowed to join in the blessing which England will as surely earn as there is an "eternal that maketh for righteousness."

I appeal to all true Englishmen—to candid friends as to generous foes—not to let this prayer go in vain. It may be that we sometimes speak in uncouth and outlandish ways; it may be that we sometimes stray in some confusion of thought and language; still it is the prayer of a rising, growing and hopeful nation. I will appeal to them to listen to the sage counsels of one of the most careful and observant of their modern politicians, who like the prophet Balaam, called, I will not say, exactly to curse us, has however, blessed us utterly. In his "Problems of Greater Britain," Sir Charles Dilke thus sums up his views on the Congress:

> "Argument upon the matter is to be desired, but not invective, and there is so much reason to think that the Congress movement really represents the cultivated intelligence of the country, that those who ridicule it do harm the imperial interests of Great Britain, bitterly wounding and alienating men who are justified in what they do, who do it in reasonable and cautious form, and who ought to be conciliated by being met half-way. The official class themselves admit that many of the natives who attack the Congress do so to ingratiate themselves with their British rulers and to push their claims for decorations. Our first duty in India is that of defending the country against anarchy and invasion, but our other greatest duty is to learn how to live with what is commonly called the Congress movement, namely, with the development of that new India which we have ourselves created. Our past work in India has been a splendid task, splendidly performed, but there is a still nobler one before us, and one larger even than that labour on the Irish problem to which our public men on both sides seem too much inclined to give their whole attention.

So careful an estimate of the work and spirit of the Congress movement cannot but commend itself to thoughtful minds.

However that may be, our duty lies clear before us to go on with our work firmly and fearlessly, but with moderation, and above all, with humility. If we might be permitted to adopt those noble words of Cardinal Newman, we may say:

Lead kindly light, amid the encircling gloom,
Lead thou me on!

The night is dark and I am far from home,
Lead thou me on.
Keep thou my feet, I do not ask to see
The distant path, one step's enough for me.[10]

After the address was over, the Congress took up for consideration. The various resolutions and adapted the following:

RESOLUTIONS ADOPTED BY THE CONGRESS

Council Reforms

Resolved that this Congress, having considered the draft Bill recently introduced into Parliament by Charles Bradlaugh, entitled 'An Act to amend the Indian Councils Act of 1861', approves the same as calculated to secure a substantial instalment of that reform, in the Administration of India, for which it has been agitating and humbly prays the Houses of Parliament of the United Kingdom of Great Britain and Ireland to pass the same into law; and further that its President, Pherozeshah Mehta is hereby empowered to draw up and sign, on behalf of this Assembly, a petition to the House of Commons to the forgoing effect, and to transmit the same to Charles Bradlaugh for presentation, thereto, in due course.

Ratification of Previous Resolutions

Resolved that this present Congress does hereby ratify and confirm the resolutions passed by previous Congress as to—

(a) to (h) the same as in Resolution III of the Congress of 1889.
(f) was made Resolution V of 1890 and (j) of 1889 took its place.
(j) is from Resolution V of 1889.
(k) was Resolution VI of 1889, very slightly modified in the preliminary words which ran: The expediency of so

modifying the rules made under Act XI of 1878 (the Arms Act) that all restrictions, etc.

House of Commons

Resolved that this Congress respectfully expresses the earnest hope that in the interest of the people of India, the House of Commons will forthwith restore the right, formerly possessed by Members of that House, of stating to Parliament any matter of grievance of the natives of India before the Speaker leaves the Chair for the presentation in Committee of the Indian Budget statement, and earnestly trusts that the House of Commons will, in future, take into consideration the Annual Indian Budget statement at such a date as will ensure its full and adequate discussion, and further authorises its President to sign a Petition, in the name and in behalf of this Congress, for presentation to the House of Commons, in accordance with the terms of this Resolution.

Excise Reforms

Resolved that, while recognising the action taken, in response to its previous prayers, in the matter of Excise Reform by H.M.'s Secretary of State for India and the Supreme Government here, and noting with pleasure the increase to the import duty on spirits, the taxation imposed on Indian-brewed malt liquors, the decision of the Bengal Government to abolish the outstill system, and the closing of over 7,000 liquor shops by the Madras Government in 1889-90, this Congress regrets that it is still necessary to urge the Government of India to insist on all Provincial Administrations carrying out, in their integrity, the policy in matters of Excise, enunciated in paras 103, 104, and 105 of the Despatch published in the Gazette of India of March 1st, 1890, especially as to subsection 4 of para 103, viz.

"That efforts should made to ascertain the existence of local public sentiment, and that a reasonable amount of deference should be paid to such opinion when ascertained."

Salt Tax

Resolved that the condition of the Finances of India having materially improved, and those special circumstances on which the Government relied to justify the recent enhancement of the Salt tax having practically ceased to exist, this Congress considers it essential that the enhancement referred to should be remitted at an early date, and empowers its President to submit a special memorial on the subject in its name and on its behalf to H.E. the Viceroy in Council.

Permanent Settlement

Resolved that having reference to the expectations created throughont the country by the Despatch of Her Majesty's Secretary of State in 1862, the principles of which were re-affirmed in a subsequent Despatch of 1865, promising the extension of a Permanent Settlement to all temporarily settled tracts in which certain conditions have long since been fulfilled, this Congress respectfully submits that the Government of India is now in honour bound to take up this question of Permanent Settlement, without further delay, with a view to practical action thereon such that fixity and permanency may be given to the Government Land Revenue demand, as explicitly promised by Her Majesty's Secretary of State more than quarter of a century ago.

Invitation to Government Officers

Resolved that this Congress, having observed with surprise a notice, apparently official, in various Calcutta newspapers which runs as follows:

The Congress

The Bengal Government having learnt that tickets of admission to the visitors' enclosure in the Congress pavilion have been sent to various Government officers residing in Calcutta, has issued a circular to all Secretaries, and heads of departments subordinate to it, pointing out that under the orders of the Government of India, the presence of Government officials, even as visitors at such meetings is not advisable, and that their taking part in the proceedings of any such meetings is absolutely prohibited."

And having also considered a letter addressed by the Private Secretary of the Lieutenant-Governor of Bengal to the Secretary of the Reception Committee, of which the following is an exact copy:

Belvedere,
26th December, 1890.

Dear Sir,—In returning herewith the seven cards of admission to the visitors' enclosure of the Congress pavilion which were kindly sent by you to my address yesterday afternoon. I am desired to say that the Lieutenant-Governor and the members of his household could not possibly avail themselves of these tickets, since the orders of the Government of India definitely prohibit the presence of Government officials at such meeting.

Yours faithfully
P.C. Lyon
Private Secretary

J. Ghosal, Esq.,
Secretary,
Congress Reception Committee.

authorises and instructs its president to draw the attention of H.E. the Viceroy to the declaration embodied in these papers that Government servants are prohibited from attending any meetings of this Congress even as spectators, and to enquire, most respectfully, whether the Lieutenant-Governor of Bengal has, or has not, correctly interpreted the orders of the Government of India.

Resolved that the best thanks of this Congress be tendered to Charles Bradlaugh, M.P., for the invaluable services rendered by him during the past year, as also to Sir W. Wedderburn,

W.S., Caine, J. Bright Maclearen, M.P., J. Ellis, M.P., George Yule, and Dadabhai Naoroji, for the unselfish zeal and ability with which they have presided over the British Agency of the Congress; further that they put on record an expression of their high appreciation of the manner in which Digby, C.I.E., Secretary of the Agency, and Surendranath Benerjea, R.N. Mudholkar, W.C. Bonnerjee, Eardly Norton, and A.O. Hume, delegates to England respectively, discharged the onerous duties imposed upon them, and of their gratitude to all those members of the British public who so kindly welcomed and so sympathetically gave audience, in over fifty public and a far larger number of private meetings, to one or more of these delegates.

Vote of Thanks

Resolved that a vote of thanks be recorded to Kumar Debendra Mullick and Brothers, Proprietors of the Tivoli Gardens, N.C. Bose and Bhupendranath Bose Proprietors of Mohan Bagan Villa, and to the Hon. Sir Romesh Chandra Mitra, T.N. Palit, Janaki Nath Roy, Gopi Mohan Roy, Harendra Nath Roy, Kissori Mohan Roy, Ramanath Ghose, and Jamadar Ghasiram, owners of houses kindly lent for the use of delegates.

Next Congress

Resolved that the Seventh Indian National Congress do assemble on the 26th December, 1891, at either Madras or Nagpur, as may be hereafter settled, in consultation between the Madras, Central Provinces and Berar Committees, and the Joint General Secretary.

Congress in England

Resolved that provisional arragements be made to hold a Congress, of not less than 100 delegates, in England, all things being convenient, in 1892, and that the several Standing Congress Committees be directed to report, at the coming Congress, the name of the delegates that it is proposed to depute from their respective circles.

British Committee I

Resolved that of the Funds now in the Joint General Secretary's hands and about to be received a further sum of twenty thousand rupees be added to the Permanent Fund and placed in fixed deposits, and that the rest of the funds accruing on account of this current year, 1890, be held by him available for the immediate purposes of the British Committee of the Indian National Congress, but to be replaced as the subscription for 1891 aie received, and, ultimately, also added to the permanent Fund.

British Committee II

Resolved that a sum of Rs. 40,000 exclusive of individual donations, is assigned for the expenses of the British Committee of the Congress and Rs. 6,000 for the General Secretary's Office and Establishment, and that the several circles and districts do contribute as arranged in Committee.

General Secretaries

Resolved that A.O. Hume and Pandit Ajoodhyanath a-e re-elected General and Joint General Secretaries for the ensuing year.

Representation in England

Resolved that this Congress does formally appoint George Yule, Pherozeshah Mehta, W.C. Bonnerjee, J. Adam, Man Mohan Ghose, A.O. Hume, Kali Charan Bannerji, Dadabhai Naoroji, D.A. Khare, and such other gentlemen as may volunteer for the duty with the sanction and approval of the Standing Congress Committees of their respective circles, to represent its views in England, and press upon the consideration of the British Public at the political reforms which the Congress has advocated.

WELCOME ADDRESS BY P.M. MEHTA

Brother Delegates, Ladies and Gentlemen,

I count it a piece of singular good fortune that I should stand before your here today to tender to you, my brother Delegates of the Twentieth Indian National Congress, the same cordial, sincere and earnest welcome, on behalf of the Reception Committee, which it was my pride and privilege to tender to you on this very Congress platform exactly this day fifteen years ago. It is a piece of still greater good fortune for which both you and I cannot but be equally thankful, that I am supported on this occasion as on the last by the presence amongst us of one than whom India had never a warmer, truer, more devoted, more self-sacrificing, more faithful and more constant friend—you see him on my right, Sir William Wedderburn—whose name is now a household word amongst us, cherished with tender respect and affection. A noble type of the high-minded and high-souled Englishman at his best, it is owing to the fact of the existence and activity of such Englishmen in the ranks of Anglo-Indians and Civilians that our hopes and our aspirations escape from despair, and our attachment and our loyalty to British rule are preserved and strengthened. It never rains but it pours, says the proverb, which in its ignorance of the scheme of providence attributes to it partiality and favouritism, and I am tempted to boast of another piece of good fortune at finding that my Chairmanship is, on this occasion, as on the last, destined to be illustrated by the presidency of another such Englishman as I have described, Anglo-Indian and Civilian, who has, not yesterday or today, but throughout a career rising from the lowest to the highest step of the ladder, uniformly and consistently realized that he best served the interests of his own country and the great Service to which he belonged, by strictly and faithfully adhering to a policy of true righteousness and sympathy. But that is another story which will be presently unfolded at due length, after I have tried, if not tired, your patience for some time longer I cannot however pass on without congratulating ourselves on the presence of a gentleman, one of the oldest and most respected Members of Parliament, who has for years, quietly and unostentatiously, but none the less nobly and earnestly, raised his voice in the interests of this country. I refer to Mr. Samuel Smith. But in the midst of these manifold congratulations, my vanity is checked by the reflection that after all, however man may propose, it is God who disposes. We looked forward at one time with enthusiastic anticipations to gaze on the kindly, radiant, and loving countenances of three, perhaps the oldest, patriarchs of the Congress. But the call of duty, which never call him in vain, has deprived us of the presence of Mr. Dadabhai Naoroji, and imperative considerations of health have deprived us of the opportunity of seeing once again the beloved and revered Founder of this body, Mr. Hume, and if I may so, his eldest son, Mr. W.C. Bonnerjee. But absent as they are, we will tell them that their names and deeds are and will for ever be cherished in our hearts with love, veneration and gratitude.[11]

And now, Gentlemen, I trust that you will not think that I unduly indulge in the inveterate habit of the people of this "Kingdom of Bombay" to consider ourselves superior to all the rest of the country when, in view of the active and passive opposition offered in past years in other parts to the measures for accommodating the Congress, I congratulate myself on the fact that the account given by Sir William Hunter in his book on 'Lord Reay's Administration,' as to the character of the relations between Europeans and Indians in this Presidency, has been amply borne out by the way in which we have been helped in securing the best sites available in Bombay for our manifold purposes. We have received kindly and generous assistance, from officials and non-officials alike, in a spirit of broad-minded liberality, justifying Sir William Hunter's observation, that "the competition of races, although as keen as in any other Provinces, is here tempered by common interests, mutual forbearance, and a certain reciprocal respect which impart a moderation to Bombay public opinion and to the Bombay Press in political crises." The Pioneer said the other day that we shall presently denounce the Government that so kindly lent us the Oval as wicked. Let me assure it that we in Bombay, however, use no violent language; and when we have to criticize Government, for even the Pioneer will not insist that it is beyond criticism, we will only call it erring and misguided.

But when I complacently congratulate ourselves on securing the best and healthiest sites for this year's Congress, I approach the question of this Pavilion and of the Encampment for your residence with some amount of nervousness. We have been told by some candid friends, or, if they will pardon me for saying so, by some critics who profess to be our friends only to be able to criticize us the more effectively, that we are only spasmodically wasting our energies, that this Congress gathering is only a show and a 'saturnalia of uncouth oratory,' and that we are wantonly and extravagently throwing away on an evanescent tamasha, monies which could be devoted more solid and useful purposes. Now this criticism strikes me, Gentlemen, as very much like the criticism applied by Revenue Officer to the impoverished ryot, when they try to explain away agrarian indebtedness by the extravagance of his expenditure on festiveland mourning occasions. As a matter of fact, the extravagance of the ordinary ryot on such occasions consists only in a few brass ornaments, a few sweetmeats, a few sweetmeats and an unlimited amount of tom-tom. So is it with us. Our Pavilion is not a Gothic temple with marble pillars and tesselated floors; it is a structure of unhewn posts and canvas, decorated with strips of cheap muslin of Congress colors to look gay. We have not housed you in palatial buildings; the canvas camp in which you are lodged has all, and more than all, the severity of military exigencies in a far campaign. To the amounts thus spent, our kind friends insist upon adding the travelling charges, as if all the Delegates would never have during Christmas stirred out of their houses to enjoy the Christmas holidays, even if they were not attending the Congress. But even taking the whole total thus added up. I venture, Gentlemen, to see boldly that all this and much more would be well spent for fulfilling the purpose for which the Congress has been organized, and for achieving the aim and end for which the Congress is constituted. To those who decry the monies spent upon it as monies wasted on a show and a tamasha, I would say that they are no more men of real insight and true imagination than those whom one of the greatest of English poets—Wordsworth—has described with such infinite pity for their incapacity to enter into the true inwardness of things:

> A primrose by the river brim,
> A yellow primrose is to him,
> And it is nothing more.

But if you realize it clearly and fully, there is no purpose more important, no mission more sacred, than the one that the Congress fulfils in the three short days to which it confines its session. It would be absurd to say that the Congress meets to deliberate and discuss and decide all the important subjects with which it deals. That task must be, and is, largely performed in the course of the years by such institutions as we may possess for forming Indian public opinion, in the common intercourse of social life, in local bodies more or less active, in the Native Press which is undoubtedly daily growing more and more capable and potent. At the end of the year, we all meet together, from different parts of the country, representatives of the people, not selected, it is true, by any authoritative or scientific process, but still representatives in all the various ways in which virtual representation works itself out in the early stages of its progressive development, representatives who are of the people and in immediate touch and cannot with them, representatives realizing in themselves the wants, the wishes, the sentiments, the aspirations of the people, representatives whose education has qualified them to ponder over gave questions of policy and principle in their application to the administration and Government of this country in all their complex relations of a foreign rule, representatives into whom education has instilled an earnest, devoted, and enlightened loyalty to the Bristish Crown and a keen solicitude for the safety and permanence of the British

Empire in which, they are firmly persuaded lie implanted the roots of the welfare, the prosperity and the good government of this country, I say, we Delegates, representative of the people, meet together at the end of the year to give voice to the public opinion of the country taking shape and formulating throughout the year, to present our Petition of Rights, our Grand Remonstrance, our appeal and our prayer for a firm and unfaltering grasp of a policy of wisdom and righteousness, for the reversal of retrograde measures inconsistent with such a policy, and for the adoption of means steadily ensuring the gradual development of free political progress,[12]

"Broadening slowly down from precedent to precedent."

Such an appeal and such a prayer can be most effectively offered at a great gathering like this by the unanimous voice of Delegates assembling from all parts of the country. If, gentlemen, we did nothing more than make this solemn petition and and this earnest prayer, we shall not have spent our monies in vain we shall not have laboured for nought.

But we are told that we have done this for long and we have done this in vain. I absolutely dispute both these propositions. Has this Congress really grown old and grey, and has it really effected nothing? I reply that the Congress has not yet attained its majority; I reply that the surest testimony to the value of its achievements direct and indirect, and the force of its influence, is to be found in the very policy of reaction and retrogression which it has from time to time provoked, the tide following each successive ebb of which policy takes us, you may be sure, further and further on the path of progress and emancipation. To estimate this position rightly, let me lay before you the confession of faith of a devout and irreclaimable Congressman like myself. I am an inveterate, I am a robust optimist, like my late friend Mahadeva Govind Ranade. I believe in divine guidance through human agency. It may be the fatalism of the East, but it is an active, not a passive fatalism, a fatalism which recognizes that the human wheels of the machinery must actively work to fulfil their appointed task. My humility saves me from the despair that seizes more impatient souls like those who have recently preached a gospel of despondency —I always seek hope and consolation in the words of the poet:

> "I have not made the world, and
> He that has made it will guide."

I derive patience from the same poet's teaching, "My faith is large in time, and that which shapes it to some perfect end."

My steadfast loyalty is founded upon this rock of hope and patience. Seeking the will of Providence, like Oliver Cromwell, in dispensations rather than revelations, seeing God's will like him in fulfilment of vents, I accept British rule, as Ranade did, as a dispensation so wonderful,—a little island set at one end of the world establishing itself in a far continent as different as different could be,—that it would be folly not to accept it as a declaration of God's will. But, as I have often said, when in the inscrutable dispensation of Providence this country was assigned to the care of England, the choice was offered to her as to Israel of old: Behold I have placed before you a blessing and a curse; a blessing if ye will obey the commandments of the Lord your God; a curse if ye will not obey the commandments of the Lord your God, but go after other gods who ye have not known.

The possession of India would be a blessing to England if administered in the spirit or righteousness; a curse if in the seductive spirit of worldliness. We cordially confess that in the main England has chosen wisely and well. The great and far seeing statesmen who presided at the consolidation of British rule in India proclaimed that the declared policy of the Crown in India should be one of righteousness, and they firmly and unequivocally announced it by the voice of the great and good Queen who then wore the Crown. But the acceptance and announcement of a policy of righteousness is one thing, its application another. The adhesion to such a policy is not determined in a day; it is not established without a long struggle between the forces of righteousness and those of worldliness like unto the struggle between Hormazd and Ahriman.

Even the chosen people of the Hebrew God continually relapsed, in spite of solemn covenants, into the worship of the gods of idolatry. Therefore it is that, while the oscillations and vicissitudes of the struggle go on, the hope expressed by the Viceroy in his reply to the address of the Bombay Corporation and echoed by Lord Ampthill before the Madras Corporation, that "there may be no two parties about England in India" is premature and practically futile. Such a hope is unreasonable and impracticable, while the pledges about equality of the Great Proclamation of 1858 are kept in the letter and broken in the spirit; while the distinctions of race, colour and creed abolished by our Magna Charta are re-introduced under the plausible guise of being distinctions based on the distinctive merits and qualifications inherent in race; while the burdens of Imperial Empire, which should be borne by the Empire including the Colonies, are disproportionately and heavily thrown on Indian finances; while attempt after attempt is made to pass on to the Indian Exchequer military expenditure supposed to be necessitated by the vulnerable position of India, but really designed to meet supposed Imperialistic exigences; while the Indian subjects of His Majesty are allowed to be deprived of their rights of equal citizenship, in the undisguised interests of the white races against the dark, in a way which responsible Ministers of the Crown had gravely declared furnished a just cause of war against the Boers; while the economic relations between the two countries are adjusted more in the interests of the predominant than of the impotent partner; while the development of the industries of the country is neglected or hampered for fear of competition with English industries; while the "consuming love" for India in the breasts of the rulers has more the colour and character of affection towards foster-child or a step-son than the equal and engrossing love for a natural son; while the results of a really bonafide and laborious Commission like the Public Service Commission, imperfect as they were, are attempted to be set aside and restricted by autocratic action, while the percentages of the admission of natives into the public service are estimated, not by the only true test of comparison with the promises made and rights established after public enquiry and deliberate action, but by the increases and decreases with those of years long previous to such pledges and promises, totally ignoring the recognition of subsequent years of "the just claims of the natives of the India to higher and more extensive employment in the public service" as stated in the Resolution of the Government of India appointing the Public Service Commission; while the people are being emasculated by the wholesale operation of the Arms Act to the future detriment of the interests of both England and India; while the small modicum of independence possessed by the Indian Universities is ruthlessly annihilated, and the Universities turned substantially into departments of Government, so that the breeding of the discontented B.A., "that distinct political danger," may be stopped or limited, and while—but it is not needful to go on any further.

We thus see that the hope of there being no two parties about England in India is not founded in the realities of the situation. It is another form of the same advice that has been also recently showered upon us by Viceroys and Lieutenant Governors, that there should be no political agitation in this country. I wish to speak with all respect for these disinterested advisers; but I cannot help comparing them to that delightful "Poor man's friend" Sir Joseph Bowley, so admirably depicted by Dickens: "Your only business, my good fellow, is with me. You needn't trouble yourself to think about anything. I will think for you; I know what is good for you; I am your perpetual parent. Such is the dispensation of an all wise Providence. What man can do I do, I do my duty as the Poor Man's Friend and Father; and I endeavour to educate his mind, by inculating on all occasions the one great lesson which that class requires, that is, entire Dependence on Myself. They have no business whatever with themselves."

This is a free but graphic paraphrase of what has been anxiously dinned into our ears recently from various quarters. I venture to say that to accept this advice would be equally demoralizing to the rulers and the ruled. It ignores all the laws of human progress, it ignores the workings of human nature it ignores environment and surroundings. We may be as well told to cease to breathe, to think or to feel. Political agitation there will always be. The only question is whether we should suppress and bottle up our feelings and hopes and aspirations and our grievances in the innermost recesses of our own hearts, in the secret conclaves of our own brethren or deal with them in the free light of open day. The former course would be preferred by the prophets of despair. We, gentlemen, prefer the latter because we have faith in the ultimate wisdom, beneficence, and righteousness of the English people. Curiously enough, gentlemen, this advice to cease political agitation found an echo, where one would have least expected it, in a corner of Bengal. To our astonishment, we were one day treated to a homily at a Provincial Conference in that Presidency on the thesis that subject races could have no politics! We were exhorted to abandon them in favour of industrial and scientific organizations. I trust, gentlemen, I will not be taken to undervalue the good work done in establishing the Association for the advancement of Industrial Science; it is already doing excellent work in conferring various industrial and technical scholarships of Rs. 100 and more.

But I may be allowed to say that when I read the report of the public meeting at which the Association was inaugurated, I could not help wondering whether our European friends who were actively supporting the movement were doing so with the hope of weaning our Bengali brethren from the bad habit to which they are supposed to be specially addicted of excessive political agitation, or whether our Bengali friends were endeavouring to coax their European friends to help them by specious professions of giving up their favourite vice and turning out reformed characters. I will abstain, however, from attributing motives as we are now perpetually advised to do by those who preach but never practise the virtue. It is needless to seriously controvert the thesis advanced by these Bengali friends, utterly unhistoric and unmanly as it is. If they will pardon me, I will only tell them how I regard them. The seem to me to be the Esaus of Bengal ready to sell their birthright for a mass of pottage. However fragrant and nourshing that pottage may be represented to be, we will not sell our birthright for it. But I am sure that there is no difficulty in retaining both the one and the other, the birthright as well as the pottage.

But, gentlemen, let us go back to the pendulum which we have left to oscillate between righteousness and wordliness for too long a time, and see how far the Congress has worked in propelling in the right direction. Never had the pendulum oscillated so violently as in Lord Lytton's time. The policy of righteousness was openly scouted. It was declared that having won India by breaking all the Ten Commandments, it was too late to govern it on the principles of the Sermom on the Mount. The country was thrown into a state of doubt and perplexity, of alarm and uneasiness. From this unfortunate position it was rescued by the advent of Lord Ripon. In him we got back the ture old English statesman, wise in his noble generosity and far sighted in his righteousness. Englishmen will never know the true value of Lord Ripon's services to British rule. He added buttresses of enduring strength to the citadel of our loyalty. It is to him we owe that in the darkest days of gloom and reaction we always confidently look forward to rays of light and hope. Except perhaps the great measure of local self Government and that of the Bengal Tenancy Act, which was intensely unpopular with the Zamindars of Bengal, he conferred no impossible boons or charters on us. He did not tell us, as the present Viceroy did, in his last Budget speech, that "I do not think that the salvation of India is to be sought in the field of politics at the present stage of her development and it is not my conception to earn a cheap applause by offering so-called boons for which the country is not ready and for which my successors and not I would have to pay the price."

Neither was it Lord Ripon's conception of statesmanship, nor did he confer any boons for which the country was not ripe. And still, to use the words of the self-same speech he heartily and genuinely sympathized with the real and progressive sympathy of true Liberalism, as Mr. Morley recently defined it in America, and not with the narrow prejudice of Conservative fear and mistrust of all progress and liberty, "with the aspirations of the Indians towards greater national unity and with their desire to play a part in the public life of the country." As these twofold sentiments are enunciated in the last Budget speech of Lord Curzon there is confusion, instead of correlation between them. Why is the salvation of India not to be sought, at least partially, on the field of politics at all times now and hereafter, if official sympathy with Indian aspirations and desire to play a part in the public life of the country is deep and genuine? How can these aspirations and desires be even gradually achieved, unless we are allowed to play at all times a modest and temperate part on the field of politics? And I venture to say that it is unfair and unjust to charge us with desiring to play any but a most modest and temperate part on the field of politics, and to warn us off altogether from it. How easily we are satisfied, when we are assured of sympathetic and righteous treatment by a frank and convinced acceptance of the principles of policy underlying the pledges and promises given to us, is shown by the fact that little as he actually did for us, Lord Ripon's name and fame are reverently and imperishably cherished in the hearts of the millions of this country.

The establishment of the Congress was almost synchronous with the departure of Lord Ripon from this country. Ever since then we have been endeavouring to formulate and place before Government measures upon which the country has come almost to an unanimous opinion as needed for the purpose of redressing grievances as well as promoting the legitimate welfare and progress of the people. It is a task which we undertook under a strong sense of duty. If, as the Viceroy eloquently said in his last Budget speech, "the country and its educated classes were making a steady advance on the path intellectual and moral progress," it would have been a grave dereliction of duty if they had not come forward on the field of politics, and, as I now repeat, what I repeated before, it they had not devoted their new culture and their energy to the task, not of supplanting their rulers, but of supplementing the endeavours of the best and most sagacious among them by proposing modifications and developments based on their peculiar, intuitive and native knowledge and information, and suggested in gratitude and loyalty by that enlightenment and education which we freely admit has been one of the most precious gifts bestowed upon us by British rule.

A wise and prudent statesman would so encourage us in performing this task by kindly sympathy and advice as to compel us, so to say, to perform with anxious care and moderation. To me it seems a grave political blunder to engender bitterness and excess by treating the Congress with dislike and resentment. It is for this reason that I deplore the attitude of our English friends towards the Congress. They have failed to understand the somewhat curious phenomenon, which they have recently observed, of some of our co-workers condemning the Congress for its disappointing inutility, and they have exultingly pointed out that this condemnation has proceeded from what has been considered the extreme wing of the Congress, and they have received these denunciations of us with cheers. But let our rulers try to realize that the men whom they cheer do not possibly desire to abandon altogether the field of politics, but may in time be carried away vainly to imagine that the failure of constitutional methods like those of the Congress was an argument to substitute others not so strictly temperate. However that may be, I repeat now, as before, that we of the Congress have always steadily and firmly conceived our mission to be imposed by duty, sanctified by patriotism and guided by loyalty unswayed by the resentment of our rulers or by the despairing counsels of the pessimists among ourselves. Therefore it is that our mission has been blest and our labours have not been in vain.[13]

I thus come back to relate the record of the achievements of the Congress. I can do so briefly, as it has been excellently summarized in the last number of "India," a paper whose valuable services to our cause, have, not, I am afraid, been so fully appreciated as they have deserved, showing how imperfect are we ourselves,—a good thing to remember, especially when we are engaged in criticizing others. Our earliest efforts were directed towards securing a platform from which we could authoritatively expound our views, and they bore fruit in 1892 in the passing of the Indian Councils Act for enlarging and expanding the Councils and substantially and practically introducing the principle of election in the appointment of their members. The voice of the Congress was potent in obtaining the Commission for enquiring into Indian expenditure. Our demand for Simultaneous Examinations for the Indian Civil Service was so far successful that Mr. Paul's motion in favour of it was accepted by the House of Commons. The strenuous opposition to reduce the motion into practice offered by the Indian Government has hitherto prevailed. We had however obtained the Public Service Commission whose recommendations, though not going far enough as we desired, and further throttled by the Government of India, still laid down principles, from which, alas, it is now attempted to retreat by autocratic action without any new public enquiry or deliberation. We have also urgently pressed upon the attention of Government, perhaps the most far-reaching and anxious problem of Indian administration, the economic broblem of the poverty of the people and its concomitant agrarian indebtedness; and though Government fight shy of the only true remedies, it is still a hopeful sign to see them labouring to discover less unpalatable solutions of the problem. Following upon the half-hearted trial of Agricultural Banks long suggested by us, we may still induce them to grant the enquiry so influentially recommended by the Indian Famine Union. Very early in our history, we proved so conclusively the essential desirability in the interests of sound and just administration of the separation of judicial and executive functions, that a statesmanlike Lord Dufferin felt constrained to admit it to be a counsel of perfection, and we have so far succeeded that now it is only on the score of expense that the change is obstensibly shelved, the real reason being the strong disinclination of District Officers to part with power once enjoyed, as if Revenue Officers did not possess power enough and to spare, with stringent Land Revenue Codes and the jealous exclusion of the jurisdiction of Civil Courts in revenue matters. One of the earliest subjects which engaged the attention of the Congress was the urgent need of a thorough reform and reorganization of the Police Force. The forecast of the Report of the Police Commission published in England has ultimately borne out the national view of the character of the force against the official view which continued to insist that the aspersions to which the police was popularly subject were largely unjust and undeserved.

In this connexion I may be permitted to say one word as to the bureaucratic policy now in vogue with regard to the Reports of and evidence were immediately issued to give time for public discussion and criticism before Government proceeded to deal with them. At St. Andrew's Dinner at Calcutta the other day, Sir Andrew Fraser indicated the new policy not only with regard to the Report of the Police Commission, but with regard also to other important subjects engaging the attention of Government, stating as an axiomatic truth that no statemen could be properly made in regard to them till the decision of the Secrtary of State for India was received. It seems to benighted non-officials like us that this course is an exaggeration of the demoralized attitude of a secret and irresponsible bureaucracy as Sir C. Dilke once called it. The Secretary of State in this way arrives at a decision under the inspiration of the Government of India without the benefit of open and public discussion and criticism. Indeed in such cases we are gravely told that it would be sacreligious to touch with profane hands the tablets sent down from Mount Sinai. The mischief thus done is so incalculable, that I would fain take the liberty to ask the bureaucrats of our Indian administration to ponder on the observations of one of the ablest and keenest of political thinkers—Mr. Walter Bagehot—"Not only" says he, "does a bureaucracy tend to under-government in point of quality; it tends to over-government in point of quantity.

The trained official hates the rude, untrained public. He thinks they are stupid, ignorant, reckless—that they cannot tel their own interest. A bureaucracy is sure to think that its duty is to argument official power, official business, or official members rather than leave free the energies of mankind; it over-does the quantity of Government as well as impairs its quality." These words were spoken of bureaucracy in civilized European countries. They apply with ten-fold force in this country with its Official Secrets' Act, which it is a mistake to suppose is inert while it does not explode in public prosecutions. The Act puts a premium on corruption, on the one hands, and, on the other, it surely and inevitably deteriorates and demoralizes irresponsible officials working in the dark. To resume our narrative of the achievements of the Congress. We were the first, in spite of spurious claims to the honor, to draw attention in view of the poverty of the agricultural masses to the need of technical and industrial education, and forced it in many practical ways on the attention of the people as well as Government. In this connexion, I trust that the scheme of an Institute of Research may not be allowed to fail on account of the death of Mr. Tata, a death the whole country deplores, but may soon become an accomplished fact, magnificent monument of the patriotism and munificence of its author. We have also pressed upon Government the great cause of Temperance. We advocated from the first reduction in the oppressive burden of the Salt tax, and the raising of the assessable minimum of the Income-tax, both which reforms have been recently carried out. I think I need not proceed further with my enumeration. It is an honorable record. It is a record which leaves no room for disappointment or despair. But further, as is again will pointed out in "India", what is particularly apt to be over-looked, is that "we are by no means sure but the greatest work of all is its negative work, where the results do not appear in any particular reform or political change." And I may well repeat here, to cheer our hearts and brace our energies, the beautiful lines quoted by Mr. Hume in his letter to us published in "India."

"For while the tired waves, vainly breaking,
Seemed here no painful inch to gain,
Far back, through creeks and inlets making,
Comes silent, flooding in, the main."

Laden with these gains, the Congress comes back to "its own native land." I well remember the day when we launched it anxiously, but hopefutly, 19 years ago. When it came back to us in 1889, a babe only five years old, it had already broadened and strengthened wonderfully. It again comes back to us fifteen years after, a handsome lad on the point of attaining his majority. It has not escaped some jealousy and rivalry. Other children whom we are assured were excessively pretty and handsome have been pressed upon us as specially deserving our love and affection. Well, Gentlemen, our hearts are large and our minds are broad, and what we have done is that we have incontinently adopted them all. One, you will see in this very pandal, a gentle and solemn little lady in a grave gathering assembling immediately after us. Another you will see, robust and vigorous, decorated with jewels and ornaments wrought in this very country, on the Oval yonder. But, Gentlemen, our affections remain unchanged from our eldest-born, and we refuse to deprive him of his rights of primogeniture.[14]

I think, Gentlemen, I have said enough to show that we have met here together from all parts of the country to pursue a noble mission, hallowed to us from a sense of duty, of patriotism, and of loyalty, all welded together by the principles of justice and righteousness which, after all is said and done, we gratefully recognize as the dominant principles of English rule in this country. We truly and earnestly respond to the words in which Lord Curzon adjured us the other day on his landing—"I pray, I pray the Native Community in India, to believe in the good faith, in the high honour, and in the upright purpose of my countrymen. Gentlemen, it is because we do sincerely believe in that good faith, in that high honour and that upright purpose, that we meet here in the open light of day to appeal to their noble and righteous impulses, by all lawful and constitutional means, so to discharge the sacred trust reposed in them by Providence, that it may redound to the glory and greatness of both countries. But I must be pardoned for saying, that when the respond to this prayer, we do not respond to it in the slavish spirit in which the great Earl of Strafford exhorted the people of England to obey the King; "Let them attend upon his will with confidence in his justice, belief in his wisdom, and assurance in his parental affections." We respond to it rather in the spirit of an ideal sketched—I will take an extremely modern instance—by a highly placed Anglo-Indian Civil Servant whom,—though you will be perhaps surprised to hear it—I venture to describe as a Congresswala in disguise, as eloquent and as far-reaching as some of our own elders, say, Surendranath Bannerjea or Lalmohun Ghose. I refer to Sir William Lee-Warner. At an Address delivered by him at the Elphistone College Union, Sir William Lee-Warner eloquently depicted the ideals towards which British rule in India was tending:

> "It is no narrow principle of a paternal Government or a rule for the benefit of the ruler which sent for the Roman with this poet's sailing orders.
>
> '*Tu regere imperio populos Romane memento,*' or which fostered differences as aiding the central authority, *Divide et impera*. Its aim is less to govern than to call forth the progressive capacity and to teach self-government. It desires to lift up the lower ranks of society and the subject to the pedestal of the ruler. 'Humanity, and 'Heaven's light our guide,' are its watch words, and they are embodied in your *Magna Charta*, the Queen's Proclamation, issued by the ruler whose authority had just been defied and restored by the sword. There are three supreme ideas of mankind, the family, the nation and humanity. The Hindu and the Greek ruler thought of the first, the Roman Empire of the second; but the British nation accepts the last and highest as its ruling idea. I venture to point out to you that from God's nature the British nation has learnt the grand idea of humanity, and that the legislation and

administration of India under the Queen bears testimony to Her Majety's desire to recognize a progressive future as before all those committed to her care. The protection of the weak, equality in the eye of the law, justice, and a common participation in the benefits, and when the time comes, in the task of good government are at least the aims which the British Government sets before it."

It is in the active spirit of this ideal that we respond, and respond, cordially, to Lord Curzon's prayer to believe in the good faith, in the high honour, and in the upright purpose of his countrymen. May we pray in return that when we ask to be allowed to cooperate in this noble task, that Lord Curzon and his countrymen will believe that we too of the Congress are inspired by duty, patriotism and loyalty.

I again tender to you my warmest welcome—a welcome mixed of gratitude for the past and high hope for the future, with patience and Perseverance for our motto. Let us take to our hearts the homely but noble words of Longfellow:

> "Let us then be up and doing,
> With a heart for any fate,
> Still achieving, still parsuing,
> Learn to labour and to wait."[15]

References

1. He was one of the prominent founders of the Indian National Congress.
2. Welcome address by Pherozeshah Mehta at the session of the Congress held in Bombay in 1889.
3. *Ibid.*
4. Presidential address by Pherozeshah Mehta at the session of the Congress held in Calcutta in 1890.
5. *Ibid.*
6. *Ibid.*
7. *Ibid.*

8. *Ibid.*
9. *Ibid.*
10. *Ibid.*
11. Welcome address by Pherozeshah Mehta at the Congress session held in Bombay in 1904.
12. *Ibid.*
13. *Ibid.*
14. *Ibid.*
15. *Ibid.*

4

Indian Nationalism

As a Member of the Local Municipal Corporation, Member, Bombay Legislative Council and Member, the Imperial Council, Pherozeshah Mehta's contribution is unique in the annals of our history. Time and again, he took up issues in the local Municipal Corporation which had deep linkage with the developmental activities of the city as well as population. As its Chairman also he saw to it that socio-economic measures received priority. Thus he gained much prominence on account of his sincerity for social measures and deep understanding of thr needs of a large section of the Presidency town.

As a Member of the Bombay Legislative Council, his contribution in socio-economic, cultural, educational and political problems facing the Presidency of Bombay was consistent and remarkable having deep linkage with his 'meaningful' uratory and cogent arguments. Very it made the bureaucracy realise about the efficacy of several measures so far neglected by it. He always sought the support of his Indian colleagues who felt much impressed with his high degree of knowledge which made his arguments strong and convincing. He took up the case of lease-holders, establishment of a Court of Wards in Bombay Presidency, Civil and Criminal judicature in Sind, Bombay Tramways Act, Budgets of the Presidency, slaughter of animals, reform in medical profession and several other problems.

In the Imperial Council he contributed much in terms of his fruitful participation in varied issues. His independence and boldness on several problems were remarkable and who-soever happened to argue with them he was given a proper reply. The officials showed respect for his arguments which contained comprehensive knowledge. 'The officials complain-ed that he had introduced a "new spirit" into the Council, but Sir Pherozeshah proved more than a match for them all. As was said of him at the time, he argument for argu-ment, invective for invective, banter for banter, ridicule for ridicule. The people of Calcutta in a public meeting assembled presented him with an address enlogising his manly attitude in the Council. The people of Bombay did the same, and the reply he gave to their address, was a masterpiece of argument, eloquence and satire, Sir Pherozeshah sat on the Imperial Legislative Council for three years but never again stood as a candidate, his object evidently being that of making way for younger men.'

IN THE IMPERIAL COUNCIL, 1894-1895.

The election took place in October, 1893. According to the rules framed under the Indian Councils Act, the non-official members of the Provincial Legislative Council had the right of sending one representative to the Viceregal Council, and their choice unanimously fell on Pherozeshah. The *Gujarati* in commenting on the appointment expressed the general feeling in terms which were by no means exaggerated:

> "The election of the Honourable Mr. P.M. Mehta to the Supreme Legislative Council by the unanimous voice of the elected members of the Provincial Council, was of course a foregone conclusion. A gentleman whom an indigenous Government would have delighted to honour by inviting him to the State Council, whom even the most enlightened constituency would have chosen as its representative to voice its grievances and requirements, and who in a free country like

France or England would have deservedly occupied the foremost position in the State has for some reason or other remained outside the Viceregal Council. . . . . The whole country from one end to the other, will receive the news of the elevation of the Honourable Mr. Mehta with the sincerest feelings of satisfaction, and we only pray that he will be spared long to continue the useful and disinterested work which his patriotic impulses have led him to undertake."

The Times of India, not always a friendly critic, wrote:

"Mr. Pherozeshah Mehta's nomination to a Companionship will be approved of by all except the Intransigeants amongst native politicians, who, being certain themselves never either to deserve or obtain distinction of any kind, pretend to think lightly of dignities and titles. Mr. Mehta has of late shown an increasing independence of the reckless rhetoricians who pretend to serve their country by embarrassing and abusing the men who are governing it, and we may be sure always will be an outspoken as well as an able critic of Government, both here and in the Supreme Council. But there is a criticism which is helpful alike to the governors and the governed. We look to him to do his part in supplying it, and it is for that reason that we are glad to see that he has been singled out for the modest distinction that the Honours List bestowed upon him yesterday."

In December 1894, the Cotton Duties Bill was presented in the Imperial Council for discussion. He put forward fairly comprehensive views and opined that Lancashire was allowed to plunder India when the Cotton Duties were abolished in 1879. He further started that an excise duty of 5% was imposed on all cotton yars. When the report of the Select Committee on the Bill was presented by the Finance Member, Fazulbhoy Visram moved an amendment in order to raise the excise limit. Mehta supported this amendment and stated.

"That principle and that policy are that the infant industries of India should be strangled in their birth if there is the remotest suspicion of their competing with English manufactures. . . . . . I protest against such a policy not only in its present immediate operation, but as establishing a most pernicious precedent."

Ultimately, the amendment was defeated by eleven votes to nine, and "for the first time in the history of British rule in India, a measure was placed upon the statute book which no one has ever dreamed of defending as being promoted in the interests of the country affected by it."

In the next session of the Council held in January, 1895, one of the first items of business was an amendment of the Deccan Agriculturists' Relief Act. It was in 1879, that the first Act dealing with certain incidents of agricultural distress and discontent was passed after an agitation which lasted for some years. The Indian Press and Indian publicists had continually called the attention of Government to the rigidity of the land revenue system, which, coupled with the ryot's ignorance and illiteracy, had reduced him to a condition of wretched poverty.

In fact several Commissions had been appointed since its enactment and each suggested its own changes in the law. Now Lee-Warner, while moving the Bill to a Select Committee, gave his reasons for not undertaking a larger measure for affording relief to the agriculturists thoughout the country as were recommended by the earlier Commission appointed by the government in 1891. At this point of time, Pherozeshah Mehta put forward his severe criticism against the limited scope of the Bill before the Council. He opined that:

"The 'soukar' is not the head and front of the offence. The Commission of 1891 has pointed out that the rigidity and inelasticity of the revenue system have much to answer for. Though it is open to revenue officers to grant remissions and suspensions, and though the Government of Lord Ripon advised a policy of well-judged moderation in this respect, in practice the rigidity and inelasticity are not slackened. As the executive will not thus move, is it not necessary that there should be some provisions in the Act by which, just as there are special courts to adjudicate equitably between the ryot and the usurious 'soukar,' there should be special courts to do the same between the ryot and the rigid state-landlord?"

As expected from the government side, Sir Antony Macdonell replied that measures were under contemplation for the equitable adjustment of the relations between the government and the ryot. In fact the government was receiving about twenty million sterling a year under the prevalent land system and it therefore showed no inclination to agree to any kind of change in it.

Another Bills presented in the Council dealt with the Cantonments Act of 1889, the amendment of the Police Act of 1861. Mehta's contribution in these two Bills was fairly unique. Under the latter Act, the Local Government had the power to quarter a punitive police force in any district, declared as dangerous or disturbed. The amending Bill sought to enable the authorities to recover the cost in certain cases from the turbulent section of the society only and not all the inhabitants of the area.

Inside the Council, the strongest critics were the Maharaja of Durbhunga and Pherozeshah, who, notwithstanding the plausibilities of the mover of the Bill, Sir Antony MacDonnell, had no difficulty in showing up the true character of the innocent-looking measure. Under cloak of redressing a wrong, it was in fact an attempt to invest magistrates with extraordinary powers in supersession of the ordinary Courts of law. They were to have a free hand in singling out individuals for punishment. The guilty and the innocent were equally at the mercy of the executive. Those who lived in the disturbed area were just as much liable to punishment as absentee land-lords, who might be hundreds of miles away. The measure was in fact nothing else than an attempt, as Pherozeshah characterized it, to convict and punish individuals without a judicial trial, under cover of executive measures for the preservation of order. This was an opinion which was not confined to noisy agitators, but, unfortunately for Government, was shared by some of its own officers. The language employed by Pherozeshah, and which raised a little breeze in the Council Hall, creating an atmospheric disturbance which was felt far and wide, was, therefore, none too strong. Said he:

> "My Lord, I cannot conceive of legislation more empirical, more retrograde, more open to abuse, or more demoralizing. It is impossible not to see that it is a piece of that empirical legislation so dear to the hart of executive officers, which will not and cannot recognize the scientific fact that the punishment and suppression of crime without injuring or oppressing innocence, must be controlled by judicial procedure, and cannot be safely left to be adjudged upon the opinions and moral certainties of men believing themselves to be capable, honest and conscientious. . . . . Empirical and retrograde as it is, this new proposed legislation would be no less demoralizing to the executive officers concerned. I have not the least desire to speak disparagingly of executive officers, most of whom, I have no doubt, are anxious to perform their duties conscientiously and to the best of their ability. But it would be idle to believe that they can be free from the biasses, prejudices and defects of their class and position."

His petulant outburst, the echoes of which were heard for a long time to come, may well be as follows:

> "As the first member of Your Excellency's Executive Council who has an opportunity of speaking after the extra-ordinary observations which have fallen from the Honourable Mr. Mehta, I desire to enter a protest against the new spirit which he has introduced into this Council. I have never heard the conduct of the administrative officers of the Government, as a whole, mentioned here without admiration of the qualities they bring to the execution of their duty, and their anxious endeavour to do their work with even-

handed justice. To-day for the first time wlthin the walls which have been distinguished by the presence, through half a century and more, of the most eminent of the executive officers of Government, who have contributed to the framing and the consolidation of the Indian Empire, I hear them all arraigned as a class as biassed, pre judiced, utterly incapable of doing the commonest justice, and unworthy of being relied on to do the duties which this legislature imposes upon them. From Your Excellency downwards, every executive officer falls under the ban of the Honourable Member's denunciations, and I for one protest against any Honourable Member so far forgetting the responsibility he owes to his position as to take advantage of it to impugn, by one general all-comprehensive accusation, not only the capacity but even the honesty and fairness of the members of a most distinguished Service—a Service of which it is my pride to have been a member. Their reputation is too well established and too widely recognized to suffer from the calumnies directed against them. The Indian Empire itself is the witness to the capacity they show in the administration of their duties; it would not last for one year if there were any truth in the accusations now made. I feel sure I can claim the concurrence of every member of Your Excellency's Council, in utterly dissociating myself from the remarks which have been made, and which I conceive to very greatly detract from the reputation which this Council has justly acquired for the dignity, the calmness and the consideration which characterize its deliberations".

He also gave vent to his feelings on the question of the restitution of conjugal rights in the Hindu community. When the Bill was discussed on 28 February 1895, Pherozeshah Mehta moved for the insertion of the clause to the effect whereby the Courts were empowered to order in fit cases that a decree for restitution should not be enforced by imprisonment. It is thus evident that with his concrete legal argument he '......... disclaimed all desire to middle with so peculiar and complex a system of social life and religion as Hinduism, as he held that whatever reforms might be desirable and necessary should be left to be developed by the action of time and education.

What he sought to do was to remove an excerscence which had been engrafted upon Hinduism by an extraneous jurisprudence, and he maintained he was representing the best Hindu opinion on the matter, the opinion which might, for instance, have been put forward by men like the late Mr. Justice Telang. He did not agree with those who believed that "the distinguishing features of the Hindu social system as regards the relations of the sexes were distrust and depression of women." The Council, however, was influenced by the strength of conservative feeling manifested in and out of it against the change, and though Sir Alexander Miller and some other official members appeared to be in sympathy with the spirit of the amendment, the only member to support it, besides the mover, was Mr. Chitnavis, and Pherozeshah found that he was really not voicing, as he claimed, the conservative and orthodox view of the matter.

He also lavied a trechant attack against the alarming growth of expenditure in India. In support of his argument he argued thus :

> "If you could reduce your military expenditure to reasonable proportions, if you could steady your forward policy so as not to lead to incessant costly expeditions, if you could get your inflated Army Home Estimates moderated, if you could devise ways by which the huge burdens of salaries and pensions could be lightened, then it is not chimerical to imagine that you could improve your judicial machinery, strengthen your police, develop a sounder system of education, cover the country with useful public works and railways, undertake larger sanitary measures, cheapen the post and telegraph, and still be in a position to relieve small incomes, to press less heavily on the land, to give the cultivators breathing time and to reduce the salt-tax."

BOMBAY MUNICIPAL CORPORATION
NATIVE GENTLEMEN AS CHAIRMEN

At the Meeting of the Bombay Municipal Corporation held on 4th September 1875, Col. H.F. Hancock proposed Mr. Dossabhoy Framjee as the Chairman of the Corporation. In doing so he said that looking to the approaching visit of H.R.H. the Prince of Wales and to the then peaceable state of party politics, it would be a peculiarly opportune occasion on which to propose a native gentleman on the Chair. Mr.Arbuthnot seconded the Proposition. Mr. J.M. Maclean, while admitting the merits of Mr. Dossabhoy, protested against his election on the ground that the time had not yet come when any gentleman could preside with advantage over such an assembly as that Corporation. A native, he argued, could not separate himself, as a European would do, from the parties into which the native members of the Corporation were broken up and therefore could not perform the duties of chairman with the vigour and impartiality that would be displayed by a European. Mr. Pherozeshah Mehta thereupon spoke as follows.

In the same impersonal spirit in which Mr. Maclean has deemed it proper to enter his protest against the appointment of a native gentleman to the Chairmanship of this Corporation, as a matter of principle, I may be allowed, Sir, also to enter a protest against the protest on the very same ground. I do trust, Sir, that in this Corporation we shall firmly lay hold of and never depart from the policy of looking straight at what is just and proper and best for the interests of that body, discarding all distinctions of caste, of colour and of creed. And in doing so we shall be only following, in our small sphere, the principle of the whole imperial policy of the British Government of India, so wisely as well as so nobly stuck fast to by the most enlightened and farsighted Anglo-Indian statesmen, in spite of resistence and temptation to the contrary. European gentlemen, Sir, from the fact of the position they occupy in this country, will always generally enjoy a leading status in the administration of Indian affairs, local as well as imperial, and native gentlemen will always be happy to yield to them that precedence to which they may be entitled by their rank, their intelligence, their education and their civilisation. And they have shown this disposition in the matter of the Chairmanship of this very Corporation. The leading community had precedence as was but just and proper; the Chairmanship of the first Corporation was yielded with unanimity and alacrity to an English gentleman. And I think, Sir, it is a graceful act on the part of the English gentlemen of this body, gracefully performed at the hands of the distinguished gentlemen bringing forward this Proposition, to nominate a native gentleman to the Chairmanship on this the first occasion of the kind. Under these circumstances, it cannot be said for a single moment that the appointment of a native Chairman reduces the European Community to a subordinate position—no such significance can possibly be attached to it. We are bound, as members of this Corporation, to see only to merit and qualifications in making our appointments, and when we find them combined in European gentlemen, we are but only too ready and anxious to recognise them, and I doubt not but that when such are found centered in a native gentleman, Englishmen will never fall behind in recognising them freely, generously and ungrudgingly.

The Proposition for the election of Mr. Dossabhoy was ultimately carried by a large majority.

BOMBAY MUNICIPAL CORPORATION

MR. PHEROZESHAH'S CHAIRMANSHIP, 1884-1885

At the Meeting of the Bombay Municipal Corporation held on 7th April 1884, the Hon. Rao Saheb V.N. Mandlik proposed that Mr. Pherozeshah Mehta be elected Chairman of that body for 1884-85. The Proposition was seconded by Sir Frank Souter and supported by Mr. Dossabhoy Framjee and Mr. R.N. Khote, the retiring Chairman, and carried unanimously. Mr. Pherozeshah after taking his seat amidst the applause of the members, said:

Gentlemen,—I thank you for the great and distinguished honour you have done me by appointing me your Chairman for the ensuing year. I have always been one of those who have been firmly pursuaded that a citizen of this no mean city could not more usefully or more honourably employ such opportunities as he may possess for public life than in taking an active and an intelligent interest in its civic administration as at present constitutionally organised. I have seen something and read something of the way in which municipal affairs are managed in other places, and it has been a subject of no little wonder to me, as it has been a source of legitimate pride, to observe how favourably the mode in which we have been conducting our municipal work compares with that of other countries more advanced and civilised than ours. You can easily conceive, gentlemen, that holding such views, how highly I value the honour you have been pleased to confer upon me and how gratefully I appreciate it! While thus sensible of the distinction, I am not unmindful of the grave responsibilities that attach to this post. But this is not the time to speculate how I may acquit myself of the duties I have undertaken. I am unaffectedly conscious of my shortcomings in that behalf. One thing only I would like to say, and that is that I will not fail in earnest endeavours to maintain the high reputation which this Corporation has acquired under the distinguished gentlemen who have preceded me in this Chair and that I will conscientiously try to conduct my Chairmanship with all fairness and courtesy.

BOMBAY MUNICIPAL CORPORATION

MR. PHEROZESHAH'S CHAIRMANSHIP, 1885-1886

At the Meeting of the Bombay Municipal Corporation held on 9th April 1885, Sir Frank Souter proposed that Mr. Pherozeshah Mehta be re-elected Chairman of that body for 1885-86 and Sir Jamsetjee Jejeebhoy, Bart. (3rd) and others seconded and supported Mr. Pherozeshah's nomination. Mr. Pherozeshah, after being re-elected said:

Gentlemen,—It is always a high honour to be chosen to preside over the deliberations of so great a Corporation as that of this City, and I am therefore not only deeply thankful to you for conferring this distinction upon me a second time, but also beeause it indicates that, in your opinion, I have not altogether failed to discharge the responsible duties of the Chair during the last eventful year and that I have done my duty, in some small measure, to your satisfaction. I am perfectly conscious of the kindly expressions—however little I deserve them—used by several of my friends in speaking on this subject, but I thank them, all the same, for their approval and confidence. It is hardly necessary for me to add that whatever success may have attended my efforts in this respect, has been chiefly owing to the cordial and cheerful co-operation and help which I have always received in the discharge of my duties from the Commissioner, the Clerk and from the members of the Corporation. While renewing my thanks for the great honour conferred upon me, need I say that I expect at your hands, once again, that support and that encouragement which you extended to this Chair during the past year, and with your assistance and co-operation, I hope to make the second term of my Chairmanship as inspiring of your confidence and as successful as the first.

At the Meeting of the Bombay Municipal Corporation held on 5th April 1886, the Hon. Mr. K.T. Telang moved a vote of thanks to the retiring Chairman, Mr. Pherozeshah Mehta, whose thorough knowledge of Municipal affairs "had proved of the greatest utility to the Corporation and to the City of Bombay." The Resolution was carried unanimously after being seconded and supported by Col. Merewether and Mr. Bomanjee P. Master, respectively. Mr. Pherozeshah in acknowledging the vote, spoke as follows.

I have to tender to you, gentlemen, my warmest thanks for the very kind manner in which you have received the Proposition moved by my friend Mr. Telang and seconded by Col.

Merewether. I will not conceal that it is a source of some pride and gratification to me that the efforts which I made to discharge the duties of the high trust reposed in me, do not appear to be entirely undeserving of your approbation. I am also much obliged to the members of the Corporation for the very cheerful and ready co-operation which they have given me in all matters appertaining to the management of the business of the Municipality and which alone has enabled me to perform my duties as satisfactorily as you think I have done. Moreover, the co-operation of the Municipal Commissioner has greatly assisted me in executing my responsibilities in a manner that has met with your approval; and I must add that it was owing to the Clerk of the Corporation that the business could be placed before us in a clear and methodical way. I have, therefore, to express to you, one and all, my deep thanks for the kindly assistance I have received from all quarters for the last two years that I occupied the presidential Chair, and during that period of time, I am proud to have heard from you with no small grantification that I acquitted myself with honour, with justice and with dignity.

BOMBAY MUNICIPAL CORPORATION

DEATH OF MR. NOWROZJEE FARDOONJEE

The Bombay Corporation adjourned on 24th September 1885, without transacting any business, as a mark of respect to the memory of Mr. Nowrozjee Fardoonjee, deceased, about whom a highly appreciative Resolution was recorded. At the outset, Mr. Pherozeshah Mehta, the Chairman, spoke as follows.

Gentlemen,—Since we last met, one of the oldest and most esteemed and valued of our colleagues has passed away from our midst; and in deference to the universal wish expressed to me—a wish with which I need not say, I heartily sympathise—I propose to adjourn this meeting without transacting any business, as a mark of respect to the memory of the late Mr. Nowrozjee Fardoonjee. I do not think there is a single member of this Corporation who remembers anything about the administration of municipal affairs in Bombay without the name of Nowrozjee Fardoonjee being associated and prominently associated with the transaction of municipal business. During that long connection with the municipality of this city, his untiring devotion, his unflinching integrity of purpose, and his uncompromising independence of character were unsurpassed. Gentlemen, I think that we shall all agree in this, that if any one individual could be said to have contributed to the success of our municipal institutions, it was the gentleman who will be no more amongst us and whose death is a distinct loss not only to this Corporation but to the whole city. Although municipal and other institutions do not depend upon individual immortality, I think the universal opinion is that the loss we have suffered in the death of Mr. Nowrozjee is a loss which will not be easily replaced. I now call upon the Hon. Rao Saheb Mandlik to move the Resolution marking our sense of the loss we have sustained by the death of Mr. Nowrozjee Fardoonjee.

The Resolution was carried unanimously and the Corporation adjourned.

BOMBAY MUNICIPAL CORPORATION

THE BOMBAY MUNICIPAL SERVANTS BILL

At it was expedient to make better provision in the City of Bombay and elsewhere, for the enforcement of regulations regarding certain classes of municipal servants whose functions intimately concerned the public health or safety, and regarding the duties, withdrawal from duty, and leave of such servants, the Bombay Government desired to introduce into the Legislative Council "The Bombay Municipal Servants Bill" (Bill No. 1 of 1890). The Bombay Municipal Corporation having received on 25th March 1890 a copy of this Act from Government for the favour of an expression of its opinion, the former appointed a Committee of six members, including Mr. Pherozeshah Mehta, to report on its provisions. The Committee in their report expressed their approval of the object and scope of the Bill and in doing so submitted a few alterations and suggestions. Mr. Pherozeshah Mehta, who disagreed with his colleagues, in a minute of dissent, wrote as follows.

1. I desire to record briefly the reasons for which I am unable to concur in the above report.

2. It is stated in the "Statement of Objects and Reasons" that "The primary object of the present Bill is not so much to introduce any new obligations, as to provide by legislation the penalty hitherto imposed under Municipal by-laws." and again, "It appears to be necessary to provide by legislation the protection which the repeal of the by-laws has withdrawn." This is scarcely correct. The defunct Municipal by-laws provided only for forfeiture of wages and a fine, a provision perfectly consistent with the general law of contract. The present Bill makes resignation, withdrawal or absence from, or neglect or breach of, duty a criminal offence punishable by imprisonment, which may extend to three months. This can scarcely be called a resuscitation of the old by-laws.

3. The provisions of the Bill go far beyond their ostensible object, as generally understood, viz., to provide against strikes. Against individual acts, the liability to forfeiture of wages would be an ample safeguard for all practical purposes; criminal punishment, if at all, should be reserved for combinations. The penal clauses of the Bill extend to the former as well as to the latter, and in so far goes far beyond the object to be achieved.

4. The Bill is also excessive in another respect. It includes within its penal operation "any wilful breach or neglect of any provision of law or of any rule or order, which, as such Municipal officer, etc., it is his duty to observe or obey." Such a provision places the most tyrannical power in the hands of Muccadams, Inspectors, and such other officers, who are not likely to exercise it in the discreetest manner. On the contrary, it will place in their hands an instrument of extortion and tyranny, which they are likly to use constantly.

5. The Bill hardly treats the Municipal servants within its operation as human beings. Under Section 3, Clause A, a Municipal servant who absents himself without permission is liable to all the penalities, except in case of illness or accident disqualifying him for the discharge of such duties. He is not excused even if, for example, the death or illness of a father, mother, child, etc., may have indispensably occasioned his absence.

6. Among the details of the Bill it is not observed that the length of notice required—two months—is calculated to entail very serious hardship. A man may lose all opportunity of bettering his prospects, if he could not leave till after two months. It must be borne in mind th.it the Bill applies not only to *mahars* and *halaiacores*, but to a variety of other people.

7. There is a recommendation made in the first report to include servants of contractors in the operation of the Act. I cannot imagine a recommendation more thoughtlessly or recklessly made. It has not occurred to the Committee that such a provision would be an engine of terrible oppression in the hands of contractors, who are not always the most honest and scrupulous of men.

8. I have also the strongest objection to such power being given to Government as is provided in Section 5. I am quite prepared to trust to the members of Government as gentlemen of honour and culture, but I am not prepared to regard them as always unerring and unprejudiced, and above the frailties which are the lot of even the best of men.

9. The Bill is a piece of that plausible repressive legislation, which experience has shown to be not only of doubtful efficacy with regard to the purpose for which it is directly designed, but is fruitful of indirect consequences entailing mischief in unexpected directions. It may or may not succeed in repressing strikes for which it is directly designed. But it is sure to become an instrument of constant and daily use in the hands

of the lower class of officers such as Muccadams and others of extortion and oppression, and in the end is likely to incite the goaded men to the very strikes, which are sought to be repressed, only that they would be of a more serious and aggravated character. In asking for such a Bill, only the fact of the late strikes is borne in mind. The lessons taught by the circumstances and causes which led to them are entirely thrust out of sight. There were two facts elicited by the Committee from the Health Officer, which the Report does not at all consider or take into account. One was that the first of the two recent strikes was owing to the extortion and oppression practised upon the men by the Muccadams; and the other, that the second strike was a factitious one instigated by the Muccudams to prevent an investigation and exposure of their misdeeds. I have shown above that the Bill goes for beyond the object in view. Its provisions will not succeed in accomplishing that object; on the contrary, they are calculated to defeat it, besides entailing other mischievous consequences. If legislation is thought to be indispensable for the object in view, the utmost extent to which it should go is to render combinations and the abetment and instigation thereof unlawful and liable to punishment.

17th July 1890. Pherozeshah M. Mehta.

BOMBAY MUNICIPAL CORPORATION

LORD CURZON'S SERVICES TO INDIA

At the Meeting of the Bombay Corporation held on 10th September 1900, the Hon'ble Sir Pherozeshah moved that an Address of Welcome be presented to Lord Curzon on his visit Bombay next cold weather. He said:

Mr. President,—I think I am at perfect accord with the public opinion when I ask the Corporation, as the representatives of the City of Bombay, to present an Address of Welcome to His Excellency the Viceroy on his visit to Bombay in November next. I am not going to speak at length as to what an Address should contain. The members will remember that in the one which we presented to His Excellency when he first came to these shores, we took the opportunity of acknowledging his great ability and experience, and of thanking him for the assurances of sympathy to which he had given expression before coming to this country. Since then one year and a half has passed away and I venture to submit that the public voice is unanimous that he has nobly redeemed the pledges he had then given. I will not go into the long series of reforms which His Excellency has inaugurated since he has been at the helm of the state. It is sufficient for me to say that in everything he has done. he has been guided by the noblest instincts of a statesman and has always recognised the fact that the people of India ought to be governed in a spirit of sympathy and consideration and with a steadfast regard for the feelings and sentiments of the various communities that inhabit this vast country. His Excellency has also shown that he has determined that justice should be the rule when dealing between all the classes of Her Majesty's subjects in India. Moreover, we all know the energy he has displayed in connection with the present famine which has devastated great portions of this country and particularly the Bombay Presidency. We also recognise with great pleasure and gratitude, the artistic interest he takes in the concerns of this historic land, among which I may mention the old public monuments and buildings which have engaged his especial attention. All these things have excited the respect, esteem and admiration of the people of all classes and creeds. I therefore think it is our duty, as the representatives of the city, to present His Excellency with an Address of thankfulness and gratitude for the way in which he has discharged the high and onerous duties entrusted to him with great tact, ability and sympathy.

BOMBAY MUNICIPAL CORPORATION

SIR PHEROZESHAH'S PRESIDENTSHIP, 1905-1906

At the Meeting of the Bombay Municipal Corporation held

on 7th April 1905, Sir Bhalchandra Krishna proposed that the Hon. Sir Pherozeshah be appointed President of the Corporation for the current year. The Proposition having been seconded and supported, was carried unanimously and with prolonged acclamation.

Sir Pherozeshah after taking the Chair spoke as follows.

Gentlemen,—I am sure you will allow me to say that I have been scarcely able to recognise myself for the last few minutes in the extremely ideal picture which has been placed before you as the person whom you are going to elect as your President. However, I am perfectly sure of one thing, and it is that I should be setting a very bad example to you for the rest of the year, if I were to make a lengthy speech in reply to the exceedingly kind observations which have fallen from the gentlemen who have proposed and supported my nomination. My friend, Sir Bhalchandra, was quite right when he said, and I confess it, that it was with considerable hasitation, that I brought myself to undertake the task which you have thought fit to impose upon me. I can assure the Corporation that I am extremely touched and am very greatly indebted to it for the friendliness of the feeling, the kindly appreciation and the generous confidence which have always been extended to me by the members of the Corporation, past and present, and which, I believe, have led you to propose me as the person to preside over your deliberations during the ensuing year. I trust and pray that you will extend to me the same friendly feeling, appreciation and confidence in trying to discharge the duties which belong to this eminent and illustrious post; and working and co-operating in that spirit I am perfectly sure, you will maintain the high and honourable tradition that has always belonged to this Chair and to this Corporation. I will only say one word more and it is that every member has a right to expect at my hands the utmost and entire fairness and courtesy in the conduct of the Chair, and I hope that when I retire from this office, you will be able to say that I have used my best endeavours to conduct my Presidentship with entire judiciousness and in a manner worthy of the great body to which we all belong.

At the Meeting of the Bombay Corporation held on 5th April 1906, the Hon. Mr. G.O.W. Dunn moved that the best thanks of the Corporation be conveyed to the Hon. Sir Pherozeshah, the retiring President, for the very able services rendered by him to the Corporation during his term of office. The Proposition being duly seconded and supported, Sir Pherozeshah made the following reply:

> Gentlemen,—I do not think that I am wanting in the power to make a speech, on this occasion but this is an exception when I do not like to speak much of myself. But from that I hope you will not think that I am less grateful to you for the kind way in which you have expressed your appreciation of the services I have been rendering to the Corporation. I am stirred by the thanks accorded to me and by the friendliness and regard shown to me by the Corporation during the time that I have been connected with this body for the last thirty-four years. I claim no credit and no member of the Corporation can claim any credit for the work he does in the cause of the city. We all love the city of Bombay and any service that we can do for it must necessarily be a pleasure to us. I do all municipal work not solely because it is thrust on me but I have taken such work upon myself as a labour of love. I will not withhold saying that if I have met with any success in the course of the last year in the discharge of my duties, that success is in no small measure due to your co-operation. My task was rendered very easy by the assistance of Mr. Wadia, the Municipal Secretary who has reduced the work of his office to a system of perfect organisation. I would also like to say a word of acknowledgment of the assistance and help of the gentleman who acted for Mr. Wadia during his short leave of absence,—I mean Mr. Masani. I have been greatly helped in my work by the exceedingly able manner in which he prepared everything for the Corporation meetings. My thanks are also due to Mr. Sheppard, the Municipal Commissioner, from

whom I have received all assistance. No President can do his work successfully unless he is helped by the gentleman who always sits on his right hand and that is the Municipal Commissioner and I was very much struck by the broad and liberal way in which Mr. Sheppard looked at every question which came before him. I have also a word to say for the Chairman of the Standing Committee. The Corporation could cope very well with the work before them only by the way in which the Chairman placed the work of the Committee before us. Dr. Dadachanjee has placed the Municipal Budget before the Corporation in a most efficient and able manner which has greatly facilitated our work. In short, gentlemen, without your co-operation one could not have met with any success.

Now leaving those matters alone. I have one more observation to make. The joint work of our joint co-operation has shown to the public of this city as well as to the public of India what a business-like body the Bombay Municipal Corporation is. It is sometimes said that we talk a great deal at the meetings. But my answer to that criticism is that to a certain extent it is necessary that we should talk and discuss all matters before us. We cannot arrive at the truth of a thing without much discussing it—might be with some confusion of thought or language. It is impossible to arrive at the right conclusion in matters of the greatest importance until we have a certain amount of talk over them—even irrelevant or confused. But we are by no means a talking body. From the reports of the proceedings in the public papers it might perhaps appear that the Corporation are amusing themselves by talking nonsense. The papers give a brief report and all the solid work the Corporation does occupy a very short space, although the nonsene is reported at a greater length. From this some draw the inference that the Corporation is doing practically nothing but that deduction is absolutely vague.

(Here the speaker quoted figures in respect of items on the agenda of the past five years and showed how expeditiously they had disposed of important matters during their comparatively few meetings.)

Continuing, Sir Pherozeshah said:—After a study of these figures no citizen can say that to be a member of the Corporation is equal to losing one's time at its meetings. The figures show that though sometimes we talk a little irrelevant, a little too much or a little nonsense, yet on the whole you will find that the Corporation has done a very great amount of work. Moreover that work has been of an eminently practical character and it had been carried out in as expeditious and as business like a manner as any Corporation of 72 members could possibly have done it. We had 49 Committee meetings in the past year when we disposed of important questions connected with drainage, water-works and other varied subjects including the health of the city and although there had been more items for discussion than formerly yet with all that the business had been got through in very few meetings each month. I therefore think that the Corporation can rightly claim to be a thoroughly practical and business-like body and the members can take credit to themselves for the way in which they discharge their public duties.

BOMBAY MUNICIPAL CORPORATION

WOMEN AS MUNICIPAL COUNCILLORS

At the Meeting of the Bombay Corporation held on 21st June 1906, further consideration was given to the following Motion proposed by Mr. Jaffer Rahimtoola at the Meeting of the Corporation held on 1st May 1906:—That the President be requested to move Government to legislate for the abolition of the disqualification for election or appointment and for being a councillor, covered by Section 16 of the Municipal Act which is to the effect that— 'a person shall be disqualified for being elected or appointed and for being a Councillor if such person is of the female sex.'

Several members having spoken for and against the Motion,

the Hon, Sir Pherozeshah said—

Mr. President—I regret to say that I think that this Proposition, which has been so indiscreetly brought before the Meeting, is not a practical one and will serve no useful purpose. I confess that last time when Mr. Jaffer was addressing us on the subject, I said to myself that it would be very unsafe to speak in public on a matter of that character. The members must have surely read what took place recently in England with regard to women's suffrage. I had hoped that this afternoon the Corporation Hall would be filled with women waving flags and vehemently urging their rights. But no such sight is presented to us—no lady present, no flag displayed, no enthusiasm shown. I have been saying to myself that discretion was the better part of valour, for, in the event of there being any such display, if they indulged in a talk, it would have been one which we would have remembered all our life. For, are we not familiar with the reports of the gathering of the advocates of women's suffrage that besieged Mr. Asquith the other day in England and made such an unbecoming demonstration? The physical, moral and intellectual attainments of those ladies are such as would frighten anybody who holds views opposite to their election. But apart from that I ask Mr. Jaffer whether the Proposition he has brought is a practical one. If the ladies themselves had come forward and said that they were desirous to co-operate with us in civic work, then, in that case I would have given my best attention to their proposal. But the very fact that ladies themselves are not desirous of taking part in our deliberations, ought, to prevent the Corporation from considering and discussing the matter. It is not a question of man being superior to woman, or woman being superior to man, but, as it is, the guiding principle in human life is the division of labour. By the process of division of labour, work is done expeditiously and economically. Women possess certain talents and certain abilities which can be better employed in certain directions whereas men employ their abilities in directions best suited to their province. It is not therefore a question of superiority or inferiority, of capability or incapability, but the point lies in the fact whether woman should encroach upon the province of man or confine herself within her own sphere of activity. In certain matters woman are better qualified and better placed than men. The functions of men and the functions of women are quite distinct. It is in consonance with human nature, human life and human activity that the division of labour is founded. Will Mr. Jaffer undertake that by the inclusion of female Corporators amongst us, our minds will not be distracted from our work? Can he give us that assurance? I am not sure that the attention of the seventy-two Corporators will not be diverted by the presence of ladies at our meetings.

If any member took too much time in talking, we compared him with a woman. Of late we have succeeded in reducing the amount of talk that used to take place at one time in the Corporation. Would it be possible to do so with success in the case of women? Is it in our power to compel a woman to cut short her remarks should she take it into her head to make a long, continuous speech? I do not think that our President will undertake to stop a woman who has once commenced to speak. Is it possible for us to frown upon a lady and if unfortunately we did not frown, we must rest assured that we would have to regret it all our life. Nature has cast us in a different mould and to a certain extent formed us in a different way. Men and women both possess great talents to suit their different environments. Women have to do their work in their homes and men, to a great extent, outside their homes. When the Act of 1872 was passed the disability of females did not go unnoticed and it was after a deliberate and mature consideration that a bar put upon their election.

It has been argued that University admit women as Fellows but we must remember that the Senate is a calm Academic body and that therefore they might be allowed to have a right in the deliberations of that body. But it is not possible for them to take part in civic affair. The rough and tumble sort of way which men follow does not sit well upon the gentler sex. There is overwhelming argument that there is no reason to reverse the deliberate decision which the legislators had come to when framing the Act. I was once charged by Dr. Master that I did know anything about what happened in Bombay. It was possible, therefore, although it has not come to my ears, that the Zenana ladies of Bombay might have met at a conclave, where Mr. Jaffer might have had the privilege of being present, and authorised him, on their behalf, to plead the cause of women members in the Corporation. I do not think any Parsi or Hindu ladies have held such a gathering, for, in the latter case, my friend Mr. Padhye would surely have given publicity to it. Mr. Jaffer has not so far furnished us with any solid argument which might be urged for the inclusion of females in this Corporation. If he convince me by sound reasoning that the presence of ladies amongst us would lead to the better transaction of business and add to the harmony prevailing at present, I would readily change my mind and vote for his Proposition. But as matters stand now, I am sorry I cannot subscribe to his opinion and will therefore vote against the Motion.

The Proposition was put to the vote and lost 9 voting for and 21 against it.

BOMBAY MUNICIPAL CORPORATION

LORD MINTO'S VICEROYALTY, HIS REFORMS AND HIS DEATH

At the Meeting of the Bombay Corporation held on 16th September 1909, the Hon. Sir Pherozeshah in proposing that an Address be presented to H.E. Lord Minto, Viceroy and Governor-General of India, on his approaching visit to Bombay spoke as follows.

Mr. President,—It was with a feeling of great joy and satisfaction that we received the news that His Excellency Lord Minto was shortly to visit Bombay which claims to be the first city in India. Even on most ordinary occasions this city would be ready to accord a loyal and cordial welcome to the representative of His Imperial Majesty the King-Emperor, but I venture to say that this occasion is not an ordinary one. Lord Minto will come to us with a high reputation as statesman and administrator. He takes rank with some of the greatest Indian Viceroys whose administrations have left permanent landmarks in the history of India. I think all members will agree with me when I say that Lord Minto's Viceroyalty will prove to be one of the most memorable Viceroyalties in the annals of British rule in this country. I remember that on one occasion Sir Raymond West in a Convocation Address pointed out that the strength and greatness of English character were described in those well-known lines of Goldsmith

> Pride in their port, defiance in their eye,
> I see the lords of human kind pass by.

Ladies and gentlemen, I should also like to refer to an interview which Mr. Macdonald recently gave to a press representative. The attitude of these Ango-Indian papers is quite inconsistent. If a visitor came to this country and expressed his views in accord with their own, then they would say that a Daniel had come to judgment. In that case it did not matter at all whether the globe-trotter had been all over India in half a dozen weeks or not. But if the visitor had the misfortune of forming an opinion of Indian problems which did not agree with the views of the Anglo-Indian Press, then the man would be put down as a monster of ignorance who, after only a six-months-and-two-days tour in this country, had the presumption to form and express an opinion on Indian matters on which he was quite unenlightened and with which he was altogether unacquainted. This has happened in the case of Mr. Macdonald who has been cried down by the Anglo-Indian Press for venturing to give expression to his views on Indian questions after a very short sojourn in this land. From a recent telegram we have learnt how M. Jaures, the leader of the French Socialists, has approved of the policy of the great statesmen, Lords Morley and Minto. I agree with the sentiments expressed by M. Jaur's but what I wish to emphasis is the inconsistent attitude of the Anglo-Indian Press. The leader of the French Socialists has never come to this country yet the Anglo-Indian Press hailed him as a Daniel who had come to judgment, simply because his views happened to agree with those of their own. I have quoted this incident only to show you that the attitude of these journalists at times is as inconsistent and strange as it is incomprehensible to most of their readers.

Ladies and gentlemen, as you are aware the guest of the evening is going back to his own country where the atmosphere is, as I have already said, surcharged with political electricity. The party to which he belongs has to fight a tremendous battle. It has taken many a long and weary years to fructify the seeds which were sown by the great Reform Bill, but the Labour Party is now gradually growing in its power and its influence which already extends to a very wide area. The conflict between the Labour Party and the other side is fraught with tremendous interest to India; for it would be on the Labour Party that would depend how the destinies of this country would be made and modified with the progress and advancement of the times.

And now, ladies and gentlemen, it only remains for me to ask you to drink to the good health of our guests of the evening Mr. and Mrs. Ramsay Macdonald. We wish them long life and prosperity and a safe and speedy return to their native country.

BOMBAY MUNICIPAL CORPORATION

SIR PHEROZESHAH'S PRESIDENTSHIP, 1911-1912

A Meeting of the Bombay Corporation was held on 3rd April 1911 the chief business being the election of the President for the current official year. There were in all three candidates, the Hon. Sir Pherozeshah, Sir Sassoon J. David and Mr. Manmohandas Ramjee and the resull of the voting was that Sir Pherozeshah secured 26 votes, David 25 and Manmohandas 12. Sir Pherozeshah being declared elected on taking the Chair, spoke as follows.

Gentlemen,—My first duty is to thank you most heartily for the great honour you have done me today by electing me your President for the fourth time:

> "The Hon. Mr. Fazulbhoy referred briefly to the question of decentralisation and with what he said and with all that fell from my honourable colleague I entirely agree. The Government, with the assistance of this enlarged Council, is quite capable of dealing with all matters of local concern, and in the interests of economy and of good administration it is most desirable that a large measure of autonomy should be granted to our Presidency. The strong views of the Government on this important question will be found in their letter to the Government of India, which is published with the voluminous report of the Decentralisation Commission."

Your Excellency, the public of this province would entirely agree with these views if the enlarged Council was so constituted as to represent the direct voice of the people, because in the matter of taxation it is the voice of the people which ought to be conclusive, and I assure Your Excellency that if it was thus constituted, nobody would have been more ready to agree with Your Excellency than I would have been. But taking things as they are, and while the Council is in the process of development, nothing would be more disastrous than to invest it with the powers of taxation. But my fears since the last two or three months have been fortunately dissipated. My alarm was completely removed when I read in the papers a short note of the Despatch which has been received from the Secretary of State on this point. Your Excellency is well aware that the Secretary of State for India has finally decided to decline for the present to give the powers of taxation to the Provincial Councils and has adduced various reasons for his decision. Among other reasons he has given one potent reason that the determining voice of the people is still not strengthened in these Provincial Councils. Your Excellency, the remarks that I have made have also a bearing to a very large extent on what is called the devolution of functions from higher to subordinate officials. I have always protested against this devolution—this giving over of the powers enjoyed by higher officials to subordinate officials unless and until such a devolution is accompanied by measures for giving active and vigilant control to the people. I would welcome such devolution of functions and powers if the officials to whom they are transferred were at the same time guided and restrained in the exercise of those powers and functions by the representatives of the people in some form or other.

H.E. The President:—Two minutes more, Sir Pherozeshah.

The Hon. Sir Pherozeshah:—Two minutes more? Then all that I can say is this that according to my watch twenty minutes have not elapsed but I accept the correctness of Your Excellency's watch. Now, instead of going on with my remarks I cannot better use the two minutes than to enter a protest against this exercise of discretion vested in Your Excellency under the rules for the direction of the Budget debate. One can well understand that when a motion on a subject is placed before the Council, ten or fifteen minutes may be considered adequate for the expression of views of each individual member. But to give twenty minutes to a member for a general debate involving all the heads of the Budget is simply to stop his mouth. I am sorry to have to make this protest, but if anybody rationally considers when a Budget has to be considered in all its heads, to stop a member from speaking for more than twenty minutes is to prevent him from speaking what he has got to say on the various heads of the Budget. I have a great deal to say about the educational policy of the Government, also about the views expressed by the Hon. Dr. Nariman on primary education, a subject on which he has spoken without understanding the merits of the question and the principle involved in the development of primary education. There are various other points on which I should have liked to speak, but I cannot do so in two minutes. All that I can do therefore is to sit down.

BOMBAY LEGISLATIVE COUNCIL

A BILL TO ESTABLISH A COURT OF WARDS IN THE BOMBAY PRESIDENCY

On the second reading of "A Bill to Establish a Court of Wards in the Bombay Presidency" moved in the Bombay Legislative Council by Sir James Monteath on 18th March 1905, the Hon. Sir P.M. Mehta made the following speech:

Your Excellency,—I am not quite sure whether I have yet recovered from the effects of the lecture, or advice, of my honourable friend Dr. Bhandarkar, which he has just administered to us. He told us in very severe terms that if we oppose any portion of this Bill or any of the provisions of this Bill we are very likely influenced by an inveterate habit of having no confidence in executive officers. Now, Your Excellency, I deliberately join issue with my honourable friend, and I ask the Council to believe that in any opposition which I have to offer to some of the provisions of this Bill, I am not actuated by a wicked desire of opposing executive officers. I believe these officers like all other people have excellent merits, but they have also the demerits and deficiencies of the circumstances in which they are placed, and it would not be wise for legislation not to take notice of the human frailties which belong to them as to all classes of people. My honourable friend Mr. Parekh was concerned with the principles which Dr. Bhandarkar laid down with regard to the way in which this world ought to be managed. I do not think my honourable friend Mr. Parekh need have very serious apprehensions as to those principles. I am not surprised however that my honourable friend, though really born in this age, may be said to belong to a very old generation. All his distinguished studies are entirely directed to the times that have gone by, and there is no wonder that the principles which he enunciates are derived from the studies of antiquities. So that it is to my mind not a very surprising thing that he should want to go back to those days when everything could be done by legislation and people could be made wise by Acts of Parliament or of the Indian Legislatures. I suppose it is quite natural for Professor Bhandarkar to regard us all as hopeless. I do not think he regards us all as moral children even, but as immoral children. It is natural for Dr. Bhandarkar, who was so distinguished a Professor in his time, to regard us all as children who should obey their instructors. But out of the class-room, we have to deal with different circumstances and hard and practical principles of real life, and I do not think it would do to allow the principles of the class-room to prevail against the hard practical principles of this life.

I should not have been surprised if my honourable friend, the mover of the Bill, had gone into some of the principles of the Bill in his speech this afternoon. But he leaves us to move amendments without giving us any idea of his arguments against them. If he had referred to these, we should have been able to present our amendments in a much more effective manner. I was surprised that he was surprised that some of the opinions expressed before his face were different from those put down in writing through those wicked people the vakils. I am not surprised that people before him should express themselves differently from the views they put in writing. I am sure my honourable friend Sir James Monteath does not do justice, in his modesty, to his awe-inspiring presence. I can quite understand that the gentleman who came to have a talk with him about the Bill was very anxious to show him that he was lost in admiration of the wisdom with which the Bill has been framed. And I am sure no one is more cognisant that the native courtesy of the Indian gentlemen, whatever his own opinions on the subject might be, would be to place them before the gentleman to whom he is talking in such a way that he would give him to understand his own views were perfectly in consonance with those of the person to whom he was talking. It seems to me it is no wonder Sir James Monteath drew the inferences he did from the conversation, but it is hardly safe to consider that these inferences would be correctly drawn.

Now, Your Excellency, I may be pardoned for saying that this is an instance of the over-legislation into which our Indian Legislative Councils are apt to be driven. I very carefully read and re-read the speech of my honourable friend in introducing the Bill into the Council, but I could not help seeing, as a man of high culture could not help seeing, that there was no immediate necessity for the passing of the Bill so far as this Presidency is concerned. It is no doubt true such Bills exist in the other Presidencies. They existed even before the beginning of the last century.

The reason was however that the circumstances of those Presidencies were so different that it was thought, in those early days, that there was necessity for the provisions embodied subsequently in the Court of Wards Acts. I have never understood why these Acts are called "Court" of Wards Acts. So far as I am aware, the word "Court," except as regards the Ancient Court of Directors, is never, employed but for a tribunal of judicial character. And why in the year of grace 1905 we should be sitting to pass an Act which is to be called a Court of Wards Act and which has not the remotest taint or tincture of anything judicial is a thing which I fail to understand. Your Excellency will remember that what is called a Court of Wards is an executive officer of Government, either a Commissioner or other officer or two or three officers appointed for this purpose. They are what would be called in Bombay settlement officers for the management of estates. We are now considering however what is called a Court of Wards Bill. This is a case of over-legislation. It seems to me that no case has been made out for this Bill, though I bear in mind the elaborate remarks of my honourable friend Sir James Monteath in introducing the Bill. The class of people for whom the Acts were passed in other Presidencies do not exist to the same extent in this Presidency, as in other Presidencies, So far as they do exist legislation deals with them, though I think perhaps that legislation may be amended to include them in a more perfect manner. But a Bill which strives to include not only these classes but classes of an imaginary character, so far as I can see after going through the Bill, I fail to perceive who are the additional persons for whom the provisions are necessary. It seems to me we are passing a separate Act which might speculatively go forward for the purpose of doing some good to some people of whom no idea is given to us. I do not know if my honourable friend Sir James Monteath is aware that the Court of Wards Regulations and Acts were simply for the purpose of protection of Government revenue. I was reading the other day a debate of the Legislative Council of the North-West Provinces which took place on a Bill in 1899 when His Honour the President pointed this out. He said—"The primary object of the Court of Wards legislation was the protection of Government revenue. The earliest regulations which were introduced and which have given the Board of Revenue and Government the powers exercised by a Court of Wards were introduced with the object of protecting the Government revenue. Since then the further idea of protecting the interests of minors and disqualified proprietors comes in. But the protection of revenue still remains at the foundation of the Court of Wards legislation." Later, as he points out, benevolence gradually insinuated itself into the legislation. I quite admit the motive of benevolence has slowly so permeated this legislation with regard to Courts of Wards that now it would be called the primary object; and it seems to me to be by far the primary object for which it is introduced. But, as it is with regard to all measures introduced for motives of benevolence, the Bill merely provides machinery which is more likely to be abused than to be used in so far as the provisions of the character to which I have referred are concerned. So far as minors and people of unsound mind are concerned I do not say it would not be a very useful provision to place them in the hands of Courts of Wards instead of the committees to which they are at present submitted. Though I think it would be unwise to take away the charge of a minor from persons about him who may be considered in the opinion of the Court of Wards capable of conducting his affairs, and place him under the, if I may say so, unsympathetic Court of Wards, and if Dr. Bhandarkar will forgive me for saying so, an unsympathetic executive officer who is appointed guardian. It may be that there are persons surrounding a minor quite capable and sympathetie and fit for the purpose. It would be very distressing if these duties should be taken from them and handed over to a hard body like the Court of Wards. It seems to me we are over-legislating in this matter when we include in the definition of landholder as has been done in clause (c) of section 2 "landholder" shall mean (i) in the case of minors and persons adjudged by a competent Civil Court to be of unsound mind and incapable of managing their affairs, a holder as defined in the Bombay Land Revenue Code, 1879; and (ii) in all other cases, a *zamindar*, *jagirdar*, *saranjamdar*, *inamdar*, *talukdar*, *malek* and a *khot* and any person not hereinbefore specified who is interested in land and belongs to a class of which the Governor in Council has declared the members to be landholders for the purposes of this Act." Now, my Lord, I should like to know who are these person. Will my honourable friend give me some indication of who are the class of of persons for whom these words are intended? I cannot make out any person not before specified "who is interested in land and belongs to a class of which the Governor in Council has declared the members to be landholders for the purposes of this Act." I went through my honourable friend's speech in introducing the Bill over and over again, for the purpose of finding out who these people could be. I failed to find anything, and that is why I am rather sorry he did not take the opportunity just now of telling us for whom this Bill is intended.

My Lord, I may be pardoned for saying that legislation is not intended for speculative objects; it is intended for certain persons and objects. But when, because you imagine there may be some persons who in future should be brought within the pale of certain provisions, you consider that therefore you are to proceed to legislate for all these speculative cases, it seems to me that the machinery of legislation is applied for a purpose which cannot be called either practical or wise.

Then, coming to the main points of the provisions of this Bill, I come to the third section which, I think the Council ought to remember clearly, is for the purpose of showing what is a Court of Wards. As I pointed out, it is not a judicial Court at all. Section 3 of the Bill says that "subject to the provisions of section 12 the Commissioner shall be the Court of Wards for the limits of his Division provided that the Governor in Council may, if he thinks fit......appoint a special officer to be the Court of Wards for a division, in lieu of the Commissioner........." So that a Court of Wards, it is declared, is only one of these officers, or only one or two joined together. Then Section 4 shows how a Court of Wards may be set in motion. "The Court of Wards may, with the previous sanction of the Governor in Council, assume the superintendence of the property of any landholder holding land within the local limits of its jurisdiction who is disqualified to manage his own property." There I should like to ask the honourable member in charge of the Bill how clause (2) of section 1 will act. Clause (2) of section 1 says the Act "shall extend to the whole of the Bombay Presidency, except the city of Bombay and Aden." Supposing a person holds property in the City of Bombay or Aden and in other parts of the Presidency, would he be subject, though residing in the City of Bombay, to this Act as regards his property in other parts of the Presidency? I think there are many points in regard to these sections that ought to be settled before we can say what is the exact application of the Act.

Clause 4 says "the Court of Wards may, with the previous sanction of the Governor in Council, assume the superintendence of the property of any landholder holding land within the local limits of its jurisdiction who is disqualified to manage his own property." I acknowledge there is a clause "provided that in the case of a landholder disqualified under clause (b) or (c) of sub-section (1) of section 5 such assumption shall be sanctioned only where the Governor in Council is of opinion that is expedient in the public interests to preserve the property of such landholder for the benefit of his family, and that the said property is of such value that economical management by the Court of Wards is practicable." Now I holds and I really mean to speak with, all respect of the powers vested in the Governor in Council; I say I have always held the highest respect for the gentlemen forming the Council of His Excellency the Governor. But it seems to me it is doing them an injustice to require them to exercise a discretion and sanction while leaving them very little indication of how they are to exercise them. It is very easy to say they are only to be exercised if it is "expedient in the public interests" to execise them. If I may say so without any want of respect to any member of Council, the time may come when members of Council will think certain things are necessary for the public interest. Supposing their successors should apply their minds in a different way, equally conscientious, and say "but there is nothing in the public interest here!" I have had some experience of these things and I find the views of members of Council very often vary very much and very widely. I think to require them to form opinions on matters that are indicated in such general words is to do them an injustice. After having laid it down in that way, we come to the principal clause, to portions of which I have very strong objections.

Section 5 says "the following landholder shall, for the purposes of section 4, be deemed to be disqualified to manage their own property." Minors, who are mentioned first, we will leave; their interests are already provided for by the Guardians and Wards Act. But while I am making this observation I should like to point out one mistake Dr. Bhandarkar made. He makes a point in favour of the Court of Wards Act by a reference to a case in which he was concerned under the Guardians and Wards Act that was expeditiously dealt with. Now would he be surprised to hear that the inquiry through which he passed was of a judicial character and not of a character described in this Act? His experience of the Guardians and Wards Act was certainly fortunate in that the inquiry in that case did not take a long time. But he seems to have forgotten that it was entirely of a judicial character. In regard to the other, section 5, disqualification is applied to females and other persons "declared by the District Court, on the application of the Collector and after such inquiry as it thinks necessary, to be unfitted to manage their own property." It seems very benevolent and nice that we should issue regulations for the direction of interests of families! How will this work, Sir? We recognise there are two minds brought to bear upon it, the Collector's and that of the Judge of the District Court. But surely, with some little experience of this country, we may also take to ourselves that the Collector may be moved in these matters by persons who are not quite disinterested, as he and the District Judge are certain to be. People who have some grudge against the family or the female will set to work, will apply to the Collector, who will be obliged to make his inquiries by his subordinate officers or probably by the police under him as District Magistrate, and what will be the state of a family's claims under these circumstances with all these inquiries carried on into their private affairs? Because an inquiry would be worth nothing unless it were carried into the private affairs of the estate in which the family is interested. To me the prospect of such an inquiry is one I cannot look on as satisfactory. There might be cases in which females wholly incapable of managing their affairs should be placed under the beneficial protection of the Court of Wards, but for one case of that sort it seems to me many would be open to annoyance and persecution. If the world could be made wise by legislation, nothing would be easier than to lay down wise principles. But the hard facts of this world do not allow it. We have to see how regulations laid down with the best intentions work in practice.

Then, leaving females, I come to what to my mind is the most extraordinary provision of the Bill introduced by my honourable friend, Sir James Monteath. I could see in his former speech that his high culture has made him aware of the inconveniences and difficulties of what may be termed grandmotherly legislation. And if my honourable friend will pardon me for saying so, I think it must have stood him in very good stead on this occasion to draw on his experience as a Revenue

Officer, which brings about views which are very different from those held by ordinary people. It could be seen from his speech that no one was more alive to the effects of grandmotherly legislation. But I would like to call it, if I may coin an English word, step-fatherly legislation. It is somewhat in the way, with which we are made acquainted by Dickens in "David Copperfield," in which the step-father looked after the interests of his step-son. After all a step-father is a step-father and he can only see things in a particular light, and he can only look in a certain way on the affairs of the minor whose interests he is supposed to be looking after. "Incapable of managing, or unfitted to manage, their own property owing to (i) any physical or mental defect or infirmity; or (ii) vicious, intemperate or wasteful habits, or such other habits as cause or are likely to cause, injury to their property or to the well-being of their inferior holders." My Lord, what a task for the Collector and the District Court! I really appeal to my honourable friend. Suppose he was sitting as a Court for deciding cases brought before him under this Section! Would not different people take different views of viclous habits, intemperate habits or wasteful habits? I do not know what "wasteful" means. I know my honourable friend makes a great deal of thrift. If a man calls in a tom-tom to celebrate a marriage half the night, he calls that wasteful. I do not call it wasteful. I think a man must have a little enjoyment sometimes. But this says not only such cases as cause injury but such as are likely to cause injury. I remember that in the course of a budget speech I made certain reflections upon the abkari policy of Government. There was a case of a liquor-shop being opened at Matheran. At that time the Finance Member was Sir Evan James, and when I was inveighing against the Government allowing such a liquor-shop to be introduced in a place like Matheran, he said "Why not let the poor man have his glass of beer?" I was taken aback; but that shows how people may vary in opinion. I ask, I appeal to, my honourable friend, how would he sit in judgment for the purposes of deciding what may be "vicious, intemperate or wasteful habits"? I no not want to run down executive officers in the slightest degree. I have the highest opinion of them.

But is it fair to ask even executive officers, incapable, as Bhandarkar thinks them, of going wrong,—would you expect even them or any other officers to say what are "vicious, intemperate or wasteful habits," causing or likely to cause injury to their property or to the well-being of their inferior holders"? I am aware in other Court of Wards Acts in other Presidencies there are similar provisions. But I think, and I think Sir James Monteath would have said, that Bombay is not to be guided by other Presidencies in matters of this character. I should have thought that we in Bombay with our culture would have recognised that there are certain things beyond the power of human judgment. I think on one occasion my honourable friend did disagree with the legislation of another Province and say he would not dream of introducing it into Bombay. I now ask him not to follow the legislation of those effect Provinces of Madras and the North by putting upon us such legislation as this is; requiring District Courts to find out persons of "vicious, intemperate or wasteful habits, or such other habits as cause, or are likely to cause injury to their property or to the well-being of their inferior holders." I know my honourable friend said in his speech that we are all aware of instances for which this Act would be useful. Would he kindly mention to us some of those instances? We know there are certain people minors and those of unsound mind, who are incapable of managing their affairs. But would my honourable friend point out any others? One Collector might run in a certain, person before a Court of Wards, because he happened to be lame or blind or something of that kind, while another Collector would pooh-pooh the idea. It seems to me these provisions should not have a place on a statute-book of a practical character. I know my honourable friend recognises that these grounds of disqualification are very open to argument and he said he was very sorry indeed to interfere with cases of that character. His words were—"In the Punjab, the United Provinces, and Central Provinces Acts conviction of a non-bailable offence is one of the causes of disqualification, but there appear to be strong objections to taking such a fact into consideration for the purpose. I admit, however, that the assumption of management on similar grounds requires to be exercised with great caution, and in particular, that there should be no unnecessary prying into private affairs or encouragement given to applications inspired by the enmity of relations." But he satisfies his mind in this way:—"In all the Acts, except that for Bengal, the power of declaring incapacity on such grounds is left to the local Government. In Bengal the adjudgment of incapacity from physical defects or infirmities is made by a competent Civil Court.

We have adopted a plan of determination which will, I hope, be accepted by the Council as providing the greatest security against abuse". Gentlemen, I should like members of this Council to say what is the security, "the greatest security" which he has provided. "We propose that the declaration should be made by the District Court on the application of the Collector,"—that is the remedy which he says would obviate the hardship of the cases to which he has referred. "The Collector will, in the instance, have to be satisfied that there are adequate reasons for interference, and he will then have to convince the District Court by evidence. It seems scarcely possible that under such a system there can be any unnecessary or arbitrary assumption of management." Now take the Bill as it stands to see how my learned friend carries out his promise in that respect. It is true he says the disqualification will have to be decided by the District Courts. But is he not playing upon words when he says "District Court"? What is the principal notion carried to our minds?—That the Court will proceed in the way in which the procedure of a judicial Court must be conducted to make it a Court that the Court will carry on its proceedings in the way of a regular judicial proceeding. But what is actually done? He leaves it to the District Court to hold "such inquiry as it thinks necessary." Why, as my learned friend is cognisant of the danger of these provisions, does he not leave it to a District Court, a judicial tribunal, to make an inquiry and pronounce a verdict? I think my honourable friend will reconsider this provision, and if it is to be retained I do hope I may appeal to Your Lordship and the members of this Council to say that these matters shall not be left to any but a regular and judicial tribunal. If these matters are important, and they are very important, why should they not be carried out with all the safeguards connected with a regular judicial proceeding? I therefore appeal to Your Lordship and the members of this Council to say, if these qualifying clauses are to be retained and people are to be dragged into Courts of Wards for defects, mental and physical, and for "vicious, intemperate or wasteful habits, or such other habits as cause or are likely to cause, injury to their property or to the well-being of their inferior holders,' at least to provide this remedy, the surest remedy against hasty conclusions, that the inquiry shall be carried out before the District Court in a judicial manner, that everyone concerned in it shall have an opportunity of placing before the Court everything calculated to help it to come to a proper decision.

Because, what a distressing matter it would be if a person were dragged before a Court and pronounced to be a person of vicious character before the world, if the proper precautions were not taken in the inquiry against him. Can, my Lord, anybody conceive a more important matters, requiring to be investigated in a judicial manner, when a man may be stamped in the face of the whole world and before his brother talukdars as a man coming under these clauses? I do appeal to my honourable friend, if he insist on retaining these clauses, to "provide the greatest security"—his own words—"against these abuses." I think the delays of Courts of Law are very much exaggerated. If they are protracted, it is a necessary evil which has to be borne because of the benefits derived from a full and costly adjudication. Therefore I say if you are to have the greatest security against abuses, with regard to which my learned friend is fully awake, at least provide that there shall be full inquiry in which everybody concerned shall be represented, and every piece of evidence shall be brought forward and a judicial opinion formed. But I say even that is not sufficient. I say there should also be a right of appeal to the High Court of the land. I say it is absolutely necessary that all the guarantees, against a wrong decision, which the legislature has provided, should be adhered to in a matter of this character. And I say no case has been made out that the inquiry in these cases should not be by a full and judicial Court, and no case has been made out why an appeal should not be made to the High Court. ....I would have made a few remarks, but I will now reserve them, with regard to sections 35 and 40, the deprivation of the power of making a will in section 38, and the power taken away from the successor of a disqualified man of dealing with the estate which he, but for the unhappy accident of his predecessor, of his father or whoever turned out to be of "vicious, intemperate or wasteful habits," might have possessed. Is this a proper matter to be included in a Bill of this character? Are you not legislating upon very different principles when you introduce this clause into the Act? I do not want to go into the case which might be made with regard to the alienation of life estates.

As it is matter depending upon principles of a far more extensive character than can be dealt with in this Bill, would it not be right that such a matter should be dealt with on its own merits? A man brings himself under this Act, and his successor is placed in the same position although he has not brought himself within any of the disqualifying provisions. And I would point out how very considerable mischief might result. I am sure my honourable friend Sir James Monteath and my honourable friend Mr. Edgerley must be acquainted with cases in which a father takes a bitter dislike to his son or to his successor who is to come from some other branch of the family, and will do all in his power to ruin his interests. He may act in such a way that he can afterwards apply to the Court of Wards and place himself under the Court of Wards Act and take his revenge upon his heir who might have to follow him. It seems to me the greater number of cases in which advantage will be taken of this provision will be cases of this character. You make a way ready for a man in that position to take his revenge. Is that the way in which a legislature should deal with a matter of this importance? It may be that the legislature should hold that estates of a certain character should be only held for life, but that is a matter which should be discussed on its own merits and is not a matter which should be thrust into a Bill of this character. Therefore I appeal to my honourable friend to omit it from this Bill, and if he thinks it is a change that is required let it be advocated on its own merits and not introduced in a haphazard manner in a Court of Wards Bill. My Lord, the other observations I have to make I will make in moving the amendments of which I have given notice.

This Bill having been read a second time, Council proceeded to consider it in detail. Several amendments were moved by Sir Pherozeshah Mehta, some of which were agreed to by Sir James Monteath whilst others were lost, and finally the Bill was read a third time and passed on 20th March 1905.

BOMBAY LEGISLATIVE COUNCIL

THE BOMBAY BUDGET OF 1905-1906

At the Meeting of the Bombay Legislative Council held at Poona on 8th July 1905, Sir James Monteath introduced the Financial Statement of the Government of Bombay for the year 1905-1906. Sir Pherozeshah Mehta made the following speech at the adjourned Meeting of the Council on 10th July 1905.

Mr. President,—I regret, and I am sure other members join with me in regretting, that His Excellency is unable to attend owing to indisposition and I hope and trust he may ever be in good health and able to attend to his responsible duties. I confess I rise with some diffidence to offer a few observations on the Financial Statement. It is a somewhat complicated budget, a budget which has been laid down on different lines from those which prevailed in former years. I am afraid that we non-official members are not such masters of Provincial Finance as Sir James Monteath who has all the figures and materials at his finger-ends and we cannot understand the figures in such a remarkable manner as he does. This is a year in which to make a survey of the financial arrangements which the Government of India have made with this Local Government. We have now entered upon the third stage of the scheme inaugurated in 1870 by Lord Mayo, which has been termed the Decentralisation Scheme. Before 1870 strained relations existed between the Imperial and Local Governments chiefly in regard to the apportionment of the local revenues by the Imperial Government. Lord Mayo introduced a system of decentralisation under which certain heads of revenue were made over to Local Governments which were besides given a large amount of independence. This system continued till 1877 when it was thought that the time had come for extending and enlarging it and of removing certain defects which had been disclosed by experience every five years, the primary object of such revision having been to secure to the Central Government what might be considered their fair proportion in the growth of assigned revenues. In the earlier revisions considerable reductions were made in the assignments, but on the occasion of the one in 1897 the aggregate change was insignificant, reductions in certain provinces having been approximately balanced by increases allowed in others. This was the opinion expressed by Sir Edward Law in March 1904, and he continued: "It cannot be said that the system of quinquennial revisions proved satisfactory for with such a short period of settlement it inevitably occurred that in the first year of the term the Local Government was necessarily feeling its way under new conditions and cautions about expenditure, whilst in the last year, if, as was generally the case, balances were large, there was a natural tendency to extravagance, lest the terms of a new settlement might reduce resources for expenditure." In 1877 the Financial Statement was in great disorder. Matters however went on with the help of the Imperial Government and in 1882 the Government of India adopted the wise policy of giving large grants and placing large revenues at the disposal of the Bombay Government. The revenues were so large that after giving the Government of India assistance to the extent of 20 lacs of rupees they were able to build up a surplus of 52 lacs of rupees, though according to their contract they were bound to keep their surplus within 20 lacs. This went on till 1887 when the Bombay Government was required to help the Government of India for financial exigencies of various kinds. The Presidency was prosperous enough to pay another large grant at the end of the contract period. This brings us to the year 1892. It was unfortunate that the Bombay Government never had the courage and enterprise to spend its surplus in any useful scheme for the welfare of the Presidency, for the result was that at the end of the five years' contract all the surpluses were carried away by the Government of India.

Then came the year 1897 when a big famine occurred side by side with an outbreak of plague. I should like to point out how the Government of India treated the Presidency at the time. In 1881 when the system of the provincial contract was considered and settled it was clearly pointed out by the Government of India themselves that, in times of famine, Provincial Governments would be called upon to contribute to the Imperial Exchequer in certain ways. Now what did the Government of India do in 1897 when plague and famine devastated the Bombay Presidency? They gave enough for purposes of famine charges, but in other respects starved the administration. Under these circumstances it was not to be wondered that the system of decentralisation of Provincial Finance, inaugurated by Lord Mayo completely broke up. The system of Provincial Contracts worked in such a manner that the Government of India themselves thought that the system could no longer be continued. I remember that in introducing the Financial Statement in the Viceroy's Council last year, Sir Edward Law pointed out that the time had come when the system of Provincial Contracts would have to be placed on a different footing. I hope with the introduction of the revised method of making assignments the Local Government will work up organised schemes for the purpose of spending the grants and will not repeat the policy which has been the bane of this Presidency for the last 20 years. In the Punjab and Bombay the settlement of 1897 was a failure mainly in consequence of the effects of famine and plague from which both of them suffered so severely, and the financial report for East-India for 1905-1906 stated that "for the last few years their finances have been in constant deficit, necessitating large annual grants from Imperial revenues to preserve nominal equilibrium." To put an end to this state of things it has been necessary to assign to the Local Governments a considerably larger share of the revenues of their respective Provinces than they received in 1897. Their assignments have therefore been increased by Rs. 36,92,000 per annum in the case of Bombay and by Rs. 16,51,000 per annum in the case of the Punjab. Moreover the Provincial shares, in the case of the heads of revenue and expenditure divided between the Imperial and the Provincial, have been so adjusted that the average Provincial annual increment of revenue will be raised from Rs. 6,30,000 to Rs. 8,55,000 in the former Province and from Rs. 3,08,000 to Rs. 6,78,000 in the latter. Initial grants of 50 lacs in each case, including special grants for plague charges, have also been allotted to start the Provinces with a liberal sum in hand at the outset of the new settlements. I regret that His Excellency has not been able to preside on this occasion, for I think, (and I think I do not reveal any secret when I say it) that the liberal settlement which has been made in regard to the Province of Bombay is largely due to the personal exertions of His Excellency the Governor, who was of course supported by his able colleague in the Council, I mean Sir James Monteath. The Financial Statement now before the Council shows that Rs. 17 lacs have been at present set aside for famine charges, but now that the conditions are normal I do not know whether Government will give an assurance to the Council as to whether this large sum or at any rate a large portion of it is to be used for some other purposes.

Besides this the Government of India have made special grants. Out of these the Bombay Presidency has got Rs. 5 lacs on account of Police charges, while the Madras and Bengal Presidencies each get Rs. 10 lacs and the United Provinces Rs. 7 1/2 lacs. I think, considering the great necessity of reorganising the Police force, the grant of Rs. 5 lacs made to this Presidency is quite inadequate. Again out of a grant of Rs. 35 lacs for primary education Bengal has got Rs. 10 lacs, Madras Rs. 6 lacs and Bombay Rs. 7 lacs, and I think in this matter also the Bombay Presidency has not got its due.

I am glad to see that a grant-in-aid has been given to the Local Boards in India. The Indian National Congress dwelt over and over again on the absolute necessity of Imperial grants-in-aid to the District and Local Boards and I am glad to see that the Imperial Government has made up its mind to make a further grant for that purpose, but I hope they will extend it to Municipalities also. The burden on Municipalities is far larger than that on the Local Boards and I sincerely trust the time will come when the Government will recognise the necessity of making a grant to the Municipal Boards also. For that reason I am glad to see in the Financial Statement before us that you, Sir, have expressed the hope that if the finances of the Government permit they will see their way to help as far as possible these crippled Municipalities.

That is a short account of the existing financial distribution. One more remark I have to make on the subject and that is that the Government of India and the Local Government have laid stress on the fact that the Presidency is very fortunate in getting a better revision in respect to the two heads of land-revenue and excise. As to land-revenue I am convinced and it can scarcely be denied that it has increased even in the most unfavourable conditions and that is not a state of affairs on which I can congratulate the Council. In this connection I wish to make an observation with regard to a certain rumour. It has been said that there are Revenue officers who think that the resolution, which has been recently issued by the Government of India as regards automatic remissions and suspensions of revenue in times of scarcity, do not take into account the fact that the assessment in this Province has been based on calculations of both good and bad years. I submit that this is tantamount to frustrating the object which the Government of India had in view when deciding upon this system of automatic remissions and suspensions. As to excise I know there is a divergence of opinion on this point between the public and the Government which is not at all likely to be easily overcome. The Government think that by increasing the duty on liquor they keep down drunkenness while the public thinks that the consumption of liquor has been steadily increasing. The Government will find it exceedingly difficult to persuade people to see the matter in their way. The interest of the contractors lies in promoting an increase in consumption whatever they may say and it is very hard to imagine that the general complaint is without any foundation. I am afraid this is a difference of opinion in respect to which both sides are ready and agreed to carry on their differences.

Then with regard to the grant of Rs. 65,000 to the Bombay University I wish to point out that if the University require a grant it is forthcoming. I do not know if Mr. Giles is aware that there was at one time an annual grant of Rs. 15,000. This was gradually reduced to Rs. 5,000 and finally taken away altogether. This was done for various reasons, the principal one being that the University ought to be self supporting. Now, such is fate, the Government has come forward again and has offered this grant. I do not know what it is intended for. It has been said it is intended for the foundation of a lectureship and professorship. But what is required in this Presidency is that it should have properly equipped and manned Government Colleges like the Eliphinstone College, and a good staff who have an inducement to stay. At present when a good man is found he is immediately required and transferred to the Inspectoris Department.

I also wish to refer to the resumption by the Government of the land which they have made over to the Improvement Trust. I was particularly astonished when the Judicial Member of the Council, the Honourable Mr. Fulton, said that it is perfectly true that the Government are resuming large plots of land and that it is perfectly legal for them to do so. It may be strictly legal, but I do not think it is necessary to tell Mr. Fulton that besides legality there should be equity and justice in the matter. No doubt it is true that there is a clause in the Improvement Trust Act which permits both the Government and the Corporation to resume certain portions of the land from the Trust if they were required for public purposes, but I think great care ought to be exercised in such resumptions, for it has been carried out to such an extent as to seriously affect the income of the Improvement Trust.

Now, Sir, I wish to speak on the matter of the Mahableshwar leases. There are very many interests in this and it is a very great pity that we should be divided on the subject of race in this country. The real wish of those who work for the welfare of this country is that these influences shall be minimised, and I shall deprecate anything which tends to widen these differences. It has been said that the Europeans have been driven out of Malabar Hill. I have heard it said that Europeans have been turned out of Cumballa Hill. It is generally understood that Government officials receive salaries which have been fixed so as to enable them to carry out their social duties, but it must be remembered that they must be prepared to pay for their requirements just as ordinary people have to do. I, Sir, do not think it is right when a man builds a house on Malabar Hill he should be required to sign a lease containing a clause that he must give it up to the Government if it be required. The conditions are not regulated by the ordinary laws of supply and demand. It is true that native gentlemen have many buildings at Mahableshwar, but I emphatically deny that there is the slightest foundation for the statement that they make any money out of these buildings. They have built the houses primarily for their own occupation and, Sir, I ask if it is right or fair to ask them to walk out because they are required for the accommodation of Government officers. It is probable that the houses built by Hindu gentlemen would not be suitable for Europeans and the Government would be chary of asking them to go out, and I am afraid they will come down on the house-owners of my community. I fail to see why

Government should resort to such measures. If they want accommodation for their officers, the Hill is large enough and the Government should build their own houses on it. I sincerely hope the Government will not give the slightest countenance to a policy which is calculated to when the distinctions of race which already exist.

You must have read an article recently published in the first Paper of Asia with regard to the annual departure of the Government to Mahableshwar. That paper carries with it the opinion of the non-official European mercantile community of the Presidency. They naturally object that the greater part of the year is spent away at Poona and Mahableshwar and only a very small portion of it is spent in Bombay. If the Government insist on carrying out the scheme to accommodate the officers at Mahableshwar in the manner they propose to do I warn the Council that the native community will join hands with the European non-official section, whose voice has, I believe, been fully voiced by the "Times of India."

I also wish, Sir, to speak on the relationship which has existed for some time past between the Government and the Corporation. The latter have always been anxious to maintain relations of the most respectful harmony with the Government, but latterly the impression has grown that the Government have not treated them in the manner to which they are entitled. For instance there is the question of stamp duties. I refer to the refusal of the Government to forego stamps on certain temporary loans. The Corporation have often to resort for raising temporary loans to debenture mortgages, and these are always subsequently made into permanent loans. By the action of the Government they have been forced to pay stamp duty over and over again. I also refer in this matter to the recent action of the Government in deducting certain charges on account of the deputation of famine refuges from Bombay from payments due to the Corporation without any previous reference to that body, and to the action of the Government in attempting to obtain from the Corporation the payment of the salary of Mr. Playford Reynolds. The

Corporation has never forgotten how it was treated in the matter of the liquor fines which item was part of its revenue. In 1878 a Bill was brought in to take that revenue from the Corporation to the Government. The allowance, contrary to all customs, was made on the amount of the revenue then without any reference to its probable future growth and so the Corporation gets Rs. 1,40,000 still although the revenue has risen to Rs. 3 lacs. Sir, I bring these matters forward to implore the Government to meet the Corporation, as they wish to do, in a spirit of harmony.

Before resuming my seat I wish to refer to the cotton-seed industry. When the schedule was made, it will be seen an attempt was made to exempt certain articles. It was then decided that pressed bales would be exempted, as thereby some of the danger caused by loose material lying about was avoided. In these circumstances the storing of the article is regulated by licenses, so that it can be known where the stores are. If the license is too heavy I have no doubt the Corporation will do something to modify it.

Mr. President, before concluding I should like to make a brief reference to the separation which is imminent. I understand, Sir, that you are leaving this Presidency within a short period. We have had our differences of opinion, but I know that you have devoted many years of your life to the Financial Department. It is possible that in such differences of opinion not hard blows but hard words have been exchanged in matters connected with Land Revenue. I wish with regard to the controversy on that subject that you had found it more consistent with your high reputation and dignity not to use the harsh language you did in respect to the arguments of one of our eminent colleagues who was actuated by feelings just as honest and conscientious as any officer in this Presidency, in the part he took in these debates. But after all has been said and done it is impossible not to recognise and appreciate that you have been a most capable, concientious and high-minded administrator and have always strenuously applied yourself to the welfare and advancement of the Presidency, in the charge of the finances of which you have been placed. You have been not only a capable and conscientious administrator, but it is a common opinion, and has come to be generally recognised, that you have always carried out the administration of the affairs of this Presidency with a kindly and sympathetic spirit. For these reasons the Council regrets your separation from the country in which you have spent the best years of your life and we wish you long life, health and prosperity in the country which you make your home.

BOMBAY LEGISLATIVE COUNCIL

HARDSHIP ON MATHERAN LEASEHOLDERS

At the Meeting of the Bombay Legislative Council held at Poona on 10th July 1905, the Hon. Mr. S. W. Edgerley moved the second reding of "A Bill to Amend Certain Enactments and to Repeal Certain Other Enactments." The Motion being carried the Council proceeded to consider the Bill in detail. The Hon. Mr. G.K Parekh moved to delete entries 5 and 6 of schedule I relating to sections 40 and 43 of the Bombay Land-Revenue Code, 1879, and he was supported by the Hon. Mr. Setalvad. The Hon. Sir Pherozeshah spoke as follows.

Mr. President,—I join my honourable friends Messrs Parekh and Setalvad in opposing the proposed amendment of sections 40 and 43 of the Land-Revenue Code. I ask Government calmly consider how inequitably the attitude taken up by them in reference to Matheran leases works on the people who have built bungalows at that hill-station. I myself own bungalows there and can therefore speak with some experience about the matter. The leases are given for the express purpose of building bungalows and it is made obligatory on the lessee to build a bungalow within a particular period. Now the very conditions of a station like Matheran make it necessary for the lessee to excavate stone and earth from his plot for the purpose of building his bungalow as it would be impossible to bring them from Bombay or any other place. And it is hard that the lessee should not be entitled to use earth and stone from his plot for erecting the bungalow which he is bound under the terms of his lease to erect. Then he is bound to erect boundary-pillars marking the limits of his plot. Moreover everyone knows that the rain-fall at Matheran every year is heavy and that the roads and approaches are washed away and it becomes necessary for the lessee to reconstruct them every year. For that purpose he has to put back stones and earth in their proper places by removing them from where they have been washed away by the rains. Yet if the section is amended as proposed, Government will be able not only to levy fees from the lessee every year for the removal of the same stones and earth but to institute criminal proceedings against him. If criminal proceedings are instituted he will be tried by the Superintendent, who is always very zealous to guard the interests of Government and who virtually is the person who starts such proceedings. True, the person so criminally prosecuted and fined may appeal to higher tribunals and ultimately have justice done. But is it right that members of the public should be put to all the harassment and expense of such prosecutions? In the case that went up to the High Court and to which Mr. Setalvad referred, Mr. Pasta was a rich man who could afford to take up the matter to the High Court. But all persons may not be in the position of Mr. Pasta and they may find it impossible to vindicate their rights. Then even in cases where no criminal prosecution is instituted Government will, under the section as amended, be enabled to recover from the lessee as arrears of land-revenue, by distraint of his properties, the fees claimed by Government for the use of stones and earth even for the purposes I have above indicated. And the lessee who disputes the right of Government to do so will be forced to use Government in a Court of Law. Now I put it to Government whether it is fair or equitable that in *bona fide* disputes as to rights of this nature Government should be at liberty to summarily enforce their view and force the subject to take up the highly disadvantageous and difficult position of a plaintiff fighting Government with all their legal and financial resources? I can well conceive the fairness of

Government saying that the lessee has no right to remove earth and stone out of his holding for using them for purposes unconnected with the lease. I quite agree that such a removal by the lessee should be prevented and brought within the section. But I do appeal to Government to consider whether it is right that they should interfere with the use on the plot itself of earth and stone taken from the plot for all lawful purposes under the lease. The judgment of the learned Chief Justice in Pasta's case shows how unjustly the section if amended as proposed would work and I appeal to Government not to press the proposal.

The Hon. Mr. Edgerley having met the objection of the honourable members by inserting the words "from his holding" after the word "remove" in section 43 Mr. Parekh withdrew his Amendment.

BOMBAY LEGISLATIVE COUNCIL

A BILL FURTHER TO AMEND THE ACT TO DECLARE THE CONSTITUTION OF COURTS OF CIVIL AND CRIMINAL JUDICATURE IN THE PROVINCE OF SIND

At the Meeting of the Bombay Legislative Council held at Bombay on 31st March 1906, the Hon. Mr. Fulton moved the second reading of the above-mentioned Bill. The Hon. Sir Pherozeshah Mehta moved to substitute in clause 2 for the words "one of the additional Judicial Commissioners shall be a barrister of not less than five years' standing," the words "the Judicial Commissioner of Sind shall be a barrister of not less than five years' standing." In support of his Motion he spoke as follows.

My Lord,—My object in moving this Amendment is to bring the Sind Courts Act into conformity with the provisions of the Letters Patent constituting our Chartered High Courts. The Statement of Objects and Reasons shows that it is the wish of Government to give to Sind a Court similar, as nearly as possible, to the High Court. The Letters Patent of the High Court, as my Honourable friend is aware, provide that that Court shall consist of a Chief Justice and other Judges of whom at least one-third including the Chief Justice shall be barristers of not less than five years' standing. The Chief Justice of the High Court must therefore be a Barrister Judge and I submit that following the same analogy it should be provided that the Judicial Commissioner of Sind, who will correspond to our Chief Justice, should be a Barrister of not less than five years' standing. My Lord, I do not deprecate the merits of the judges drawn from the Covenanted Civil Service. I have the highest respect for the ability and capacity of Civilian Judges and some of our best judges have been provided by that service, for example, Sir Raymond West and Sir Maxwell Melvill, two of the finest judges that ever adorned the High Court Bench. But, after all, these are exceptional cases. Civilian Judges labour under one very great drawback with regard to the discharge of judicial functions. They have never practised at the Bar and those who are really conversant with the practice of that character know full well that nothing fits a man for the judicial bench so well as having practised at the Bar. It gives him a knowledge and a grasp of appreciation of evidence with which he has to deal, and which he could not get, however long he may be sitting on the Bench and however complicated may be the questions which he has to decide from time to time. However high the abilities of the judicial members of the Civil Service, it has always appeared to those who have practised in their courts that there is just something wanting in them in consequence of their not having practised at the Bar. There is also another reason which has very largely been put forward by the English mercantile community as a reason for having in all the Chief Courts a Barrister Judge as Chief Justice. It is that a Barrister Judge is generally, I will not say always, because there are exceptional cases, more conversant with Commercial Law than Civilian Judges. The Civilian Judges do not come in contact with commercial cases so much as a Barrister Judge who has practised in any of the High Courts in the Presidency and therefore it is that the Barrister Judge has a large grasp of questions relating to Commercial Law than the ordinary Civilian Judge is likely to possess, for the simple reason that he has not to deal with commercial cases in the various districts of the Presidency. Such questions do not arise except in mercantile and seaport towns. Persons practising in the Court of these places are far more likely to have a grasp of Commercial Law than the Civilian Judge.

But it might be said, we have already provided that one of the three judges shall be a Barrister. To that I would answer that it is the Chief Judge of the Court that gives the stamp to the Court. We see it in the High Courts of the various Presidencies that it is the Chief Justice that gives the stamp and character to the Court over which he presides. It seems to me that a Barrister Judge would be in a position to give a stamp of that character much more efficiently than a Civilian Judge.

It is for these reasons that I think it necessary to move that the Judicial Commissioner, and not one of the additional Judicial Commissioners, should be a Barrister Judge.

But, my Lord, while I move this Amendment I am not very sanguine of its success for the reason that this question some time ago was very largely agitated in Bengal and Burma when it was proposed to fill the post of the Chief Judge of Burma by a Civilian. The Chamber of Commerce and almost every one protested against the appointment being filled by a Civilian Judge and prayed that it should be filled by a Barrister Judge, but the Government of India were inexorable. I do not know how that circumstance will affect the considera-tion of this question by your Lordship's Council. But I do assert that the reasons for selecting a Judicial Commissioner from practising Barristers are very strong and I think it my duty to place it before this Council to be dealt with as they think proper. I therefore move that for the words "One of the Additional Judicial Commissioners shall be a Barrlster of not less than five years' standing," the words "the Judicial Commissioner of Sind shall be a Barrister of not less than five years' standing" be substituted.

The Hon. Dr. Bhandarkar:—Your Excellency,—All Barrister Judges are not good nor are all Civilian Judges bad. If the amendment had been in the following form, namely:—"one of the three Commissioners shall be a Barrister of not less than five years' standing," thus leaving it to Government to make the Chief Commissioner or one of the judges a Barrister instead of "the Judicial Commissioner of Sind shall be a Barrister of not less than five years' standing," I should certainly vote for it.

The Hon. Sir Pherozeshah:—I shall be willing to accept Dr. Bhandarkar's modification of my Amendment.

The Hon. Mr. Fulton:—We have given consideration to Dr. Bhandarkar's Amendment, but we have decided that we are not able to accept it at present because this clause has been submitted to the Government of India. The change proposed is not material, because at present, as the law stands, it is quite open to Government to appoint barristers to all three of the judgeships, if they like; but there are orders of the Secretary of State on the subject which limit their discretion in the matter. So far as the law stands they can do exactly as they please, and even supposing they make the alteration proposed by Dr. Bhandarkar they would still be very much in the same position; but it might be taken to indicate a charge of policy. Until it is proposed to change the policy, which at present is not contemplated, I am unable to accept the Amendment.

Dr. Bhandarkar and Sir Pherozeshah thereupon withdrew their Amendments.

In moving to omit the whole of section 9E in clause 4 of the same Bill, Sir Pherozeshah Mehta said—

My Lord,—I attach some importance to this Amendment because I believe that, if my honourable friend in charge of the

Bill had considered this section more carefully, I think he would have come to the conclusion that this section is objectionable on two grounds. Firstly it is undesirable in itself, and secondly it does not do what he thinks it does do.

Clause 9E runs:

> "Section 182 of the Code of Civil Procedure and section 356 of the Code of Criminal Procedure, 1898, shall not apply to any proceeding in the Court of the Judicial Commissioner. In that Court the Judge shall, as the deposition of each witness proceeds, make a memorandum of the substance thereof which shall be written and signed by the Judge with his own hand and shall form part of the record. Where the Judge is unable to make such a memorandum, he shall cause the reason to be recorded, and the memorandum shall be made in writing from his dictation in open Court."

Now the reason for introducing this section has been stated by my honourable friend in the Statement of Objects and Reasons. There he states that "it is proposed to apply the provisions of new section 9E to criminal cases as well as civil. As Sessions cases in Karachi are almost entirely tried by jury and there is no appeal on a question of fact, the verbal accuracy of the Judge's record is not of so great importance. It is desirable where possible to conclude jury cases in a single day's hearing. There are many cases in which a second day would be unnecessary if the time spent in recording the evidence in full and afterwards reading it over to the witness were saved. Judges entrusted with the work of a High Court may presumably be trusted to make an adequate record of the evidence."

Now, my Lord, these sections—the one in the Civil Procedure Code and the other in the Criminal Procedure Code—lay down minute regulations for the purpose of recording evidence as given by a witness; and what happens is, if the evidence is not given in English, the deposition of the witness as given in his own language is taken down and then read over to him.

He thus has an opportunity of seeing whether a correct record of his evidence is taken down, so that when he has signed it, it is an admission of the witness himself as to what he meant to say and what he actually did say. Now what is the position with regard to the High Court? In the High Court it is not, as my learned friend puts it, that the High Court simply makes a memorandum of the substance of the evidence given by a witness. In the Civil Procedure Code a section is provided in Chapter XLVIII which contains special rules relating to the chartered High Courts. Section 633 says:—"The High Court shall take evidence and record judgments and orders in such manner as it by rule from time to time directs." I ask my learned friend's attention to this. The High Court under this section has the power of framing the very same rules which are embodied in section 182 for recording evidence. As clause 9E stands, it takes away from the Judicial Commissioner's Court such power altogether. It gives no power to the Court to record evidence in the manner in which the High Court may, if it chooses, by rules which it has power to make, record it. The Sind Court even if it thinks that evidence should be taken down in the manner provided for District Courts under the Civil Procedure Code, it will not have the power to lay down a rule providing that it shall be done in that manner. The High Court has got the power of framing such a rule and it is instructive to see how the High Court has exercised that power. It has found it desirable to make rules for the purpose of taking down evidence of witnesses in the same manner as provided in the Civil Procedure Code.

You will find the rules at page 224, section 269 of Volume 1 of 1901, of Rules and Forms of the Bombay High Court. The rule in question runs:—"Upon the hearing of any suit the evidence of the witnesses shall be taken down in writing by, or in the presence and under the superintendence of, the Judge or one of the Judges, not ordinarily in the form of question and answer, but in that of a narrative, and the notes so taken shall be sufficient for all purposes and shall form part of the record." This does not go quite into the minuteness of section

182 of the Civil Procedure Code. Section 182 provides that "in cases in which an appeal is allowed the evidence of each witness shall be taken down in writing, in the language of the Court, by or in the presence and under the personal direction and superintendence of the Judge, not ordinarily in the form of question and answer but in that of a narrative, and, when completed, shall be read over in the presence of the Judge and of the witness, and also in the presence of the parties or their pleaders, and the Judge shall, if necessary, correct the same and shall sign it." All these details have not been embodied in the High Court rule but that rule is substantially a reproduction of section 182. It lays down that the evidence and not merely the substance of it shall be taken down. The clause as it is now in the Bill is really most objectionable. Under section 9E section 182 shall not apply to any proceeding in the Court of the Judicial Commissioner and that Court will not even have the power to determine for itself whether it shall or shall not follow substantially the provisions of section 182 as the High Court has done. In that Court the Judge shall, as the deposition of each witness proceeds, make a memorandum of the substance thereof, which shall be written and signed by the Judge with his own hand and shall form part of the record. Now, my Lord, I have the greatest repugnance to that phrase "substance of evidence." Substance of evidence may mean anything. I have had pretty long experience in the mofussil District Courts and the High Court, and whenever the word "substance" is used, what is taken down is of the most meagre character. I know there are judges who take down a correct substance of the evidence. But whenever you give power to a judge to take down merely the substance of evidence, it is almost impossible for any one to judge from such memorandum what the witness did really say. And questions constantly arise in Civil as well as Criminal Courts as to what it was the witness actually did say on a particular point.

Sometimes it is of the very greatest importance in the case. There being a memorandum of the "substance," one side says, "Oh, the witness did not say what was taken down, or he did not make this specific statement." While the other side says, "Oh no he made that specific statement," Under these circumstances the Court finds itself on various occasions quite helpless to ascertain what the witness did actually say. From my own experience I can say that it is most desirable to follow the strict provisions of the Civil Procedure Code. I have often heard laymen saying that this is waste of time. A similar observation is often made with regard to appeals. They say that appeals should be done away with. Those who have really studied the subject recognise that, though it looks as if unnecessary time is taken up by appeals, in the end and in the long run it secures what is of far greater importance, namely, the strict administration of justice. Those who say that there ought not to be so many appeals little realise that it is owing to the existence of permission to appeal that the judge takes far greater care in the way in which he conducts the trial than if no appeal were allowed. In the majority of cases the judicial officer tries them with far greater care and accuracy than would be done if his mind was free from the burden of thought that whatever his decision might be it could not be appealed against. If the evidence were taken down in the way the witnesses endeavour to put it before the Court, if what the witnesses did actually say were taken down in their own words, I think it will ensure a more careful adjudication of cases than would otherwise be the case. Therefore, I appeal to my learned friend not to take this retrograde step of accepting "the memorandum of the substance of evidence", but to abide by the provisions of the Civil Procedure Code which have been very carefully considered and which apply to all District Courts in the Presidency. If he is not, however, prepared to go so far, then I would ask him to give power to this Court to make rules for the purpose of taking evidence in the same way as the High Court of Bombay has power to make rules on the subject. So that it may be open to this Court to provide as the High Court has practically done that evidence shall be fully recorded as provided in section 182 of the Civil Procedure Code. "The memorandum of substance of evidence" is an elastic phrase which in most cases may mean almost anything. Therefore

I ask my learned friend to consider one of the two alternatives. I think he will be doing a great service to the cause of the judicial administration in Sind if he followed the provisions of the Civil Procedure Code.

My honourable friend has said we are going to raise the Sadar Court to the status of a High Court. Now Courts are not raised like that by Acts of Parliament. They must have old traditions to regulate them and they must have surroundings for the purpose of maintaining their real status. The traditions of a High Court cannot be created; nor can environments. A High Court like that in Bombay has traditions which have come down not only from its own past history, but traditions which it has so to say inherited from the Courts in England. These traditions come to High Courts and no act of the Legislature can provide them. The environments of a large city like Bombay with its large and public-spirited population cannot be created all of a sudden in other places. I am quite willing to admit that Karachi is fast rising in importance with its growing trade and population. Perhaps my honourable friend Mr. Webb may say I cannot appreciate Karachi in its true light. But I do not think he will deny, that, although Karachi has rapidly developed, it has not quite come up to the status of a city like Bombay with its large population, commercial activity and its public spirit. Europeans, who are in a very large preponderance, contribute largely to this and the native population is also advanced. You cannot create all these things in a Province like Sind. Therefore, I think it will be very desirable to apply to Courts there the procedure laid down for District Courts. Now all District Courts so far are regulated by the provisions of section 182 and the corresponding provisions of the Criminal Procedure Code. I think it would be really doing benefit to the Province of Sind if those provisions were allowed to be applied to the new Court. For these reasons, my Lord, I move the Amendment that section 9E should be eliminated.

The Hon. Mr. Fulton:—There appears to be some misunderstanding. What we intend to do is to get rid of the reading out of the evidence. Now in the District Court of Karachi the evidence is given generally in the Sindhi language or in some vernacular language. It is translated into English as the language of the Court and when the evidence is given by a witness it is translated by the interpreter and the Judge writes it down. At the end of the evidence the Judge hands over his note to the interpreter. The interpreter reads it and translates it sentence by sentence and the witness finally says it is correct. The intention was merely to drop this last item, viz., of reading out the retranslation into the vernacular, and in other respect it was not desired to alter the method of taking down the evidence or to authorise the Judge to take down anything less than he takes down at present.

H. E. the President then asked Sir Pherozeshah Mehta whether he pressed for a retranslation.

The Hon. Sir Pherozeshah:—Personally, I am strongly of opinion that it would be a desirable thing to enforce the provisions of the Civil Procedure Code; but if Government are not willing to go so far, then I would pray that they give power to the Court to make rules for taking down evidence, and drop altogether the words "substance of evidence" which are objectionable.

H. E. the President:—Do you wish that the evidence should be recorded in narrative form?

The Hon. Sir Pherozeshah:—Yes, my Lord.

The Hon. Sir Pherozeshah then expressed his willingness to withdraw his Amendment in view of a modification of Section 9E proposed by the Hon. Mr. Fulton.

The Hon. Mr. Fulton:—Your Excellency, it is proposed to omit section 9E and to substitute the following new section for it.

"9E. The Court of the Judicial Commissioner shall record evidence in such manner as it by rule with the sanction of the Local Government from time to time directs. Section 182 of the Code of Civil Procedure and section 356 of the Code of Criminal Procedure, 1898, shall not apply to any proceedings in such Court after such rule has been sanctioned."

His Excellency the President put the motion that the clauses should be amended accordingly; this was agreed to and clause 4 with the new section 9E was passed to stand part of the Bill.

BOMBAY LEGISLATIVE COUNCIL

A BILL FURTHER TO AMEND THE BOMBAY TRAMWAYS ACT—SIR PHEROZESHAH STRONG PROTEST

At the Meeting of the Bombay Legislative Council held in Bombay on 16th March 1907 the Hon. Mr. Fulton proposed that Rule 23 of the Standing Orders be suspended under Rule 49 to permit him to move a very short Bill amending two sections of the Bombay Tramways Act of 1874, as it had been impossible to give the customary fifteen days' notice. H.E. the President, Lord Lamington, then suspended the Standing Orders and the Hon. Mr. Fulton rose to move the first reading of the Bill and in doing so said:—The matter is one of urgency ....and if none of the honourable members object I shall ask Your Excellency still further to suspend the Standing Orders so as to allow the Bill to be read a second and third time at this meeting and passed.

The Hon. Sir Pherozeshah thereupon spoke as follows:

Your Excellency,—It is most unfortunate that this Bill has been brought forward without the slightest notice being given to the Corporation. When I lay before the Council all the facts connected with this question, I think it will be admitted that it is very necessary that the Corporation should have an opportunity of expressing their opinion on it. The Hon. Mr. Fulton has read to us Mr. Rimington's letter and a memorandum of the Municipal Commissioner. Now the Corporation has never been informed of what had been stated in the said memorandum. The matter has not been brought before the Corporation. In a great undertaking like the Tramways Company's contract the Corporation should, in connection with all important points like those involved in this Bill, have the fullest opportunity of giving their opinions and to state what experience they have had in the matter which would enable the Council to judge properly on those points. The Hon. Mr. Fulton is perhaps not aware that a Committee of the Corporation has been sitting to consider all questions arising in connection with the Tramways and this Committee has had to deal with various questions relating to the width of the roads and concessions to be made to the Tramway Company for the purposes of running the cars in streets which had been acknowledged necessary to be widened before they would be allowed to lay single lines and in some places double lines. It is most important that the city should not have lines running in streets which are not wide enough to have traffic of this character; but the Corporation have done their best to make all reasonable concessions which could be granted to the Company in order to enable them to run through various parts of the city which otherwise it would have been impossible for them to do. In dealing with these concessions the Committee of the Corporation considered very carefully what was the width of the carriages and overlapping portion beyond the rails. It was on the basis that such over-lapping portions were 14 inches that we granted many concessions with regard to streets that were not otherwise wide enough for the purpose. This is a serious question and the Corporation having made concessions upon that basis and that basis only, I strongly submit to Your Excellency that the Corporation should have an opportunity of saying what they wish to say upon the changes now proposed. Mr. Rimington proposes to have no limit whatever and to leave it to the discretion of the Commissioner from time to time to say what should be the over-lapping area. It seems to me this would be a procedure of the most unsafe character. Commissioners come and Commissioners go. Some stay for a few months and others longer. They are not permanent officials bound to continue for any specific length of time and the experience which one might bring to bear upon the question might not be of a character sufficient to justify his being entrusted with the power of exercising his discretion on a question of this magnitude. A Commissioner might come who would say "let it be 18 inches over-lapping" and another would say "there is no harm in 20." To this it may be answered that the word "Commissioner" under the Tramways Act really represents the Corporation. But it is an open question whether the "Commissioner" there is only the mouth-piece of the Corporation or has the power of exercising his own discretion. The Corporation has always claimed that the Municipal Commissioner in these contracts is only the mouth-piece of the Corporation. But it cannot be concealed that the contention has been raised whether the powers given and discretion vested in him are given and vested only as the mouth-piece of the Corporation or whether he can act upon his own independent authority. True the Corporation has power by a majority of three-fourths to pass a vote of censure upon the Commissioner and thereby remove him. This is, however, an absolutely impracticable thing to do under ordinary circumstances. I have never known such a case to arise but the possibility can always be contemplated of a Commissioner taking it into his head and saying "Power and discretion are entirely given to me and I will do what I like without reference to the Corporation." The city would in such an event be placed in a difficult position. I appeal to Your Excellency to refer this matter to the Corporation for their consideration. The Corporation in their relations with the Tramway Company have tried to do their best in the interests of the city and to meet the requirements of the Company as generously as possible. I can speak from personal experience, for I am Chairman of the Committee which for three years has been dealing with questions arising out of the Tramways. I say emphatically that the Corporation have dealt in the most reasonable manner with the Company, having in view the necessity for the expansion of the city and the facilities that ought to be given to the travelling public. We have not stood upon technicalities or objections of a trifling character and we have tried to meet the wishes of the Company in a very fair and generous spirit. Under these circumstances, I think it is due to the Corporation that this matter should not have been brought before Government before the Corporation had had their say on the matter.

I venture to think that Mr. Rimington should have sent to the Corporation a copy of the letter addressed by him to Government and stated that this application was being made and the Commissioner should also have sent to the Corporation a copy of his memorandum and then the Corporation could have taken the necessary action. Of course it will be said that the Corporation can still approach Government with their views but I ask honourable members of Council to remember how difficult the situation becomes when once Government have definitely committed themselves to a proposal by embodying it in a Bill. I desire to cast no reflection upon the members of Government, but I am only speaking of human nature as it is. Having once been committed to certain lines it is very difficult to effect an alteration. My experience of this Council has been that Your Excellency and Members of Government are always ready to listen to our representations in the most generous manner, but I do think in this matter that it is unfair —if I may use the word—to the Corporation, that this should not have been sent to the Corporation before the Bill was formulated. The plea of urgency has been introduced, but there would have been no urgency if the Tramway Company had carried out that which they undertook to do within a certain time. There have been bitter complaints about the delay in the work, and having delayed the matter themselves they now urge the plea of urgency. I ask that the matter may be referred to the Corporation in view of the circumstances which I have stated.

The Hon. Mr. Fulton :—After hearing the remarks of the Hon. Sir Pherozeshah, I have not the slightest objection to referring the Bill to the Corporation. We were not aware that it was at all contentions. We propose to hold another meeting about the middle of April and perhaps the Corporation can let us have their opinion by that time.

The Hon. Sir Pherozeshah:—We will try to deal with the matter without loss of time. The Corporation will consult the wishes of Government in this matter.

The Hon. Mr. Fulton:—The Government have no strong wishes on the point except to further the general convenience of the people of Bombay. I move that the Bill be read a first time.

The Hon. Sir Pherozeshah:—Certainly. I do not object to that.

H.E. the President then moved that the Bill be read a first time. The Motion was carried and the Bill was read a first time.

The Hon. Sir Pherozeshah:—Perhaps it would be best not to appoint a Select Committee just at present, if the Bill is coming on in April.

H.E. the President:—Yes, until we receive an opinion from the Corporation there is no use in appointing a Select Committee.

The Hon. Mr. Fulton agreed to the course proposed.

At the Meeting of the Bombay Legislative Council held in

Bombay on 18th April 1907 under the presideney of the Hon. Mr. Fulton, Sir Pherozeshah moved that the second reading of the Bill further to amend the Bombay Tramways Act be adjourned to the next Meeting of the Council in June. He said that circumstances had so taken place that it had been absolutely impossible for the Bombay Corporation to deal with the matter.

The Hon. the President:—That is another way of not allowing the electric trams to run.

The Hon. Sir Pherozeshah:—I am sure the tramways will then be in the same position as they are at the present moment.

The Hon. the President:—I understand that the electric trams are meant to be run in May, if there is no legal difficulty in the way.

The Hon. Sir Pherozeshah:—That is in the papers. But I have been reading in the papers statements of that character for the last six months.........

The Hon. the President:—What you mean to do at present is to move that the matter be adjourned to the next Meeting of the Council?

The Hon. Sir Pherozeshah:—And that in the meantime a Select Committee may be appointed. There is a good deal of matter to be placed before a Select Committee.

After further discussion the Hon. the President put the Motion for adjournment to the vote and declared it lost.

The Hon. Sir Pherozeshah asked for a division. The Council divided, there were 7 for and 10 against the Motion which was therefore lost.

The Hon. Sir Pherozeshah:—I enter my strong protest against the way in which this matter has been dealt with in the

Council. I came on the distinct understanding that if the Corporation were not able to move, the matter was to be held over till the June meeting. I accordingly sent no notice of amendment.

The Hon. Mr. Fulton then moved the second reading of this Bill and inquired whether any gentleman wished to say anything about it.

The Hon. Sir Pherozeshah:—I have a good deal I could say, but I would fain spare the Council if I know what the wishes of Government are in regard to adding the words "without the consent of the Corporation" at the end of section 6. I could go into the history of the question, if necessary. We are anxious to promote the convenience of the public—is a term which can be considered in two ways. In promoting their convenience for two months we might be doing harm to them for future years. Will Government agree to the insertion of the words "without the consent of the Corporation" in section 6?

The Hon. the President:—Why not add the words to section 6?

The Hon. Sir Pherozeshah:—Yes, that would not complicate matters.

The Hon. the President:—The Commissioner has not submitted to the Corporation his sanction in this particular instance.

The Hon. Sir Pherozeshah:—That is what I have been surprised at and it is the more important because the Tramway Company have never complained that we have not treated them with great consideration. I will appeal to the Hon. Mr. Dunn, who is on the Committee, and who knows exactly what has been done, whether we have not always treated them most reasonably.

The Hon. Mr. Dunn:—I can substantiate that. The Committee have always been most anxious to meet the Tramway Company in every possible way. We have always met them in a most sympathetic spirit.

After further discussion the Bill was read a second time.

The Hon. Sir Pherozeshah:—I propose as an amendment that the words "without the consent of the said Corporation" be added to section 6 of the Tramways Act of 1874.

The Hon. Mr. V.D. Thackersey seconded the amendment. Several honourable members having spoken, the Hon. the Advocate-General moved that instead of the words "without the sanction of the Municipal Corporation" the words "without the sanction of the Municipal Commissioner" be inserted.

The Hon. Mr. Cameron supported this amendment.

The Hon. Sir Pherozeshah:—...........As regards the point made by the Hon. Mr. Rahimtoola and the Hon. Mr. Cameron about the powers given to the Municipal Commissioner in the Act and in the concession, I may say that powers with regard to certain details of administrative action have been given to the Commissioner, though ultimately he has to come to the Corporation for sanction. The concession does also give powers straight to the Corporation leaving aside the Commissioner for various reasons. As for instance, in the matter of taking tolls, fares, etc., the Company has to obtain the approval of the Corporation, and the Commissioner has got nothing to do with it. Then again the Corporation only has the power to make special arrangements for the use of tramway lines for Municipal purposes. But the most important part of the objection is founded upon a clause in the concession, which has been taken from the Act and which provides that the public have every right to use the roads made by the Tramway Company. Article 6 of the concession lays down that nothing shall take away the right of the public to pass across any part of the road over which a tram line is laid. The great risk lies not on the outer sides of the terminus, but on the double tracks—on the space between the two lines. If that space is very narrow and is encroached upon even by inches it affects the safety of the public. I may say it is necessary to put in the words "Municipal Corporation" in the section. Ultimately the Corporation passes everything, and in either case the Commissioner cannot set aside a resolut ion of the Corporation. I submit that when we are laying down a matter of this sort, it is right that the power should be given to the Corporation.

On a vote being taken the Hon. the Advocate-General's Amendment was lost and the Hon. Sir Pherozeshah's was put to the vote and carried.

The Bill was eventually read a third time and passed.

BOMBAY LEGISLATIVE COUNCIL

FAREWELL TO THE HON. MR. E.M.H. FUTON, C.S.I.

At the Meeting of the Bombay Legislative Council held on 18th April 1907, the Hon. Sir Pherozesh spoke as follows at the end of the session.

Before the Council adjourns I should like to express our deep regret that we are so soon parting with the Hon. Mr. Fulton. Throughout your tenure of office, Sir, you have ever shown the greatest courtesy and consideration to eveyone in the transaction of the business of this Council. I have had the pleasure of serving under you as Chairman on several Committees and never was Chairman more anxious to give a reasonable hearing to one side and the other. Speaking both for myself and for those of my colleagues who have served on Select Committees, I can say that we are deeply grateful to you for the uniform kindness and courtesy which you have ever displayed. One matter in regard to which we are all especially grateful to you is for your sustained and active interest in the cause of buildings for primary schools in this city. The question had been before the public a long time before your arrival in

Bombay and the interest with which you took up the question, contributed in an enormous degree to the solution which was ultimately arrived at, and which brought good healthy buildings for the primary schools in Bombay within practicable sight. On behalf of myself and the Council I wish to say how deeply we regret having to part with you and I tender to you our best thanks for the interest you have taken in the public matters of the Bombay Presidency.

The Hon. Mr. Fulton having replied the Council was adjourned sine die.

BOMBAY LEGISLATIVE COUNCIL

THE BOMBAY BUDGET OF 1907-1908.

Crushing Reply to Hon. Mr. Logan's Insinuations

At the Meeting of the Bombay Legislative Council held in Poona on 22 June 1907, the Hon. Muir Mackenzie introduced the Financinl Statement of the Government of Bombay for the year 1907-1908 when the Hon. Mr. Pherozeshah Mehta made the following speech.

Your Excellency,—I rise to offer a few observations on the Budget under circumstances which, I am sure, my hourable colleagues will admit, can well claim and deserve their commiseration. I feel very much like the Red Indian Chief of whom we read in novels, who jumps into the arena, arrayed in a variety of warlike accoutrements and who finds to his dismay that he is stripped of them, one by one, by the people around him. I came here with arranging a number of topics in my mind on which I hoped to address the Council. But my dismay may be conceived when I found one honourable member after another getting up before me and anticipating them one after another. My honourable friend Mr. Setalvad has been the worst sinner in this respect. I have been calling the attention of the Council for a series of years to several educational topics of more or less importance. Mr. Setalvad has cooly appropriated nearly every one of them. The Hon. Mr. Ibrahim and others who followed him have treated me nearly as badly, so much so that I was seriously considering whether I might not distinguish myself this year by exercising the self-restraint of refusing to plough the sands as I have done for so many years and remain silent altogether. But my honourable friend Mr. Logan has come to my help in my dilemma and made it impossible for me not to rise to offer a strong protest against the unfounded and prejudiced observations which he has allowed himself to offer from his place in the Council. I confess I was astonished that the Hon. Mr. Logan should have thought it right to make so personal and offensive an attack as he has done against members of this Council as honest and sincere as he considers himself to be. Not that he has enlightened the Council by anything new or original. He has only trotted out all the old fallacies and arguments with which we have been perfectly familiar in this Council for many years. They have been exploded again and again in this Council and elsewhere.

But they will not die even hard. My Lord, the Bombay Revenue-officer, like the Bourbons, "never forgets and never learns." Time after time have lessons been administered to him, but he has been proof against them all. Has the Hon. Mr. Logan forgotten altogether the history of these counsels and lessons? Does he not remeber the lecture administered by the Commission appointed to inquire into chronic agricultural indebtedness of the Deccan rayat? Has he forgotten how they pointed out that one of its main causes was the inelasticity of the Bombay Revenue System? The Bombay Revenue-officer, then as now, My Lord, kicked against what he contemptuously described as the meddlesomeness of a Commission unfamiliar with the profound mysteries and beauties of the Bombay System and sat down to indite a portentous minute of protest and resentment against the ignorant deductions of an alien Commission. Then again I suppose the Hon. Mr. Logan has no memory for the conclusion of the Famine Commission presided over by Sir Anthony McDonell who pointed out that the Bombay

Revenue System and its principles of assessment were reducing a large percentage of the agricultural population to the condition of day-labourers. The findings of Mr. Maconochie's Commission, surely, are too recent to be forgotten, even though the Hon. Mr. Logan and these of his way of thinking may querulously and stoutly repudiate or explain them away. Coming to more recent times when one would have thought the dire existence of prolonged famines would have sobered him, we still find the Bombay Revenue-officer resisting any improvement.

My honourable friend may take it that the public of this Presidency has not and will not easily forget the obstinate tug-of-war which has waged over the subject of the amendment of the rules relating to suspensions and remissions and the vexed point of individual inquiries to which the Bombay Government clung so pertinaciously. The whole world knows that had it not been for the pressure put by the Government of India, our present improved system of granting remissions and suspensions would never have come into effect. In saying so, I ought perhaps, My Lord, to beg the pardon of the Financial Member, for I am not unaware that there were exceptions and that there were not wanting experienced and large-hearted Revenue-officers who condemned the prevailing policy and strove and struggled to get it discarded. The valuable services which such men rendered during the late famines did not escape warm recognition and appreciation from the grateful non-official members of this Council. All this refers to the general policy and principles of the Bombay Revenue-officer. His practical ways and methods have not been better. The Kabilpore case in which the late Sir Herbert Birdwood distinguished himself when acting as District Judge is not yet altogether forgotten, nor is the castigation administered by Chief Justice Sir Michael Westropp when the case went up in appeal to the High Court nor the scathing condemnation of the grasping conduct of Revenue-officers. The Report of the Maconochie Commission shows that they are what they were then. They will never learn. My Lord, I do not propose to deal in detail with what has been advanced by the Hon. Mr. Logan. It has been repeatedly dealt with before, and, now as then, the Revenue-officer will never be convinced. It would be useless and ineffective to combat the intolerant prejudices and bigoted sentiments regarding the agricultural condition of the people and the principles of revenue assessment to which he has so long been consistently and steadfastly wedded. It is a pity to reflect that no amount of authoritative investigation or counsel has ever been able to dissociate himself from his own ingrained ideas and prejudices.

My honourable friend has talked of famines and political propaganda, and he told us that formerly revenue was paid with marvellous punctuality. He tried to make out that it was not so paid now in consequence of political propaganda. The Hon. Mr. Logan has not adduced a shred of evidence to bear out his conclusion. Surely the real explanation lies on the surface without resorting to offensive allegation about political propaganda. It is a well-known fact that there had been no famines in Gujarat for a long series of years before 1896-97 and since then recurring periods of scarcity and famine overwhelmed the province. Is it a wonder, then, that even though heavy, the rayats could and did pay their assessments before 1896, and that they could not do so during the lean years? It has been dinned repeatedly into our ears that in fixing assessments, good and bad years were taken in account, but with such alterations of long periods when the province was free from famine, where were the materials for taking an average? It was idle to talk of such things for the purpose of justifying the wringing out the full assessment from a rayat utterly impoverished by successive blows following one upon another. With such facts, where was the use in dragging in the bug-bear of political propaganda to explain a phenomenon so perfectly simple? My Lord, it was unpardonable for the Hon. Mr. Logan under such circumstances to make offensive insinuations about blaming those "who inculcated habits of dishonesty and contumacy to the people." My Lord, the Hon. Mr. Logan in this connection talked of "the orators," evidently intending to include some of us as these unscrupulous "orators". It cannot but be a matter of regret that any member of this Council should have allowed himself to give expression to such insinuations. I say, My Lord, such observations should never have been made by a responsible officer of Government speaking at this Board. Not a fact, not a particle of evidence has he advanced in support of his imputations. My Lord, I cast these imputations back in the face of him who makes them. I say it is utterly untrue that "orators" have inculcated habits of dishonesty and contumacy to the rayats. It is a pity that the Hon. Mr. Logan should not have had the courage to name even a few or one of the "orators." The fact is that, freed from the control of the Civil Courts and practically irresponsible and altogether autocratic, the Bombay Revenue-officer is absolutely intolerant of criticism unless by way of praise.

He has so got into the habit of thinking that he alone understands everything, that he is impatient of contradictions and thinks it impertinence and something worse for anybody however sincere and disinterested to meddle in what he considers his own peculiar province. It never occurs to him that he is only betraying prejudice and bigotry. Let me tell the Hon. Mr. Logan that we have pleaded and shall always plead the cause of the rayat, and for that matter of the landlord and the sowcar when we believe that they are oppressed and ill-treated and have grievances which demand redress. And let me also tell the honourable member that the men who do so are as honest and sincere and perhaps even more distinterested and public-spirited, as he believes himself and his brother officials to be; no "political propaganda" and no "orators" are at the bottom of the impoverishment of the agricultural population and their inability to pay their dues in times of distress, but it is the rigid and oppressive way in which the Bombay revenue system has been worked for years and years. It is sad, My Lord, to contemplate that the Bombay Revenue-officer still clings to his old traditions of repression and rigidity and that nothing has been of avail to turn him from his old bigotries and prejudices bearing so hardly upon the agricultural population of which he fondly hails himself to be the mabap but is really the stern collector of as large a revenue as possible. I will only saya passing word as to the clam set up by my honourable friend to be the only person, along with the Hon. Mr. Drew and perhaps with the Hon. Mr. Barrow in this Council to represent the interests of the rayat and that we represented the sole interests of the landlord.

My Lord, it is not easy to conceive how an official can be said to represent the rayat's interests when his main and principal function is to extract as much revenue as possible. But for ourselves, My Lord, we claim to represent the interests of both the rayat and the landlord, when they can indeed be differentiated at all. We think it our duty to speak out for all interests, even of the sowcar, who was described in the Viceroy's Council by Sir James Westland as one of the most useful instruments to bring the rayat's assessment into the Government treasury. It is said against him that he charges higher rates of interest than Government charge on their tagavi advances. No wonder that is so, when we remember the stringent powers and processes which Government have reserved to themselves to recover them. My Lord, the Hon. Mr. Logan talked of a prosperity Budget, as showing that the country was more prosperous than ever before. My Lord, this is one of the most superficial arguments that can be imagined to prove by itself the country's prosperity. True the Imperial Budget shows large surpluses, but by themselves, they prove nothing. We have to examine the character of these surpluses, how and whence they are derived, before we can hold that a surplus means general prosperity. If it is essentially derived from taxation directly or indirectly imposed, if it is the result of an artificial system of currency bearing hard on the people and indirectly taxing them, then a surplus is no sign of general prosperity, but only a burden a source of impoverishment. There may be thus an overflowing surplus, but the condition of the rayat may still be increasing in indebtedness and poverty. As I have said before, My Lord, I do not propose to enter into detailed arguments touching all these questions raised by my honourable friend. I know they will leave him as unconvinced as before and they would, moreover, far exceed the limits even of a Budget speech in Council. I have now done, My Lord, with the Hon. Mr. Logan.

I will now proceed to offer a few remarks on what fell from my honourable friend Mr. Armstrong. We know that the Hon. Mr. Armstrong always puts his points so soberly and carefully that they can be dealt with only with courtesy and respect. He will permit me, however, to point out that his remarks about municipal matters savour of the general fallacy into which public criticism of a certain class regarding municipal administration is frequently guilty. Every fault of omission or commission is laid at the door of the Municipal Corporation, when it really ought to be carefully discriminated between the different municipal authorities which the law has constituted. Very often the Municipal Corporation has to complain as much as the public of Municipal executive and has in reality struggled long and hard to set it right in spite of ignorant or interested misrepresentation. But the blame is nearly always laid on their shoulders. I hope and trust that this undiscriminating confusion will cease, for it otherwise deprives the Corporation of the valuable support of public opinion in many an effort to make Municipal Administration careful and efficient. With regard to the Hon. Mr. Armstrong's comments on the water-supply of the city, there was an undertone of unfavourable criticism against the inaction of the Corporation in dealing with the question. In the first place, the recent fire near the Crawford Market involving a portion of Sitaram Buildings, was not due to the insufficient or defective supply of water. Water there was in abundance, but time was lost in opening the proper sluice-valve which should have been open. The fault lay with the executive of the Water Department and the Corporation has undertaken a strict, thorough, and speedy inquiry into the cause of the mismanagement. As to the supply itself, people have forgotten that it was the Corporation and its private members who, even against the hesitation of the Municipal executive, firmly pronounced for providing a constant and full supply and undertook the vast scheme which resulted in the present Tansa Lake. It was the Corporation which roused the executive with great difficulty to work a special staff for testing and preventing the enormous leakage of the supply through the mains, which was for long incredulously denied by Commissioners and Water Engineers and which on actual testing, has been now discovered to be beyond what they dreamt of. They are now carefully considering the question of the duplication of the Tansa main which is beset with more difficulties, sanitary and otherwise, than most people are aware of. But even so, the Corporation are quite prepared to undertake it if careful consideration shows it to be necessary or desirable.

With regard to the question of town-duty on sugar, the Corporation have had no opportunity of dealing with it. It was only the other day that the Chamber brought it to the notice of that body. Till now it was with the Commissioner. But in justice to Mr. Sheppard, the Municipal Commissioner, I should like to say that he pointed out to the Chamber a very simple way of removing the difficulties of the merchants but which they do not care to accept as to the total abolition of the duty; the policy of the Corporation has been to reduce or abolish in the first instance the duties on necessary articles of food. Sugar is not a necessary article of food in the same sense as, for example, grain is. The question, therefore, must be considered from all sides and cannot be dealt with solely with regard to the alleged grievances of the merchants who, instead of facilitating the task of collection and refund by simple precautions, created difficulties by the innumerable devices resorted to by the middlemen employed by them to perpetrate frauds of the grossest description.

The one other point to which the Hon. Mr. Armstrong referred was about the provision of overbridges, and I am in full sympathy with what he has stated. The railway crossings are no doubt a nuisance and a scandal and it is time that necessary overbridges should be provided in the City. The most important of them are, I believe, five or six and I trust they may be soon undertaken. But let me say that in this respect the City has to complain not only against the Railway

Companies, but also against the Government itself. Because these railways are practically Government concerns, and it seems to me that the Government should have recognised that there were legal and moral obligations to build them. They ought to have recognised that as the Railway Companies came into the City for their own purposes to make profits, the City should not be made to suffer inconvenience. It cannot be gainsaid that the burden of providing overbridges lies upon the Companies. I remember looking up the English Railway General Clauses Act. As Your Lordship knows that a large number of railways in England are dealt with by Private Bills with their own clauses and conditions. But the legislature has provided that where there are no private Acts there should be clauses for the building of the overbridges. In the Railway General Clauses Act it has been laid down that every railway coming into a City must provide culverts, bridges, etc. That is the principle upon which the Government ought to recognise that it owes to the City the obligation of providing for it the conveniences which are required for its traffic. I hope Your Lordship's Government will take up the question in earnest and will find means to accelerate and dispose of it in as speedy a manner as possible.

The Hon. Mr. Muir Mackenzie in his reply to the several members who had spoken on the Budget said:—The remarks of my honourable friend Mr. Logan led to a lively rejoinder from the Hon. Sir Pherozeshah Mehta. It was quite interesting to have our solemn deliveries varied with a little salt.........I cannot imagine that the Hon. Sir Pherozeshah was correct when he turned overwhelmingly on the Hon. Mr. Logan and said that the "orators," whose utterances stimulated the revenue-payer to the dishonesty indicated, were, in the fiery utterance of Sir Pherozeshah, "us". There are orators outside this Council who say exceedingly unscrupulous things.........But I feel no necessity to bolster up the Hon. Mr. Logan who is well able to take care of himself.

H.E. the President, Lord Lamington, in concluding the

debate said:—......I regard with very great satisfaction the interesting passage of arms which took place between the Hon. Sir Pherozeshah Mehta and the Hon. Mr. Logan. In these days when we know that proposals are mooted to increase and develop the utility of the work of these Legislative Councils, one pre-eminent feature which must ever be borne in mind is that they must be vitalised, as it were, both official and non-official members taking part in debate, exchanging arguments and entering generally into the contest of words. And so long as the arguments are fairly stated and refuted in good spirit, I regard it as a matter for satisfaction when I find any member in this Council taking up arms whether on behalf of or as a critic of the Government. Of course, it is rare indeed that Government finds a champion outside its own ranks, not because such do not exist, but because by the very nature of the case it is not the method of governing here to produce them. It is only in a country fully possessed of representative institutions like Great Britain where you have two opposing parties, indulging in true criticism of each other's proposals. Consequently I say that it is not often Government finds a supporter amongst the non-official element, ann therefore on an occasion like this when members meet on terms of equality I am delighted to find Council champions for the action of Government, and equally delighted to hear vigorous critics deliver critical and trenchant opinions. In this particular case we may say that whatever strong blows were dealt by the two honourable members, we may take satisfaction that each of them was armed with triple brass so that no one need take alarm less they should do one another serious injury.

At the Meeting of the Bombay Legislative Council held at Poona on 20th June 1908, a year after the above-mentioned incident, the Hon. Mr. Logan, while speaking on the Provincial Budget, craved His Excellency the President, Sir George Clarke's permission "to refer to an episode which occurred last year when the Hon. Sir Pherozeshah took the occasion of certain comments of mine in answer to the Hon. Mr. Parekh to make an attack on me of a somewhat personal character, which I have had no earlier opportunity of answering." "I am under the great disadvantage," he continued, "that the Hon. Sir Pherozeshah is not here today, and for this reason I will shorten my remarks to the smallest compass necessary to justify my own position, and will give nobody an opportunity of saying that I am attacking the honourable member behind his back. It will be remembered that I stated that the land assessment was really very light and left a high margin of rental. The Hon. Sir Pherozeshah Mehta talked of a great many things in his reply, but he did not say anything to meet this point, except that my statements were old fallacies which had been long exploded. Old, Sir, they may have been, for the facts have been notorious these forty years; but fallacies they are not. They have been established in the most authoritative way by the Government of India.........The Hon. Sir Pherozeshah was particularly violent in repudiating a remark of mine, that the agitation against the land-revenue was a political one. But unless the honourable member understood the word 'political' in a sense different from the usual one, it seems to me that he was very courageous in repudiating the political connection ....In the Deccan at least the agitation is closely connected with the political campaign of the Poona Extremists. They frequently address meetings of agriculturists, and as an illustration I may mention that about a week before the Hon. Sir Pherozeshah Mehta was denouncing what he had the presumption to call my 'unpardonable insinuations' on the subject, one of the most notorious of these Extremists was addressing a meeting at Satara.........I think I have now said enough, Sir, to show that the statements I made last year were in accordance with existing facts, and I consider that the Hon. Sir Pherozeshah showed a want of sobriety in denouncing them as he did."

The Hon. Mr. Setalvad who also spoke felt bound to refer to what had fallen from his honourable friend Mr. Logan about the passage of arms the previous year between him and the Hon. Sir Pherozeshah Mehta. "Mr. Logan has stated," said Mr. Setalvad, "that when he spoke of orators and political agitators and their connection with the contumacy on the part of the rayats to pay the assessments, he had in mind some mischievous agitation in the Deccan and that he did not insinuate anything against any honourable member of this Council and the attack therefore made on him by Sir Pherozeshah was unmerited and unjustifiable. Now, whatever the intentions of my honourable friend Mr. Logan might have been, I am afraid that he has forgotten the language that he actually used last year." Then referring to the words used by the Hon. Mr. Logan in the previous year, viz., that "The interests of the rayats are not independently represented here by any person except myself, the Hon. Mr. Drew and perhaps the Hon. Mr. Barrow. The landlord's interest is practically the sole interest which is represented by the Indian Members. It is because these landlords' interests are so well represented in this Council that we hear so much about these matters"—Mr. Setalvad said—"Can language be plainer than this? Did not Mr. Logan here refer to non-official Indian members and question their honesty of purpose by saying that they supported landlords interest and sacrificed these of the rayats, whose only friends, he said, were himself and Mr. Drew and perhaps Mr. Barrow? It was these unworthy and utterly unjustifiable charges and insinuations against non-official members that my honourable friend Sir Pherozeshah promptly repelled and took exception to, and not Mr. Logan's denunciation, if any, of the mischievous Deccan agitator. And I venture to think that what Mr. Logan calls Sir Pherozeshah's attack on him and of which he complains was perfectly justified and well deserved and that Sir Pherozeshah had not, in saying what he had said, lost his sobriety as suggested."

The Hon. Mr. G.K. Parekh who followed Mr. Setalvad submitted that it appeared very clearly that, when Mr. Logan was referring to the people who were responsible for inculcating contumacy and to those who represented the interests of the richer classes and not the interests of the rayats, he was alluding to his colleagues in the Council.

After speaking at length on the same incident, the Hon. Mr. D.A. Khare concluded his remarks as follows:—"The Hon. Mr. Logan has a right to think that what he says, he says honestly; so we also say that what we say here we say honestly. We are not posing as disguised champions of particular interests, and I trust that every member will give another member the same credit which he wants to take to himself for honesty of purpose and disinterested motives."

The Hon. Mr. Logan:—Your Excellency,—May I be permitted to close this controversy as a personal one between Honourable Members and myself by saying once for all that in speaking last year of orators who inculcated dishonesty and contumacy among the people, I did not refer to anything that has ever happened in this Council and I cannot understand how Honourable Members should have supposed that I did. Why, Sir, the country is covered with orators. I did not restrict my remarks to Poona as the Hon. Mr. Khare now professes to understand. I referred to agrarian agitation throughout the Presidency, but I did not refer to anything that has happened here.

Thus, after all the members concerned having had their say, this unpleasant controversy was here brought to an end.

BOMBAY LEGISLATIVE COUNCIL

THE BOMBAY BUDGET OF 1909-1910

At the Meeting of the Bombay Legislative Council held at Poona on 19th June 1909, the Hon. Sir John Muir Mackenzie introduced the Financial Statement of the Government of Bombay for the year 1909-1910. The Hon. Sir Pherozeshah Mehta made the following speech.

Your Excellencey,—I am very thankful to you for giving me now the opportunity for making a few observations, not upon the Budget but upon the general principles and policy which has guided this Council under its present constitution.

But before I do so Your Excellency will allow me to thank you for the very liberal manner in which members are supplied with Government papers, Press Communiqués, etc. I assure Your Excellency that this assistance has been invaluable to us. Formerly we had to make inquiries in all sorts of places and then we were not always satisfied that we had got the information we wanted, but under Your Excellency's new policy, members have been greatly assisted and I thank Your Excellency for adopting a measure of this character. My honourable friend Sir John Muir Mackenzie will forgive me if I say that I feel a little disappointed at the very brief remarks he has made before the Council on this occasion. My disappointment arises not inconsiderably from the circumstance that we know of the graphic power of description, the great use of language, and the generous appreciation of the work done which my honourable friend has often shown and in consequence of which I hoped that on his occasion, which Your Excellency has described as the closing scene of the reformed Council under the Act which came into operation in 1893, he might have given us a graphic summary of the work done by this Council and especially by non-official members and the impress their work has had upon the Budget which the Government has been able to lay before the Council on this occasion. I think on this occasion the opportunity might have been taken to recapitulate what has been done in the direction I have pointed out.

Your Excellency, the observations I am going to offer, I hope, will not be taken in the light that I offer them as adverse or hostile criticism of the Government. I shall certainly offer some criticism in the course of my remarks as to the way in which the efforts of non-official members were sometimes met and to their non-success; but Your Excellency, I will at once say that in offering that criticism, taken by itself, I shall be presenting only one side of the shield.

No one recognises more than I do that the true genius of British statesmanship contains within itself the power to recognise at the proper time—though perhaps slowly and cautiously—such drawbacks and failings as may present themselves and moves up to the requirements of the time and the march of progress. Your Excellency, the approaching reforms in this Council prove what I say. It is sometimes said that the grant of these reforms is the result of agitation but every student of history knows that agitation may be dealt with in one of two alternatives. There is the statesmanship which meets agitation by simple and pure repression; there is the statesmanship which tries to meet it by marching up, as I have said, to the requirements of the time and trying to lead up to reforms, such as we have got for the removal of the defects and drawbacks which may have presented themselves in the course of administration. That is what has taken place in regard to the march of Indian events and I have no doubt we shall all be much inspired in the future in the work of bringing into operation the reforms in the interests of this country, in the true interests of the connection of this country with England by, if Your Excellency will permit me to say so, the sympathetic guidance of statesmen like yourself. I have no fears for the future and if I look back to the past—as I am entitled to do for I have been a member of this Council ever since the present Act came into operation in 1893 and I have been able to watch its work perhaps more nearly than many other members—I say we may well look forward to a period of greater usefulness than even the past has provided. When we began in 1893, with the new functions which devolved upon us, there were forebodings that we should not be able to exercise those functions in a satisfactory manner. Even such a distinguished thinker as our late colleague Dr. Selby ventured to argue that when under the system of nomination we had got such good men as Ranade,Tyabji and Telang we could not expect to get even similar men by election. I then ventured to point out that this system of election had a magic in itself and worked upon those elected in a way that nomination could never do. Still we approached our duties with timidity and some misgiving but I am sure that the work which has been done has been neither useless nor vain.

Taking the judicial department, for instance I think the Hon. Mr. Webb will gladly recognise that an important reform in his province is due to the non-official members. From the very year 1898 we urged Government to reconstruct the Sadar Court of Sind. The Appellate Side was under a single Judge. The reform was first urged upon the Council by my old friend Odhavram Mulchand, the first member from Sind. I helped him and as a result—though it was a very slow process and took more than ten years to persuade Government to undertake it—the recognisation was carried out, and Mr. Justice Fulton steered a Bill through this Council putting the administration of justice in Sind on a sound and satisfactory basis.

Then, Your Excellency, there were a great many things even in the High Court of Bombay that required looking into. There was the question of the appointments of the Clerk of the Insolvency Court and of the Administrator-General. The Clerk of the Insolvency Court was allowed to drew thousands of rupees a month from the fees that came in instead of drawing a salary. Sir Richard Temple's Finance Commission pointed out that the work could be properly done by an official who would be well paid on a salary of Rs. 600 a month. From the first, my friend Mr. Setalvad, fresh from the High Court, urged this upon the Council. It required many efforts and many years before it was carried out, but I am glad to say Government decided to take the fees themselves and pay the Clerk a salary thereby saving a very large amount of money. In the same way the Administrator-General was allowed to draw thousands of rupees though his services could have been adequately paid for by a moderate salary, and I am glad to say that now a salary is paid for the office instead of the holder being allowed to draw the fees.

Then, Your Excellency, I may record one failure on our part in getting what we strenuously tried to get in this Presidency and that is the separation of judicial and executive functions. I took one of the first occasions which presented itself, I think it was in 1893, of urging upon Government to do this and I pointed out that the scheme could be carried out not only economically from a financial point of view but satisfactorily from the point of view of administrative efficiency. On that point, as I have said, we have to record a failure. That is surprising seeing that when owing to stress of famine exigencies Government were for a time obliged to relegate the judicial duties of revenue-officers to subordinate judges, it was proved to work satisfactorily. With that experience to guide us, it is a source of disappointment that this Government has not been forward in urging the Government of India to experiment in this Presidency along with the sister Presidency of Bengal. Your Excellency will perhaps remember that the Viceroy's Council, when it last considered the matter, selected the Bengal Presidency for the experiment instead of the Bombay Presidency a position we in Bombay resent.

Then there is one point on which I think I can congratulate myself and the other non-official members and that is the old thorny question of the police charges of the City of Bombay. I urged upon Government that it was an anomaly that the Bombay Corporation should be called upon to pay the cost of the police when the whole of the police administration was in the hands of Government. After a long struggle, I hope I may be allowed to call it a struggle, the Bombay Government made an arrangement, largely owing to the efforts of our late colleague Sir Steyning Edgerley, under which Government took over the police charges and imposed upon the Corporation primary education, medical relief and other minor charges. It was one of those questions requiring sympathetic treatment and required a lot of care on the part of the unofficial members. Then Your Excellency will permit me to refer to some points with regard to education. I do not know whether Your Excellency is aware that the Bombay University had in the beginning a grant of Rs. 15,000. Then Government, in the name of the needs of primary education, reduced it to Rs. 10,000 and again the claims of primary education and financial exigencies brought it down first to Rs. 5,000 and then to nothing, I struggled to prevent what I then thought meant the separation of Government from higher education, for Government's action was universally interpreted to mean the adoption of a set policy of dissociating Government from higher education. I protested against such a policy being adopted in this or any other parts of the country. Since then Government have fully realised that such a policy was not a policy beneficial to the best interests of the country, and they have, I am very glad to say, returned to the older policy and raised the grants so that instead of Rs. 5,000, Rs. 10,000 or Rs. 15,000 Government have given Rs. 50,000, Rs. 60,000, Rs. 1,00,000, Rs. 2,00,000, Rs. 3,00,000 for the purpose of the University and I think Government ought to be congratulated upon acting in that manner. I see there is no University grant this year but this is I take it, due to the exigencies of the year and will be made up in future years.

Then, Your Excellency, I may refer to the Fergusson College. When we urged Government to give a grant we were told that they did not wish to interfere with private enterprise. Private enterprise I might say without being invidious is a term which has been used in various ways. It was sometimes been used to defend depriving Government colleges of their grants and sometimes to defend depriving private colleges of their grants. The Fergusson College was deprived of the grant it used to get and I believe that it was the Government of Lord Harris which began by giving a grant of Rs. 3,000 which I think ultimately came up to the full amount aided colleges can claim, Rs. 10,000. In mentioning Fergusson College I may also state that I join my honourable friend Mr. Setalvad in deploring that Government will not grant to Gujarat and Sind Government Colleges as they have done to the Deccan. Government have established a model college in Bombay and given another one to the Deccan, and Gujarat and Sind ought to have Government colleges also. We have been told that Government are leaving it to private enterprise, but I pointed out many ago that such a policy had not succeeded and that the only remedy was the provision of model Government colleges in Gujarat and Sind in the same way as in the Deccan.

Then, Your Excellency, we may take some credit for inducing Government to take a step in advance with regard to the question of the construction of primary school buildings in Bombay. For a long time Government would not listen to us, but ultimately they awoke of the necessity of the occasion and appointed a Committee to consider the matter. Now, a scheme has been settled for spending ten lacs on such buildings, Government and the Corporation sharing the cost equally. I am glad to confess that in this matter Government have met the wishes of the Corporation in a liberal spirit.

Then, I think, this Council and especially its non-official members can lay claim to making Government take a firm and decisive step in another direction, and here I beg to congratulate Your Excellency's Government on what has been done with regard to the salaries of primary school teachers. To my friend Mr. Setalvad is due the credit of bringing this question before the Council. In 1893 he drew the attention of the Council to this matter by pointing out that primary school teachers were paid salaries lower than even ordinary peons and labourers. These teachers were paid for many years Rs. 5 or Rs. 6 a month, and a large number called pupil teachers were paid Rs. 3 to Rs. 5 a month. Your Excellency could well imagine, with the knowledge which you can bring to bear upon educational questions, what sort of teaching pupils in the primary schools could have received under those conditions. Government pleaded all sorts of excuses and the Finance Member pleaded two things; (1) the state of the Provincial finance; and (2) the calls upon their purse in various other directions;—and the somewhat surprising excuse that was brought forward of the law of supply and demand. I have heard with surprise the plea; "If you can get teachers for Rs. 3 and Rs. 5 why should you pay more?" Now, this is a plea which is far from convincing. Although you may get a certain kind of men for Rs. 3 and Rs. 5, it does not follow that they can really do the most responsible work which the teachers have to do of training the minds of the young. I admit with great pleasure that Government have thoroughly realised the importance of this question, and I think

Your Excellency's Government is to be congratulated for taking a firm and decisive step in raising the salaries of these teachers. I am perfectly certain that this process will be continued until the teaching in primary schools is placed on the basis on which it ought to be.

I also congratulate Your Excellency's Government upon the recent resolution which has been issued with regard to the establishment of a training college for primary school teachers in Bombay itself. This has probably followed upon the recommendation made by the primary education Committee to the effect that it was absolutely necessary that such a college should be established in Bombay. It is of no little credit to Your Excellency's Government that they have lost no time in framing a scheme and forwarding it to the Corporation for securing such a good purpose. I have no doubt that the Corporation will approach the question in the same spirit in which Your Excellency has launched this project.

We have done one other good thing. Lawyers are now in discredit. But, if that is so, there is no doubt that law teaching should be put upon an improved and proper footing. For years we had urged that the Government Law College should be put upon a proper basis and our efforts met with no success. And Your Excellency will allow me to point out that when we did win success it was not in a way upon which Government can be congratulated. At that time a scheme was started for a private Law College with my late lamented friend Mr. Justice Tyabji at its head. A committee was formed and the University was approached to grant it recognition. The recognition was granted. When Government saw that after all a private college was to be established they thought the time had come when a step should be taken forward. This could only be done by establishing aproper Government Law College. Then they brought in a scheme under which the present Law College exists.

I think, Your Excellency, I have indicated some of the salient reforms brought about by the exertions of non-official members under the Heads of Justice and Education. There are many other minor questions, but I do not propose to take up the time of the Council by dilating upon them. I now come to the most important Head of the Budget—the Revenue Head, and it is in connection with that department that I really hoped my honourable friend Sir John Muir Mackenzie would state what had been done by non-official members in the interests of the Presidency.

Your Excellency, it is with a great deal of astonishment that I have seen recently a claim put forward in public that so far as the interests of the rayats and the agricultural population of this Presidency are concerned it is the Government officials—the revenue-officers—who ever look after their interests in this Council, and that much could not be expected from non-official members in that direction who rather than look to the interests of the rayats are more bent and interested upon looking to the interests of the money-lenders, the sowcars, and the landlords. Your Excellency, I have said, I have seen with great deal of astonishment that plea put forward. I will ask the members of the Council to look to the records of the Council from the year 1893. I venture to say that no claim ever put forward was more unfounded so far as the revenue-officers were concerned and more libellous so far as the non-official members were concerned. From 1893 non-official member after member has striven hard to draw the attention of the Government to the hardships and difficulties under which the rayats have laboured, to the pressure which was tried to be put in the collection of revenue and to the rigours of the rigid system of revenue collection and, which, not only the official members who have worked on Government Commissions but also officials outside the Presidency have admitted, was responsible to a very large extent for the indebtedness of the Bombay rayat. Your Excellency, the Deccan Agriculturists' Commission pointed out that it was largely to the rigidity of the system of revenue collection in Bombay that the indebtedness of the Deccan rayats was due. Sir T.C. Hope, one of the most distinguished Revenue members of the Bombay Government, who afterwards went to the

Viceroy's Council, admitted that the indebtedness of the rayat was owing in a large measure to the rigidity of the Bombay system of land-revenue collection. Again, the Famine Commission reported to the same effect. I admit that the Bombay revenue-official never admitted the pertinency and soundness of the view taken by officials from other parts of India, charging them with knowing nothing about the Bombay revenue system, and pertinaciously maintained that the Bombay system was the best system under the sky. But even on these questions I am glad to congratulate the Government on the gradual improvement that has taken place in this direction through the exertions of non-official members. Government has at length yielded to public criticism and given up their favourite system of remission and suspension remission of land-revenue during times of famine Time after time, we pointed out the futility of attempting individual discrimination in granting remissions and suspensions. But nothing could move them from it until the Government of India passed its orders on the subject, and now we have a system, which, as the Hon. Mr. Parekh has admitted today, has worked liberally and justly in this Presidency. But it was not a little due to the persistent efforts of the non-official members that improvement has been effected.

I think Sir John Muir Mackenzie will remember that the abolition of the Survey and Settlement Department was very largely accelerated by the pressure put upon Government by non-official members, though I see with some nervousness that in the recent Report of the Land Records Department, proposals are made, which, if carried out, would mean the resuscitation of the old Survey and Settlement Department. I hope my alarms are not well founded but I fear these proposals if adopted would do away with the good work which was done with the abolition of that Department.

Then, Your Excellency, if the Hon. Sir John Muir Mackenzie will allow me, I will draw attention to the efforts made by the Hon. Mr. Parekh in bringing to the notice of Government the way in which famine measures were administered in some of the talukas which he represented. We were told in this Council the statements were exaggerated, if not altogether unfounded. Lord Northcote, the then Governor, told Mr. Parekh that if his statements and allegations were in any way well founded, he should present them in the shape of a statement and prove them. The Hon. Mr. Parekh with a persistency and tenacity all his own did so and collected a mass of facts, with the result that Government appointed Mr. E. Maconochie, then, I believe, serving the Government of India, to conduct an inquiry. The inquiry was held—and speaking from memory —I think I am correct in saying that many of the allegations and statements regarding the hardships suffered by rayats were borne out by the view which Mr. Maconochie took in his Report. His Report went up to the Collector with the inevitable result that he was convinced that Mr. Maconochie was all wrong. It next went up to the Commissioner, who happened to be Sir Frederick Lely, and though he said that several of the statements were exaggerated, he wound up as follows:

> "The Commissioner thinks the inquiry has done good by bringing to light irregularities which may now be rectified for the future. It has also shown that even the superior authorities did not thoroughly realise the deterioration of the taluka and its consequent inability to stand the shock of famine. This has since been represented to Government in Mr. Mehta's Revision Report and its forwarding memoranda. It is creditable to the public officers of the taluka that so little real hardship has been proved or even alleged. The Aval Karkun Himatram Ganpatram has incurred suspicion, but in the Commissioner's judgment there is not sufficient ground for punishing him. Others, including manv talatis have made mistakes, some from sheer stupidity, some from excess of zeal in carrying out what they thought the wishes of Government, and some though overwork at a very difficult time. Further than this the Commissioner does not think it is possible to go."

I may point out that Government did go a little further

and said that taken as a whole the Hon. Mr. Parekh's statements were not really satisfactorily proved. But in a case of this character it is to the Report of an indepedent Commissioner and to the Report of the Commissioner of the Division, Sir Frederick Lely, that we should look for judgment in the future. There is no doubt, however, that Mr. Parekh did very valuable service when he brought to the attention of Government the hardships which were inflicted upon the poor rayats in the taluka. I am glad to be able to acknowledge that as a result of what Mr. Parekh did, Government though it shock its head at him took strong measures to prevent any such thing recurring in future.

There is one other point to which I will refer in regard to the land-revenue administration. I have said that it is with surprise that I have read of the claim which has been put forward by revenue-officials of the Presidency that they are the protectors the interests of the rayats than the non-official members of the Council. Your Excellency, whoever will read the record of the proceedings of this Council of 1901 relating to the Land-Revenue Code Amendment Bill will see that it was the non-offiial members who fought the battle of the rayats against the officials in this Council. That Bill, which was subsequently passed, endeavoured to assume that the State was the sole landlord of the soil in the Province. But the older class of administrators from Mountstuart Elphinstone downwards had always admitted that Government had 'Rajbhag' or were joint-landlords and entitled to a certain share of land-revenue only. They never asserted that the State was the sole landlord in the Province. The Land-Revenue Code Amendment Act tried to assert that Government was the sole landlord and we fought against that. It was never meant by the stalwart administrators of old that the soil of the Province should pass into the hands of a class of agricultural tenants who should hold land temporarily during restricted periods of short leases. The old system was that which the State itself impressed upon the occupancy of the land a permanent tenure hereditable and transferable. It gave dignity self-respect and status to the rayat, and the Act really aimed to destroy that status and we fought as had as we could against such a revolutionary project as the Bombay Government then entertained. We have been twitted with doing what had never been head of, namely, withdrawing from the Council on that occasion. But, My Lord, the non-official members did this in consequence of the way in which the Bill was pushed through this Council. The only Council which has ever met at Mahableshwar was to introduce this Bill in hot haste. By a suspension of standing orders it was pushed on early in the rains in the Poona sessions, and the deliberate object of this haste was stated by the Revenue Member in charge of the Bill to be take advantage of the forfeitures which would necessarily occur in the stress of the famine that was then raging. We prayed to Government not to push on a Bill of that magnitude with such haste. There was, however, such a growing agitation against the measure in the Presidency that ultimately Government had to issue a resolution stating that they were not going to take advantage of famine conditions and make forfeitures and issue restricted short leases which they were asked by the Bill to legalise. As the Bill to was to be pushed through in that manner we resolved not to take any further part in it. I am glad to say that our efforts in that direction have not altogether proved in vain. The agitation which then took place and the expression of feelings of all classes of the people have led the Bombay Government to adopt a wise policy of not working the Act to any large extent to forfeit occupancy rights and grant short term leases. I have more than once asked Government for a report showing the action taken by them in that respect, and in 1906-1907 I was very glad to see from the report of the Government that their action was very wisely restricted. Your Excellency, our efforts to stop that legislation was not succcessful, but ultimately Government saw the wisdom of not pushing the thing too far.

Your Excellency, I had intended to say a word with regard to the efforts and action of the non-official members with regard to another branch of the administration, namely, Excise. But I approach that question with a great deal of trepidation. I see that looseness of statement does not go unpunished. I have not had the opportunity of referring to papers and documents as I could have wished, and I think I would fight shy of that perilous question. But one thing I may be permitted to point out, and it is that though it is perfectly true that the abolition of drink cannot be the aim of Government, still the point of view from which the question of Indian temperance is necessarily looked at by people in this country is different from the point of view which is held in more temperate climes where drinking—moderate or excessive—has been a part of the life of its people. Not only the question presents itself in a different manner altogether, but the large majority of the population—Hindu and Mohammedan population—all hold that drink is a religious prohibition. They approach the question from that point of view. It is not a question of restricting excess. But in India the question is the passing away from total abstinence to a gradual increase in the vice of drunkenness. I think it is one of the questions in which Indian temperance reformers cannot but view with alarm the introduction of the vice among the proorer classes. I am glad to see that Your Excellency's Government is in full harmony with the views of those who think that the cause of temperance should be advanced as steadily and as strongly as possible, and I have no doubt that under Your Excellency's sympathetic guidance the action of the department will tend to the direction in which measures will be taken to prevent the increase and growth of the vice which is abhorrent to the sentiments of the people of this country.

Your Excellency, I have been already too long. I hope I have shown sufficiently that the efforts of the non-official members have not been altogether in vain since the Reform Act of 1893 came into existence. This brief view of past history is calculated to inspire hope for the future.

And I confidently trust that under Your Excellency's liberal, high-minded and sympathetic guidance the extended Council which will now come into operation will have before it a future as beneficial and brilliant, nay, more so than has been the case in the past. The curtain is falling upon the present Council and I wished very much that there had been a word of appreciation from my honourable friend Sir John Muir Mackenzie in presenting the Budget to cheer us on for the future.

However that may be, I am sanguine from past experience that the country may well expect that under the new India Councils Bill just passed, the non-official members will devote themselves to promote its best interests with patience, with sobriety and with unselfish integrity of purpose.

BOMBAY LEGISLATIVE COUNCIL

SPREAD OF EDUCATION: GOVERNMENT'S DUTY

At the Meeting of the Bombay Legislative Council which was presided over by Sir George Clarke, Governor of Bombay, and held at Bombay on 15th March 1911, the Hon. Rao Bahadur G.V. Joshi moved:—"That Government be pleased not to raise the scale of fees in Government High Schools." On this Motion The Hon. Sir Pherozeshah spoke as follows.

Your Excellency,—The question of fees in secondary schools is in itself a very important question, but it has been rendered considerably more important in consequence of the close connection with the larger question of educational policy. Your Excellency, in offering a few remarks on a question which becomes in this way of great importance, I will implore Your Excellency, not to think that the remarks come from one who is offering them in the spirit of an unwise politician. In the recent books which Mr. Valentine Chirol has written on Indian unrest, or rather I should say, the letters which he wrote to the London Times and published in the form of a book, he says:

> "That the powers of the University Senates have not been unduly curtailed is only too clearly shown on the other hand by the effective resistance hitherto offered at Bombay to the scheme of reforms proposed by Sir George Clarke. To the most important features of the scheme, which were the

provision of a course of practical science for all first year students, a systematic bifurcation of courses, the lightening of the number of subjects in order to secure somewhat more thoroughness, and compulsory teaching of Indian history and polity, no serious objection could be raised, but the politicians on the Senate effectively blocked discussion."

Now, Your Excellency, I need not be so modest as to say that I am not included in this class of politicians on the Senate. As your Excellency is aware I took an active part in the discussions in the Senate, but I do implore Your Excellency to believe that in taking the part which I did on that occasion, I was not actuated, as insinuated in the remarks of Mr. Chirol, by the perverse prejudices of that obnoxious individual the Indian politician. I implore Your Excellency to believe that in the remarks which I propose to make on this occasion I am actuated by the same regard for the welfare and progress of this Presidency and for the welfare and progess and development of education on its true lines in this Presidency which, I am perfectly confident, actuates Your Excellency and Your Excellency's Government in making the proposals for the various educational reforms which you have put forward. It is very often said that you must not ascribe motives. It is a phrase which is very loosely used. For, I think, if motives are nothing more than intentions drawn from acts or actions it is impossible in properly discussing a subject not to refer to such intentions as disclosed by actions. Even in matters of criminal jurisprudence, courts of law resort to motives to see why certain acts or actions have been performed. When it is said that you must not ascribe motives all that we really ask for is that you should not seek for intentions except as far as they are disclosed by acts or actions.

Now, in proceeding to offer my remarks I ask this Council to consider in the first place one thing. In the Press Note to which my honourable friend Mr. Sharp, the Director of Public Instruction, has referred, and which I have carefully studied over and over again, and in the remarks which he has offered to the Council on this occasion a great deal of reference is made to the unlimited liability which is sought to be imposed upon Government in the matter of various classes of education. It is said that the time has come when Government cannot undertake an unlimited liability to provide for all the demands that might be made upon them in respect of education. Now, Your Excellency, I want to ask the Government who issued the note, and my honourable friend Mr. Sharp, where is it that Government have ever been asked to undertake any unlimited liability? In my long experience of public affairs, all the demands I have ever heard made, have been extremely modest demands to increase the ratio of educational expenditure which has always compared and still compares most unfavourably with the ratio in almost every other country in the world. On the contrary, the position of those who say that Government ought to undertake a serious liability with regard to the secondary education, as well as with regard to the primary and higher education, is this. In other countries of Europe what has been the provision for secondary education? Who have been the people who have made the largest and the most liberal provision for the secondary and higher education? Take England. The noble institutions for secondary and higher education there are provided, by whom? By the Kings, by the high State dignitaries, by the high ecclesiastics, by the great landlords—in fact by all those people who in the older days when these institutions were established, were in the position of, if I may use a comprehensive term, great landlords and the possessors of the great wealth of the country, because in those days wealth went with land. Those were the people who founded the noble benefactions which now serve even in a rich country like England people who come from by no means an impoverished class with secondary and higher education. I will ask Your Excellency to consider carefully in coming to a decision on points of unlimited liability, who stands in this country in the position of Kings, great landlords, the great State dignitaries and the great ecclesiastics, but the Government? It is the Government in India who is the great and universal landlord. The Government as constituted in this country occupies the same position which the great landed aristocracy, those great magnates and dignitaries of England once occupied. Therefore it is that we have always contended that a special and peculiar liability rests upon the English Government in India to make liberally and generously the same provision which was so liberally and so generously made in England. That is the function which we ask the Government to perform in this country.

But how have they performed it? I know Your Excellency is impatient of going into past history, looking to the present and the future only for doing active, useful and valuable work. I confess I do not look upon that proposition in the way in which Your Excellency looks at it. Very often if we look into the past and go into the history of the question we can properly judge what ought to be done in the present and what ought to be done in the future. I ask—what has been done by Government in respect of primary and secondary education? I will confine myself to this Presidency. Years ago, Your Excellency, I may be allowed to presume to say that an humble individual like myself publicly implored Government to take a larger view of their responsibility in regard to this matter and not to be content with schools ill-equipped, ill-furnished and ill-tutored without hostels or residential quarters. I remember that at the time of the Education Commission which is called Sir William Hunter's Commission, an important minute was furnished by one of the best members of this Council—I mean Sir Raymond West—pointing out how meagre, how slender, how unproportioned was the provision for secondary education in this Presidency and adding a prayer for an advance of a far more rapid character both in the improvement of the schools and in the facilities for developing secondary education than existed at the time. Have Government discharged the duty which I say lay upon them? Till they have done it I venture respectfully to say that the time has not come to speak of throwing unlimited liability on the shoulders of Government in respect of secondary or any other sort of education. Why? What is it that even the Press Note discloses as the reason for increasing the high school fees? It is that the surplus may go to the improvement of the present schools. I waded through the Press Note in vain for some statistics to show what was the alarming demand for admission to Government high schools. I wish in the Press Note the results of some inquiries had been stated—inquiries as to the number of students that would be allowed in the different high schools in the Presidency. So far as the numbers that were fixed by Government in the older days are concerned they are by no means of an overwhelming character. I do not know how far they are going to modify them now, whether they are going to increase or diminish them. But what I venture to place before this Council is that till Government have discharged the normal obligation, that lay upon them, of making normal provision for the spread of secondary education I repeat again that the time has not come of talking of placing an unlimited liability on the shoulders of Government.

Your Excellency,—there is a wider question of policy to be taken into account, as has been hinted by my honourable friend Mr. Parekh, in considering what ought to be undertaken in this country under the circumstances and conditions in which it is placed in respect of secondary education. I have been familiar for years together with the talk of encouragement to private enterprise. It is not a new cry that has been now taken up. The Hon. Mr. Sharp says that one of the objects of the proposal is to clear the ground for private enterprise. It is a cry which, I must confess, I have heard over and over again. There was a time during the regime of Your Excellency's noble predecessor, Lord Reay, when this cry was taken up with great earnestness and with great energy. We people, of the educated classes, have been charged with not coming forward to give advice from our own experience to Government on matters of policy and we have been told that we have been only destructive critics and that we have never put forward constructive proposals. If facts are looked to, I venture to say that the imputation has never been deserved, and, Your Excellency, in this question of educational policy it has been less deserved than in any other direction of political, intellectual or social activity. So far back as twenty years ago we pointed out that this cry of encouragement of private enterprise must be very cautiously dealt with. We pointed out that the desire of Government to shift from their shoulders the task of developing secondary instruction on to the shoulders of private enterprise was fraught with grave political danger and capable of doing grave political mischief. Your Excellency will see that I am not saying this simply for the purpose of this debate, but I have here in black and white an Address which I gave as President of the Bombay Graduates' Association and in which I earnestly drew the attention of Government to the grave impolicy and political blunder of dealing with that cry except in a guarded manner. We cried very loud in the wilderness on that occasion. What has been the result? Though Government were not able to make over the established high schools in the different districts to private enterprise they still continued to show enormous indifference to the claims of secondary education.

H.E. the President:—The honourable member has already exceeded fifteen minutes.

The Hon. Sir Pherozeshah:—The subject is so large that—

H.E. the President:—I am glad to give you a few more minutes.

The Hon. Sir Pherozeshah:—I am afraid I have not done with even one-third of what I intend to say. I an so full of this subject and it is a matter of such importance that I thought I might not lose this opportunity of putting forward my views.

H.E. the President:—I will give you a few more minutes, Sir Pherozeshah, I may say that under the terms of the Resolution, we are concerned more with the present and the future than with the past.

The Hon. Sir Pherozeshah:—My belief is that if you want to act will in the future you must not forget the past. I quite see that I should not take up the time of the Council by exceeding the time limit. I must seek a future occasion for the purpose of getting out all that is in me with regard to the important questions which are raised in the course of this debate and dealt with in the Press Note issued by Government. My honourable friend Mr. Sharp in dealing with the matter brought in important questions of policy, which require to be fully dealt with. It is not possible to do it in the time limit and I will not take up the time of the Council any further. I will take another opportunity of putting forward my views.

The Resolution was put to the vote and lost.

BOMBAY LEGISLATIVE COUNCIL

THE SLAUGHTER OF CATTLE

At the Meeting of the Bombay Legislative Council held at Poona on 26th July 1911, H.E. Sir George Clarke, Governor of Bombay, presiding, the Hon. Mr. Abdul Husein Adamjee Peerbhoy moved:—"That the Governor-in-Council may be pleased to enforce existing legislation, if any, and to introduce such further legislation as may be necessary for restricting the slaughter of cattle, for purposes other than that of human consumption, i.e., for trade purposes, such as for extracting fat, hides, bones and horns." The Hon. Sir Pherozeshah Mehta spoke as follows.

Your Excellency,—Whatever may be the fate of this Resolution, which my honourable friend Mr. Abdul Husein has brought before this Council, whether it is or it is not found practicable to carry out the proposal it formulates, I still hail and welcome this attempt on the part of a Mohammedan gentleman as indicating that even the Mohammedan community is not averse to join in practical and temperate endeavours to solve an economic problem of great importance and seriousness. It is impossible not to recognize that in this country a very important portion of the mass of the people object to the slaughter of cows both on religious and economic grounds.

It is no doubt thought that the movement which is now prevailing to a very large extent in this country was inspired by religious feelings and formulated on religious grounds, but it is not imporbable that if we go back for enough, the religious feelings were themselves the outcome of economic necessities, when cattle formed an important portion of the agricultural wealth of the country and the preservation of this agricultural wealth was considered to be a problem of the greatest interest and value to the country. But however that may be, there is no doubt that there has been a large decrease in the number of horned cattle in the country. That is a problem of a serious character and requires to be dealt with in a large and statesmanlike manner. To my mind it is a noteworthy thing that a Mohammedan gentleman comes forward to help to solve this problem and proposes ways and means, and in spite of the fact that my honourable friend Moulvie Rafiuddin Ahmed seems to imagine that his action is likely to be misunderstood by the Mahommedan community, I take it that the Mohammedans themselves are reasonably desirous of co-operating in the solution of this great economic problem, apart from its bearing on the question of the slaughter of cattle for human food. Therefore it is that whatever may be the fate of this specific Resolution which the Hon. Mr. Abdul Husein has brought forward, I hail it as an attempt on the part of a Mahommedan gentleman to join with his Hindu brethren in solving a problem seriously affecting the prosperity of the country.

The Hon. Mr. R.P. Karandikar moved an amendment, viz. "That the maintenance and rearing of cattle claim larger attention of Government in the interests of agriculture".

The Hon. Mr. Abdul Husein then asked permission to withdraw his Resolution in favour of Mr. Karandikar's amendment, which was granted. The amendment therefore became the substantive proposition which being put to the vote, was lost.

BOMBAY LEGISLATIVE COUNCIL

THE REGISTRATION OF MEDICAL PRACTITIONERS

At the Meeting of the Bombay Legislative Council held at Bombay on 21st November 1911, the Hon. Mr. R.A. Lamb moved the first reading of the Bill for the registration of medical practitioners in the Presidency of Bombay. The Bill created a Medical Council which would control the keeping of the Register and would have power to remove from it the name of any medical practitioner who was guilty of any grave misconduct or unprofessional act. The privileges which the Bill conferred on registered practitioners were as follows:

1. No person who was not registered was to be considered to be a "legally" or "duly qualified medical practitioner" under any Act in force in the Presidency, or was entitled to give any certificate required by any such Act.

2. No person not registered was to be appointed to be medical officer in any hospital or dispensary not supported entirely by voluntary contributions.

3. Registered practitioners were to be exempted from serving on inquests.

The Hon. the Surgeon-General H.W. Stevenson and other honourable members having spoken on the Bill, the Hon. Sir Pherozeshah made the following speech.

May it please Your Excellency,—It was impossible not to listen to the speech of the honourable gentleman who just sat down without being equally interested and amused. My Indian colleagues in the Council took up cudgels on its behalf for the Ayurvedic system of medicine and spoke up vigorously. My honourable friend Colonel Jackson has retaliated by telling us many interesting and amusing stories as to how the Indian *vaids* and *hakims* treated cases here and there which have come to his knowledge. But I wonder whether he has ever heard the other side and the number of stories told by Indian patients of the remarkable and startling manner in which now and then they have been treated by qualified medical practitioners. I was very much interested to hear a remark from the Hon. the Surgeon-General who told us how one of those unqualified men, who had a patient suffering from tuberculosis, gave him some cough mixture. I believe the story is perfectly true; but I ask him, has he heard stories of what are called qualified medical practitioners who do exactly the very same thing and who when patients have gone to them for serious chest diseases, have treated them as cases of cough and cold. I know several stories of that character.

But after all this impassioned eloquence of the Hon. Col. Jackson, I put it to the Council if we are not drifting away from the true meaning and purport of the Bill. When the honourable members were speaking on the Bill I was rubbing my eyes over and over again to find out what was the real connection between the arguments that were urged and the real substantial meaning of the Bill before the Council. I am afraid so far the discussion on the Bill has proceeded on entirely wrong and irrelevant lines. I will ask my Indian colleagues to consider in what way is it that it really affects the *vaids* and *hakims*. To my mind it is quite clear that they are left out in the Bill as they have ever been before. As a matter of fact, they have never enjoyed the privilege of giving certificates. What is there in the Bill which takes away in any respect from the position which they now occupy? They are left entirely to their own devices as at present without let or hindrance. Now I think that the very first speakers—the Hon. the Surgeon-General and the Hon. Col. Jackson—are to some extent responsible for confirming my Indian colleagues who followed them in imagining that this Bill was really aimed against *vaids* and *hakims* for their speeches endeavoured to justify and show the necessity for adopting measures for disqualifying the indigenous medical practitioners. Even my honourable friend cannot be quite acquitted of the same charge. In his short dispassionate speech, he threw out only one justification for the Bill,—a justification which amounts to this that Bombay should suffer for the sins of Bengal. He said that in Bengal there have sprung up several institutions which turn out irregularly qualified medical men, and those institutions have in recent times multiplied to such a very large extent that it is possible that they may invade this Presidency. I do not think the honourable member has been able to convince the Council that such an infection has reached or is very likely to reach this Presidency. But if the object of the Bill is to prevent this, then there is a necessity of checking the practice of *vaids* and *hakims*. But turning to the sections of the Bill you will see that in no instance the *vaids* and *hakims* are really touched.

BOMBAY LEGISLATIVE COUNCIL

THE BOMBAY BUDGET OF 1912-1913

At the Meeting of the Bombay Legislative Council held at Poona on 8th July 1912, the Hon. Sir Richard Lamb introduced the Budget of the Government of Bombay for the year 1912-1913. The debate on it contiuned till the following day when Sir Pherozeshah spoke as follows.

Your Excellency,—I only propose to say a very few words on the Budget on this occasion. I join my voice to the complaint which has already proceeded from the non-official members of the Madras Legislative Council that the arrangements, which were propounded by the New Reforms Act and which were supposed to be framed with a view to bring non-official members into closer touch with the preparation and discussion of the items of the Budget, are, as the non-official members in the Madras Legislative Council called it, more or less of a farce, not in the way of inveighing against any individual person, but under the stress of circumstances which could not permit the non-official members to take that part in the framing and discussing of the Budget which it was at first thought the new rules would allow them to do. Perhaps, Your Excellency, I would explain what I mean to convey by giving a concrete instance of this year. As soon as the

Budget proposals were ready, we immediately proceeded with the appointment of the finance committee. When the finance committee was formed I, as one of its members, received the Budget proposals on a Friday and was asked to attend the meeting of the committee to consider them on the following Monday. I think it would be recognised that it is almost impossible for a non-official member to master the proposals prepared after careful consideration by the Finance Member within the time which was thus given to the non-official members. I did not attend the meeting on Monday, because I thought it was perfectly useless to do so and because I had another important engagement on that day. I thought the deliberations of the Committee would at least take such time as would enable me to go through the proposals and to be present on the following Tuesday or Wednesday to take my part in its deliberations. Unfortunately the Committee wound up its affairs on that very Monday, and nothing remained to be done but to sign the final report made by the Committee. It is perfectly true that when the Budget came again before the Council after it had been referred to the Government of India, it was open to the members to bring forward resolutions on specific items. But I think it will be admitted that the procedure by way of resolutions is one which is most cumbrous and hampers non-official members to a very great extent in going over the various items, and even if they confine themselves to two or three principal heads, they find it is absolutely impossible to cover the various topics and subjects. In the old days when this arrangement did not prevail, there was a great advantage in the general debate which was allowed on the Budget during the rains in Poona. It was a custom hallowed by practice and, I must say blessed over and over again by Governors and Viceroys who encouraged the general discussion of the policy of Government. Unfortunately Your Excellency has ruled that this debate must be confined within the narrow limits of items in the Budget itself. From the reports which I have read in the papers as to what fell from the Hon. Sir Richard Lamb yesterday. I find that he enjoined members to confine themselves to the relevant matters in the Budget only. I confess for one that the twenty minutes allowed even for that purpose are not sufficient for covering, what you might say, two or three important heads. For instance, I should have liked to make some remarks about the head, "land-revenue." I should have liked to explain what took place on the previous occasion on the Council as regards restricted tenures. But it is always impossible for members to place their views before the Council so as to be understood and followed without going through the historical account of what has happened in the past. That would in itself take more than twenty minutes. In the same way I should have very much liked to speak on the educational heads of the Budget and discuss the policy of Government as regards primary education, secondary education and the higher University education. But it always strikes me that it is utterly impossible to do justice to anything that you might desire to place before the Council within the space of twenty minutes. The honourable non-official member of the Madras Legislative Council, who has raised this point, suggested that the finance committee should be made the standing committee throughout the year, and I put it to Your Excellency and the Council if a remedy of that sort may not prove an efficient and practical one. From the remarks which fell from the Hon. Sir Richard Lamb and which I read in the papers, I find that he himself says that the discussion of various items of the next year's Budget are already proceeding. If that is so, it is very desirable for this finance committee to be converted into a standing committee, so that its members may have an opportunity of discussing these questions as they arise, and may not have to wait till the end of the year. I do not blame any one for this result, because so far as the way in which the finance committee can work is concerned, it is restricted by the preparation of the Budget locally as well as by the necessity of sending it for consideration by the Government of India. It seems impossible, if the present arrangement is followed, that justice can be done either by the members of the Government or the non-official members. They are limited by the requirements of time for passing the proposals from one person to another. The only remedy for this at present seems to be that the finance committee should be transformed into a standing committee, before whom the Finance Member should bring forward his proposals as he himself considers them and then send them on to the Government of India. It appears to me that some remedy must be found to give effect to the one great object of the reforms which, as Lord Morley distinctly put it, was to enable the non-official members to be in closer touch and contact so as in a manner to take a really efficient and active part in the preparation and consideration of the Budget.

BOMBAY LEGISLATIVE COUNCIL

A BILL FURTHER TO AMEND THE CITY OF BOMBAY IMPROVEMENT TRUST ACT, 1898

At the Meeting of the Bombay Legislative Council held at Poona on 9th July 1912, the Hon. Mr. M.B. Chaubal moved the first reading of Bill VII of 1912—a Bill further to amend the City of Bombay Improvement Trust Act, 1898. The Hon. Sir Pherozeshah spoke as follows.

May it please Your Excellency,—In rising to offer my observations on the first reading of this Bill, I confess I heard with astonishment the speech made by the Honourable Member in charge of it. Your Excellency, I cannot help firmly but respectfully complaining bitterly of the treatment which, as set forth by the Honourable Member himself, has been accorded to the Municipal Corporation of the City of Bombay in regard to the preparation of this Bill. From the account given by the Honourable Member of the way in which the amending Bill was prepared, it was perfectly clear that everybody who has anything to do with it—the Improvement Trust, Government and even the Municipal Commissioner,—has been over and over again consulted in the preparation and revision of the Bill. But the Corporation, which has most to do with it, has been left out of account except in regard to the question of financial readjustment. Your Excellency,—so far as this

Improvement Trust Act Amending Bill is concerned, the Corporation and the Corporation above all, is the body which is most intensely and actively interested in it. That is the body which supplies not only the sinews of war, but is also responsible not only for the legitimate financial operations of the Board but even for its blunders and errors. For, Your Excellency, under what are called the bludgeon clauses of the Act, it is the Corporatinn which makes good any deficiency or failure of the Improvement Trust in making necessary payments to the people entitled to them. It is, therefore, the Corporation which is the body most vitally interested in the matter. I bitterly complain that in the preparation and revision of the Bill, everybody even those who were least interested in it were consulted, and it was the Coporation and the Corporation alone that was left out of account.

Now, Your Excellency,—what is the position which the Municipal Corporation occupies in this matter? But before I go to that point I cannot help making one further remark, and it is that the Corporation has been treated in the apportionment of powers and burdens as Prince Hal described Falstaff's meal of bread and sack—the tiniest bit of bread and an intolerable quantity of sack. My honourable friend almost made it a boast in his opening speech that the Corporation had not been forgotten in the distributions of loaves and fishes and increased powers at least in two instances had been their share. What are they? The first one is this. Under the present Improvement Trust Act the Corporation and the Muncipal Commissioner exercise a predominant voice over the action of the Board in framing improvement schemes and one of the sections of the Act requires that when an official representation, as provided in that section, has been made to the Board, they are bound to take up that scheme if they find that the representation with regard to the sanitary condition of the area concerned is correct, and that their financial resources enable them to undertake the work. That is the provision in the present Act. It is proposed under the amending Bill to take away the obligation thus imposed on the Board requiring them to undertake a scheme for which they have received an official representation and in its place to give the Coporati on only a right of appeal to Government against the refusal of the Board to undertake it. In other words, the Bill takes away by far the larger power hitherto enjoyed by the Corporation under the section of the Act and gives them the solace of an appeal only in its place, and yet the honourable member says, we are increasing the powers of the Corporation because in case the Board do not take up such a scheme as presented by the Corporation, forsooth the Corporation has under the amending Bill the power to appeal to Government.

The second matter in which the power of the Corporation is alleged to be increased is with regard to the acquisition of lands with buildings upon them. The honourable member said that at present when the Board require for their purpose any Municipal land with buildings upon them they have not to pay for them. Now, it is proposed that the Board should be required to pay for them, though they may take away vacant land and streets, not for the purpose of adding to the streets, but for any purpose for which the Board may require it in connection with their schemes. Your Excellency will see how unjust the provision is. Up to now the Board had power to acquire streets and land vested in the Corporation only for inclusion in a street, but under the provision of the amending Bill a street or vacant land can be taken away not for the purpose of adding it to other streets—because if that is done it would eventually again become the property of the Corporation under the Act—but for any purpose for which the Board may require it, including sites for building.

BOMBAY LEGISLATIVE COUNCIL

Bill No. XIV of 1912.—A Bill to amend the Bombay Land-Revenue Code, 1879, the Khoti Settlement Act, 1880, and the Gujarat Talukdars Act, 1888, and to repeal the Bombay Land Record-of-Rights Act, 1903.

At the Meeting of the Bombay Legislative Council held at

Bombay on 6th January 1913, the Hon. Sir Richard Lamb introduced the above mentioned Bill and moved for the first reading of it. The Hon. Mr. D.V. Belvi said:—"It is very surprising to me that an amending Bill of this portentous length should be hurried in this manner, for when considering a measure of this kind, we have to see at the first reading whether it would not be more advisable to introduce a Bill re-casting the whole law regulating the collection of revenue from landed property in this Presidency. On these grounds I move under Rule 7 that the further consideration of this Bill do stand over till the next session of the Council."

The Hon. Sir Pherozeshah thus supported the Hon. Mr. Belvi's motion:

Your Excellency,—I think every member of this Council will join with me in congratulating the honourable member in charge of the Bill for the lucid way in which he has explained the principal clauses and the amendments that have been proposed. There can be no doubt that he has put very clearly before the Council the divergence between the registered occupants and the beneficiary owner and has certainly made out a case for some legislation on the subject. But the question goes further. How is this divergence to be remedied? The honourable member in charge of the Bill has pointed out the way in which the remedy has already been put in practice. I quite unde-stand the attitude of my honourable friend Mr. Barrow and of the Hon. Mr. Curtis who now poses in the character of a reformed person for he is no longer the revenue-officer who will never learn and never forget, but is one who has learnt to reform and learnt to progress. But I am not surprised to find that the Hon. Mr. Barrow and the Hon. Mr. Curtis are quite satisfied with the amendments that are proposed for they have seen them worked in actual practice, and I have no doubt that the opinions they have formed have been formed after a careful study of the amendments and after a personal experience of their actual working. But the law requires that there must be further guarantees for legislation besides the opinions and the experience of the Members who have put the measure in practice. Of course, if they are satisfied that their opinions are sound and correct they would in all probability turn out very good when put to further tests. But that does not do away with the absolute necessity of proceeding with the new measure in the manner required by law and of seeing that all the guarantees for a proper investigation have been complied with. What are the facts brought out by the Hon. Mr. Belvi? He says that the Bill has not even been translated in the vernacular. I confess I am surprised to learn that that has not been done. My Lord, I do maintain that this is one of the provisions which should be scrupulously carried out in regard to all the measures of an important character. The amendment of the Land Revenue Code is certainly not a matter of slight importance. Both the codes of 1865 and 1869 were passed after a careful and lengthy discussion of the various principles which they involved and I am perfectly certain that my honourable friend Sir Richard Lamb will admit that no modification or amendment of the Code should be put on the Statute Book until every opportunity is given to all the parties concerned for careful criticism, investigation and representation. I beg to submit that these guarantees have not been fulfilled in regard to this measure. My honourable friend Mr. Barrow may say that the people are satisfied with the way in which the Executive have tried to meet divergence between the registered occupant and the beneficiary holder. But we want something more in the Council than the opinions of the officials. They may be satisfied, but it is absolutely necessary that people—the *rayats*—who are most interested in the matter should have an opportunity, in the first place, of understanding what is proposed to be done and in the second place, of submitting their criticism after a careful examination of the various provisions of the Bill. Those guarantees have not been carried out and I put it to the Council whether it is right to hurry through a Bill of this character merely on the sentimental grounds which have been put forward by the Hon. Mr. Curtis. Now, what will take place if you pass the first reading of the Bill now? A select committee will immediately be appointed which will proceed to consider the Bill in February and upon the receipt of their report the matter will be brought forward in the Council in March. That, I do submit, gives no opportunity to the parties concerned, as I have already stated, in the first place, to understand what are the provisions of the Bill and whether the remedies that are proposed are right remedies for the evils which exist, and, in second place, to submit their representations. There are two courses open to Your Excellency. The first is that which my honourable friend Mr. Belvi has proposed viz., to adjourn the consideration of the first reading till the next sessions of the Council. There is another way which might be applied to nearly all legislative measures of importance. In the Imperial Legislative Council I know the practice always was to introduce a measure of an important character for the first reading in the Council, and then not to proceed to appoint a select committee but to adjourn the further consideration in order to let the public consider it and send in representations containing their criticisms on it, till the next Sessions of the Council. Then it was that the Council proceeded to appoint a select committee which at that time was in possession of all the views available to carry on its work with expedition. I submit, Your Excellency, if Your Excellency's Government is desirous of proceeding with the first reading of the Bill today, then no select committee may be appointed till the next Sessions of the Council, which would be held at Poona in the rains. That will give time to the people to study the Bill, to consider what the various amendments are and to send in their representations in time to be placed before the select committee that will be ultimately appointed. I venture to say that you must not expect ordinary common people to try and understand measures of this character with the same rapidity and with the same grasp as the trained Revenue Officers can easily command. I can easily understand that the Hon. Mr. Barrow or the Hon. Mr. Curtis can rapidly go through the provisions of this Bill and say whether they are good or not. But that is not so in the case of common people who take slightly to this thing and require time for the proper understanding of a measure like this. I appeal to Your Excellency to take one of these two courses, either to allow the first reading of the Bill to be adjourned—though perhaps it may be objected to as it has already been brought forward—or the Council may accept the first reading, but Your Excellency may not put forward the proposition for the appointment of select committee till after a certain interval of time which would really be the next Sessions of the Council at Poona. I venture to submit that either course will meet the exigencies of the situation. I again appeal to Your Excellency's Government not to hurry through this important legislation merely on the strength of official opinions because I think these opinions require to be supplemented by the opinions of other people who are vitally interested in the amendment of the Code and who are entitled to form opinions on it. I do not deny that it is very probable that ultimately the Council may take the view that the measures that are proposod are of a beneficial and acceptable character, but it is absolutely necessary that all guarantees provided for a full investigation of the measure by the people vitally interested in it should be strictly carried out, for though that might involve some delay, such an investigation would enable the Council to consider fully the representations made by the people.

The Motion for adjournment was lost and the Motion for the first reading of the Bill was proceeded with. The Hon. Sir Pherozeshah said:

Your Excellency,—I should like to offer one observation with regard to the remarks which fell from my honourable friend Mr. Barrow. I think he missed the point in what he said in regard to the argument whether it was urgently necessary to pass the first reading in the Bill at this stage. We quite admit—or at least *I* for one quite admit—that probably the opinions that have been passed by the revenue-officer have been correct ones with regard to the people whom the Bill will mainly affect. But the argument that I wish to make and which my honourable friend Mr. Barrow missed was "Let the people speak for themselves; you don't speak for them". My honourable friend Sir Richard Lamp said that he was convinced that the amendments in the Bill were accepted by a large majority of the people whom it will affect. The argument I put forward was that the legislature requires that those who are interested in it must be allowed to speak for themselves. Now, in regard to the working of the present system the Hon. Sir Richard Lamp spoke of the inconvenience and delay which occurred in collecting Government Revenue on account of the divergence between the registered occupants and the actual holders of land. This struck me as rather strange, for we read in the Administration Reports year after year that the major portion of the land revenue is collected without any difficulty whatever. The question then is, how is it that the revenue has been collected so easily? The answer would be that we are proceeding upon the Record of Rights. If that is so we have already before us a system which could be worked without the existing legislation depending upon the Land Revenue Code in the first place and on the Record of Rights in the second. I quite admit that it is desirable—it is almost necessary as the Hon. Mr. Parekh very briefly pointed out—that the Code should be amended in the direction in which it is proposed to bring together the real occupants of the land within the purview of the law. I quite admit that there is necessity for legislation, but the question is whether the measures that have been proposed by the executive for the purpose of remedying the evil are thoroughly well devised for the purpose for which they are meant and whether they would not create difficulties that are not foreseen. It is all very well for my honourable friend Mr. Khandalawalla to say that the Bill only involves a few questions of definition. But I submit that these questions of definition of occupants, superior holders, inferior holders, tenants, etc., are bristling with all sorts of difficulties, and it is a question whether new definitions would not lend us in difficulties which are not seen now. These definitions are of such a character that unless they are based upon far-sighted observation they are bound to burst out in other directions creating new difficulties and raising new objections. It seems to me that in the absence of further representations the Select Committee will find considerable difficulty in the way of settling these definitions in the various directions with regard to the people who have real interest in the occupation of land. Barring that I think it is not only a desirable but a necessary piece of Legislation to meet the divergence between the real occupant and the nominal occupant.

The Motion for the first reading of the Bill was carried and the latter was referred to a Select Committee.

At the Meeting of the Council on 13th March 1913 the Hon. Sir Richard Lamb moved the second reading of this Bill and the Hon. Mr. S.B. Upasani moved for an adjournment of same. The latter's motion was supported by the Hon. Mr. G.K. Parekh and was opposed by the Hon. Mr. G.S. Curtis. The Hon. Sir Pherozeshah then said:—

Your Excellency,—I cannot help prefacing what I have to say with the remark that I entirely disagree with the honourable member who just sat down when he said that the mover of the proposal for amendment is only making an unnecessary fuss. Well, that is very idiomatic English, and so far as it is idiomatic, we can endorse it, but so far as sentiment is concerned, I venture to say that there was not a grosser misdescription of the action of the honourable mover of the amendment than that given by the Hon. Mr. Curtis. On the contrary, when you examine the question properly, you will see that the Hon. Mr. Upasani has been far from making any unnecessary fuss about a measure of this character. The Hon. Mr. Curtis thinks it is a measure of very little importance and that if you bear in mind one or two little principles, everything contained in the Bill is at once as plain as daylight. Your Excellency, I was glad to hear my honourable friend Mr. Curtis complimenting this Council on the development of increased intelligence which it is bringing to bear on the questions which come for discussion before the Council, though I cannot say that I can entirely go with him when he ran down the character of the discussion in the older Councils. But, Your Excellency, it seems to me that the point of the Hon. Mr. Curtis' remark really comes to this; that revenue officers who have devoted a large portion of their time and whose duty it is very largley to deal with these matters have considered and taken all the time they required for the purpose of considering bills of that character, and that the Council would do well to allow those revenue members to do their thinking for them. This is a proposition, Your Excellency, to which it is impossible for any member of this Council to give his acquiescence. However, competent revenue officers may consider themselves to be in regard to matters of this character, the business of the members of this Council,—the duty which is imposed upon them,—is by all means to give due weight to the representations made by revenue members, revenue officers, but to come to a final judgment upon their individual examination and consideration of the questions involved in any measure that may be brought before them. Now, Sir, I venture to say that this Bill before the Council is a Bill of very great magnitude and of very great importance. The Hon. Mr. Curtis said "why, look at this phenomenon that the Hon. Mr. Parekh who has devoted a lifetime to the consideration of revenue questions has very little to say against it." I think my honourable friend Mr. Curtis will bear this in mind that Mr. Parekh himself has explained how it is that he has not been able to give the fullest consideration to the measure before us. He pointed out that it not seldom happens that measures and sections look innocuous at first sight and that they seem to have nothing serious in them, but it is only after very careful consideration and going into the different meanings of the amendments proposed that something is discovered which involves questions of very serious importance indeed and of very great magnitude. I venture to assert, Your Excellency, that this is a measure of that character. Not only members of this Council, but the general public interested in the agricultural condition of this country really have had no time to go through the perplexing amendments of a large number of sections which are included in this Bill. The result is, as the Hon. Mr. Curtis has pointed out, that it is perfectly ture that we have not been able to put our fingers readily upon some of the most contentious issues which are involved in this Bill. Now take the first one to which the Hon. Mr. Parekh has alluded. The Hon. Mr. Curtis said that so far as sub-divisions were concerned the Revenue Departments have been helpless and that has been going on for a long series of years, and what they are going to do now is to accept the existing state of facts. But Your Excellency will see that it is really an admission on Mr. Curtis' part that it is a question of very serious importance—this question of the minute sub-division of survey numbers. He himself, if I have understood him rightly, is against minute sub-division. He has referred to the lecture recently delivered by Mr. Keatinge before the East India Association in London in which that gentleman deplores in the strongest terms the minute sub-divisions of the areas of land in this Presidency, thereby preventing really any method of agricultural improvement by the appliance of capital and various other measures which could be adopted if the measurements of land were much larger than they are now. The Hon. Mr. Curtis deplores this state of things and yet he at once proceeds to justify this Bill which I venture to say will facilitate still further the system of minute sub-divisions.

The Hon. Mr. Curtis:—How?

The Hon. Sir Pherozeshah:—How, because under the section

you will recognise and give legislative countenance to the sub-division of the area of a survey number. I say it is a most serious state of things, if this Act in the slightest degree involved what is deplored as existing in this Presidency against all the interest of agricultural improvement. Well, if you do that, if you place facilities in the way of revenue officers to recognise every sub-division, well, Your Excellency, I venture to say that the agricultural condition of this Presidency will be worse than it has ever been before. That is one of the most serious questions which have to be considered in connection with this Bill. When you are in this amending Bill giving these facilities, it seems to me that surely it is time that the question should be considered in its fulness, and I venture to suggest we should devise means whereby this amending Bill instead of giving facilities should raise difficulties in the way of those minutest sub-divisions which have been going on, it is said, for the last 40 years. I say that the wiser and more economic policy to be adopted under the circumstances is not to give powers or further facilities for sub-divisions, but to devise ways and means, and I hope the ingenuity and the ability of the revenue officers is not unequal to the task to devise some measures for the purpose of preventing this sub-division which is likely to be most disastrous to the economic and agricultural interest of this Presidency. Surely, I ask the Hon. Mr. Curtis if this is not a question which requires the fullest and the most careful consideration before any step is taken, which, I say, will end in the disastrous result of the most uneconomic way of conducting agriculture. That is one question, I think, which may well require, not two years, as Mr. Curtis scornfully spoke about the debates of past years about revenue codes, surely it is one of those questions to which we should apply ourselves in all seriousness and consider whether we might not do something better than helplessly accept this Bill. I submit, Sir, this Bill really has not been given a sufficient time for consideration. It is very seldom that you see a Bill of this character involving questions affecting the whole agricultural condition of the Presidency put forward in the way in which this Bill has been done. I now regret more than ever the decision which the Council came to on the last occasion when it rejected the motion for the adjournment of this question. I now see even clearer than I did before that it was absolutely desirable and necessary that fuller time should be given both to the members of this Council and to the agricultural population to consider the various details which are involved and which are incorporated in such a way that it is very difficult to find out what it really all means. You will remember that when you mean to amend a Bill of the character of the Bombay Land Revenue Code you have in the first place to examine all the amendments of the old sections. Of course I can very well imagine that the revenue officers, whose duty it is every day of their lives to look into these matters, have all these things at their fingers' ends, but it is very difficult for members of this Council who, of course, by no means devote their entire time to all matters placed before them from time to time that they should have sufficient time to arrive at some judgment in regard to the proposed changes. But leaving the members of this Council alone, so far as the agricultural population is concerned, we know very well how difficult it is for small landholders immerged in their own business and in their own task of cultivating the lands to understand and see what it is that is being done in the Legislative Council in regard to their condition. These things can only reach them very slowly. It is a long time before they can bring themselves to consider what are the changes which are going to be carried out and what might be the consequences after they are carried out. To them it is impossible to apply the test which Mr. Curtis applies to members of this Council. If he only marks one or two things —one or two principles—then he will understand the whole of the proposed amendments. I submit that it is only fair, it is only due to the large agricultural population who are by no means educated, ready to take up new ideas, that they should have ample time for the purpose first of making out what the proposed changes are, and what are likely to be the consequences of those changes. Now, it is impossible to say that ample time has been given to consider the Bill. Of course, it has been published before, but it was brought to the newly-elected Council which sat in January, and here we have a Select Committee sitting upon it almost at once, a report made, and brought in the middle of March. I submit, Your Excellency, that the time which is thus given for consideration to the public is extremely inadequate, and I think it is perfectly right that my honourable friend Mr. Upasani should bring forward a proposition for adjournment which should enable more time to be given to the consideration of the various questions involved in this Bill.

There is another point to which I should like to invite Mr. Curtis' attention and the attention of the members of this Council. There are clauses which point out that if there is any alteration in the use of the land, then a new assessment may be made even before the thirty years' period of the lease. Now what is meant by the change in the use of the land? I have seen some representations and some criticisms in the Press by those who want to know what is to be called the change in the use of the land. Is the employment of one sort of crop against another which may have existed at the time of the settlement to be considered a change in the use of the land? Supposing we have been sowing one sort of crop and now we take to another, is it to be considered a change in the use of the land or not, and if that is to be considered a change, are Government entitled, under those circumstances, to re-assess the land even within the period of thirty years.

It is an important question. Of course, under the Land Revenue Code, we know perfectly well that if land employed for agricultural purposes is diverted to non-agricultural and other things, it is liable to a fine. Now this is a matter which requires to be explained. I am almost certain that very few *rayats* have really understood that there is such a change proposed to be brought about by the instrumentality of this Bill. Surely they ought to be allowed time in the first place, and then come to this Council to say whether they consider it desirable or undesirable. Therefore, when you consider all these points, it seems to me that this Bill is really of very great importance, which may almost bring about a revolution in the agricultural condition of this Presidency. And a Bill of this sort, it seems to me, is one which requires the most careful and sustained consideration which can possibly be given to it. As I have said, the time allotted to this Bill is really much too limited for the purposes to which I have drawn attention, and I appeal to the Council to see that a Bill of this importance which indirectly but really affects the agricultural interests of this Presidency is not allowed to be hurried through without the fullest consideration, and I therefore strongly support the Motion which my friend Mr. Upasani has moved.

The Motion when put to the vote was declared to have been lost and the second reading of the Bill was proceeded with and carried and the Bill was then considered clause by clause. That being done, at the Meeting of the Council on 14th March 1913, H.E. the President put the Motion for the third reading of this Bill. The Hon. Sir Pherozeshah thereupon spoke as follows.

Your Excellency,—As I propose to vote against the third reading of the Bill, I should like to make a few observations on the Bill before it is put to the Council. My Lord, I still adhere to what I said yesterday that a Bill of this magnitude should not be pushed forward in the haste which I consider this Bill has been subjected to. I know that this criticism on my behalf and those who take the same view has been regarded with a great deal of impatience by Revenue Officers, and I also know that my honourable friend Mr. Curtis in phrases, which I am sure are as elegant as they are idiomatic and forcible, has told us that in criticising the Bill, as we have done, and in criticising the method by which it is pushed forward, we have been making unnecessary fuss. I was rather sorry to find that my honourable friend Sir Richard Lamb, who is always sober in his expressions, has accused me of having been guilty of perversion of terms. My Lord, so far as this assembly is concerned, we have been some times exposed to this sort of criticism, and we have learnt to take it with equanimity and even cheerfulness. I certainly have learnt to do so, and I hope the newer members of this Council will also come to harden themselves in this respect, as I have done. But, My Lord, I still maintain, in spite of the reiteration of my honourable friend Sir Richard Lamb that the Bill only affects the procedure of collecting the assessment, I still venture to submit that it does in an indirect way very largely affect the policy, which is only the sound policy for the progress and improvement of agriculture in this Presidency. I know both the Hon. Sir Richard Lamb and the Hon. Mr. Curtis insist upon this circumstance that the Bill only recognises existing facts. That may be so, but in recognising existing changes, you may also do this, that by giving legislative sanction to those existing facts you may give an impetus and you may accustom people to regard small divisions of land as something which has been sanctioned by law and approved by Government. I submit that such a tendency, if created, will be most unfortunate to the agricultural progress and improvement of this country. As I have pointed out yesterday, if any steps were to be taken, they should have been in the opposite direction. The old sections 98 and 116 of the old Code distinctly point to a policy of not recognising small sub-divisions of survey numbers, and it would authorise measures for the purpose of preventing the minutest sub-division. I submit, that those safeguards in the Act have really been weakened by the modifications which have been introduced by the Bill before the Council, and so far, I consider that it is most unfortunate that the *rayats* of this Presidency should now labour under the impression that the Government themselves and the legislature also have joined in sanctioning the minutest sub-divisions of land. That is a point of view from which I consider that this Bill will have the most unfortunate result on the land policy of this Presidency, and therefore it is that I am unable to vote for the third reading.

Several honourable members having spoken H.E. the President Lord Sydenham said:—Before putting this Bill to the third reading I should like to make one or two general remarks. I can assure this Council that if I thought that there was anything in this Bill which would tend to stereotype that sub-division which is going on in India, or to increase it, then I should be as ready to oppose the third reading as my honourable friend Sir Pherozeshah............But I am glad to know that my honourable friend Sir Pherozeshah, with his great influence, shows that he has been giving his attention to what may become a burning question before long. I think he told us that he made several speeches on the subject. I wish he gave me private references to those speeches. They would be of interest not only with regard to land in India but with regards to lands in other countries also. In any case we can all feel sure that when Government comes to deal with the question again, it will have the perfect support of the Hon. Sir Pherozeshah Mehta in ending or at all events always limiting the excessive sub-divisions which are now going on..............

The Motion for the third reading of the Bill was then put to the vote and carried.

References

1. These references are from the speeches and writings of Pherozeshah Mehta edited by J.R.B. Jeejeebhoy. I feel much beholder to him. H.P. Mody has written a comprehensive biography of Pherozeshah Mehta and a few details have been used in this work.

5

The Assessment

Pherozeshah Mehta was a remarkable leader of the Indian National Congress for three decades. One of the prominent founders of this political organisation as he was, he played his political role in the Bombay Corporation, Legislative Council and the Imperial Council. He was a fine orator and with his rich legal background, he could argue well and very often he silenced the British bureaucrats with his comprehensive views on several issues.

He spent his whole life for the upliftment of his people specially in the field of education. He fought for universal education and argued that it was the only best way for the economic upliftment of the people. As a prominent member of the Bombay University Senate, he suggested several reforms in the department of education.

As a Congress leader he always showed keenness to improve its stature and made the Raj realise that it was the only political organization in our country which could negotiate with the Viceroy regarding constitutional concessions. It was a long journey under respective Viceroys and some of them did not like the political programme of the Congress. But the Congress leadership managed and controlled by leaders like Dadabhai Naoroji, Surendranath Banerjea, Gopal Krishna Gokhale, Pherozeshah Mehta, Lajpat Rai, Bal Gangadhar

Tilak and others traversed about thirty years, before the global war, with success on several issues.

Indeed Gokhale and Mehta who represented the moderate views always adopted constitutional methods and opposed the extremist approach of Tilak, Aurobindo, B.C. Pal and others. They opined that at this point of time, the Raj, at any cost, would not oblige them to grant them as much as they desired. Any kind of extremist approach, they opined, instead of promoting their political interest, would damage it.

On his sudden demise, several leaders paid glowing tributes to him. V.S. Srinivasa Sastri, D.E. Wacha and Dr. Scott greatly enlogised his services to the nation.

It was a sound instinct that led Sir Pherozeshah Mehta to reject official preferment when it come to him. He would no doubt have been a most successful and distinguished servant of the Crown and benefited his country to the greatest extent that was possible to an Indian official. But his conspicuous talents and extraordinary personality were peculiarly fitted for eminence in non-official life, and there can be no doubt now that they could not have yielded to India half the benefit they have actually done if their possessor had chosen to be a Judge of the High Court or even a Member of the Executive Council. There is a certain sort of talent which, though of high quality, requires for its fullest display pre-existing organization, opportunities and channels of exercise ready made, the discipline of established things which provides work for every hour and constant scope for the beneficent use of authority. Office is the most appropriate destiny for a person endowed with it. The gifts of Sir Pherozeshah were of a different stamp. They could in a sense make their own environment. Thrown on the trackless sea of public life without chart or compass, he was able in storm and in sunshine to steer clear of rocks and shoals, and though he never reached the Happy Isles which are beyond human ken, he must be reckoned amongst the great pioneers who made the voyage comparatively safe for the adventurous people to whom the quest has irresistible attractions. No one in official bondage could have given to the City of Bombay fifty years of uninterrupted and dis-interested service or have fought repeated battles for civic freedom and wrought such an intimate connection between the fortunes of that great city and his own name as to compel an Anglo-Indian paper to write of him: "The Bombay Corporation is Sir Pherozeshah Mehta and Sir Pherozeshah Methta is the Bombay Corporation." No one in official bondage could have kept the western presidency within the limits of moderation and loyalty to the British Throne in the troubled times that followed the Ilbert Bill or the Bengal Partition. The political school represented by the Indian National Congress has been moulded into its present shape by firm-minded and far-seeing patriots, amongst whom from the beginning Sir Pherozeshah was one of the most influential and in later years almost the most influential. When it was threatened with dissolution some years ago, anxious Congressmen all over Indian looked to him almost instinctively, as children in a house might to their father when the wind howled outside and the rain beat on the roof.[1]

It is a great pity that he has been taken away at this critical hour in the fortunes of India when her final place in the British Empire is under serious consideration. His unrivalled power over his countrymen and his unique position in the non-official world of India rendered his goodwill and co-operation so useful to the highest authorities that it is no wonder Lord Curzon and Lord Sydenham regretted to have been deprived of them for a time. Of strength of will and courage of conviction he had more by far than the common share. These qualities preserved for him the respect and homage of his compatriots even during the periods when he had apparently lost his popularity. It used to be said even of his ablest personal foes that, whatever they spoke and wrote of him ordinarily, their address when face to face with him was couched in accents of deference. Few could resist the persuasiveness and versatility of his conversation or the charm and finished courtesy of his manners. Once at a meeting of the Subjects Committee of the Congress in Bombay, answering a charge that used to be brought against him during successive years of autocratically preventing the framing of a constitution for the great National Assembly, he asked a Punjab veteran: "Why did you not call me to account there and then?" The old man answered amidst laughter that he had been cowed down by Sir Pherozeshah's personality. "'My personality!" answered he, looking smilingly round, "how can I help it, gentlemen?" The wrath of his assailants was turned away and nothing more was said on the subject at that sitting. Another picture of him that dwells in the memory relates to the famous Calcutta Congress of 1907, when the passions of a certain section of Bengalis had been worked up to a high pitch and chose the great Bombay autocrat as one of the victims of their fury. When the Subjects Committee assembled, his forceful figure was seen on the dais in proximity to that of the President. Young Bengal thought that the Grand Old Man was in the shadow of a malignant planet, and cried out repeatedly: "Down with Sir Pherozeshah!" But there he sat, calm and unmoved, with the unconcern of a lion until the excerations died down. He exhibited the same composure and self-command in the still more exciting scenes at Surat.

His personality, imposing as it was, could not account entirely for his vast influence. People met in him a person of matchless debating power, mastery of details which the ablest officials might envy, and that overpowering interest which earnest advocacy commands when it is for unselfish causes. I have watched him more than once in the Legislative Council, always keen and on the alert for points of order and procedure, not slow to signify his approval or disapproval as speaker after speaker turned, as if by facination, to where he sat to find out what impression he was producing. Even the President of the Council was not altogether exempt from his interruptions. On one occasion, when the Land Revenue Administration of Bombay had been severely criticised by the Hon'ble Mr. Goculdas Parekh, an official member, who had been strung to the quick, forgot himself so far as to say that the ryots were becoming more and more contumacious because their friends and supporters in the Council and outside

were inculcating habits of dishonesty. When Sir Pherozeshah's turn came to speak, the scene in Council was worth seeing. He was obviously agitated, and while the house listened with tense feelings, went into the history of Bombay assessments and remissions, showed how the Government of India had to intervene to rescue the ryot from the oppressiveness of the Bombay revenue official, and wound up finally by raising his voice and exclaiming with a minatory gesture: "As for inculcating habits of dishonesty, I cast the accusation back in the teeth of him who made it." When I related the story to Mr. Gokhale, he clapped his hands in admiration and said: "Only Mehta could have done it; he never fails to rise to the occasion." It was this manly outspokenness of utterance and the tone of equality with the highest in the land that came naturally to him, which had sounded so unfamilar and so unseemly in the ears of an earlier generation of officials when first Sir Pherozeshah's voice was heard in the Imperial Legislative Council in the last years of Lord Elgin and the first years of Lord Curzon. General Sir Henry Brackenbury gave the member from Bombay lofty and patronising advice in the approved official style, and Sir James Westland complained of "the new spirit" that had been introduced into the Council. The expression was seized by the Bengal public who were delighted to find an Indian that could stand up to exalted officials and tell them unpleasing truths as man to man. A public reception was given to him in Calcutta and an address was presented in which the phrase "the new spirit" figured prominently. This demonstration, remarkable as coming from the inhabitants of Calcutta, was mainly due to the exertions of Mr. W.C. Bonnerjee, most generous of friends and stout-hearted to patriots. Twice afterwards in Bombay Sir Pherozeshah was the recipient of addresses voted by the public in appreciation of his eminent services. Such striking recognition has fallen to the lot of few public workers in India. A long career of fifty years lived in the full glare of the public eye could not but bring Sir Pherozeshah now and then into collision with those that wield the destinies of the country. On such occasions Sir Pherozeshah did not flinch in his determination to withstand the policy and measures of officials. The opposition which he led to the notorious Bombay Land Revenue Bill of 1901 attracted a great deal of attention at the time because, after the failure of a heroic effort to get the consideration of the Bill adjourned, he and some of his followers, including Mr. Gokhale, left the Council meeting as a sort of demonstration, declaring that they would not, even by their presence, participate in the enactment of so harmful and so unpopular a measure. In one of those fits of wrong-headedness which at happily race intervals possess the officials, he was excluded from the place of precedence that was his due on the occasion of the visit of Their Imperial Majesties as Prince and Princess of Wales, although he had been elected President of the Bombay Corporation for the year expressly for the purpose of welcoming. Their Royal Highnesses as the foremost citizen of the foremost city in India. Popular feeling was roused in an unsual degree, and the Bombay Government saw the wisdom of retracing their false step before it was too late. Another time certain high officials openly joined a caucus which tried to keep Sir Pherozeshah out of the Bombay Corporation where, it was alleged, he exercised an overpowering and unwholesome dominance. Once more a wave of popular indignation swept off Sir Pherozeshah's assailants, and he stood vindicated as the father and champion of the Corporation. It was about this time that the centralising tendency of Lord Curzon imposed a standard time on all India. But the cities of Calcutta and Bombay in undiscriminating opposition to everything that emanated from him, would have none of it. Sir Pherozeshah stood out for Bombay time and it is owing to his ucompromising attitude on the occasion that the visitor to Bombay still sees the municipal clock over Crawford Market show a time much behind that which he observes at Victoria Terminus. Notwithstanding these episodes, however, the European community of Bombay, both official and non-official, true to their sportsmanlike qualities have always been generous in recognising Sir Pherozeshah's great qualities and eminent services, and given due meed of gratitude and praise for his unswerving loyalty to the British connection, and his powerful advocacy of the virtues of the British Empire in critical times. Not the least remarkable feature of his remarkable ascendancy over the Bombay Corporation was its complete immunity from imputations of jobbery or personal aggrandisement of any sort—an example of shining purity for all aspirants to distinction in the sphere of local self-government.

It is one of my most vivid and inspiring memories, the evident pride with which, in one of his confiding moods, he told a small party at his own tea-table that Thursdays were consecrated to "my Corporation." No fee, he said, could tempt him from Municipal business. He has been often compared by English friends to Chamberlain and Gladstone, One hesitates to assert where pesonal knowledge fails. But there can be no doubt Sir Pherozeshah was one of the strongest and wisest men of his time, exercising a powerful influence to noble and unselfish ends. India has recently suffered great losses—Ganga Prasad Varma, Satish Chandra Banerjee, Gokhale, Sir Henry Cotton and now Sir Pherozeshah Mehta. Who next? We cannot stay the hand of Death. All we can do is to treasure the memories of the great dead, to recall their virtues and so far as we may, benefit by their example.[2]

At the special meeting of the Bombay Municipal Corporation held on Wednesday the 10th November, at Mr. D.E. Wacha's request the President read his speech. In this Mr. Wacha said:

> With a heart sick and full of the deepest sorrow at the swift and sudden death of my life-long friend and co-worker, it is difficult for me to find words to speak with anything like fulness all that I so poignantly feel at the present time. Our friendship began at school when we were boys of six, and nothing came between us from then to the time he passed away—a big span of 64 years—to mar it even in the slightest degree. It was unbroken and uninterrupted. And, now, I feel his loss sadly and consider myself left lonely and stranded. But whatever my personal loss and grief, it must sink into the larger grief in which the whole Indian nation is plunged. Universal sorrow prevails all through

the country and commingled with the gloom of the terrible war, the end of which none of us can foresee, the shadow of his loss had further darkened the whole Indian world like an eclipse. Thousands of brave men have shed and are shedding their blood in the cause of the world's freedom. Daily do we read of the marvels of heroism achieved by Britain's noblest sons and by our own countrymen in the various sanguinary fields of battle. But India has lost her valiant son Pherozeshah on the field of "fruitful strifes and rivalries of peace". He gave the best of his life-blood, his great talents and his indomitable energy, uninterruptedly for full forty years to the cause of his motherland with a courage, independence, untiring devotion and unexampled selflessness which are today the admiration of millions of his countrymen. It is not for me to relate the immeasurable services rendered by him to the city of his birth, and to its Municipal Corporation, in particular, during half a century. They are writ large in the civic history of this city. The hero of a hundred fights in this civic chamber, he earned the hegemony of the Corporation and maintained its reputation for the highest efficiency by his ungrudging spirit of self-sacrifice, by his disinterested services and by his undoubted abilities given to the cause of his city from week to week, month to month, and year to year for fully forty-five years. It is an unprecedented record in the history of this city, nay in the history of whole India, and no tribute from our faltering tongues today can ever repay the gratitude under which he has left us.[3]

HIGHER POLITICS

And what shall I say about his other and greater work, unparalleled and unprecedented in the annuals of British Rule in India. In the great Indian field of high politics, of popular instruction, of popular freedom of thought and speech, of liberal culture and other reforms of the highest importance to the welfare of the country, he worked incessantly with a singleness of purpose—the greater good of the Indian people—without any other hope of reward than that of his own conscience. The last few years of his life had been those of his widest influence and his highest reputation as a great statesman of unusual brilliancy, of almost unerring sagacity and clearest foresight. But this is not the place and the time to offer that fullest appreciation of his great and invaluable services to his country. I only content myself by observing that gifted as Sir Pherozeshah was and endowed with such versatile talents, universally recognised, he would have made his mark in any country of the civilised West, and his lot been cast there and most specially in that great mother of Parliaments, the British House of Commons, with its rich and historical traditions of seven hundred years. (Hear, hear.)

It has sometimes been said by those who absolutely knew next to nothing of his real feelings and sentiments, of his pure patriotism and burning desire to see the people of this country lifted to higher level in the scale of the great nations of the world, that he was a most difficult man to deal with. But I can boldly say without the least hesitation and with a knowledge of his innermost heart, that perhaps no man was more misunderstood than he. The great majority of Anglo-Indians, official and non-official, who a few years ago saw in him nothing but a relentless democratic swordsman who wielded his sword most uncompromisingly, have of late acknowledged him to be the embodiment of a vigorous yet dignified policy which, while raising the prestige of political life in India, has at the same time brought the rulers and the ruled to understand each other better. Even his political opponents have respected his courage, his penetrating judgment and his dignified firmness. By his great urbanity and genial nature, he gained the affectionate regard of all classes and communities and of friends and foes alike. Underlying, as is alleged in some quarters, his autocracy, there was something that touched the very chords of public life. Thus it was that he became the idol of the whole Indian nation, and thus it was that he was unreservedly confided in alike by his countrymen as by the Government. I can only conclude by saying of him what Shakespeare has said of

Henry V:

Hear him debate of commonwealth affairs,
You would say—it hath been all his study
Turn him to any cause of policy,
The Gordion knot of it he will unloose,
Familiar as his garter; that when he speaks,
The air, a chartered libertine, is still,
And the mute wonder lurketh in men's ears,
To steal his sweet and honeyed sentences.

Sir Pherozeshah is no more. His place is void. He bloomed like the secular aloe tree of which the poet has sung. It will be some generations before another like him shines as brilliantly as he did on the Indian firmament. He has gone to join that chorus of the immortals of whom George Eliot has so beautifully sung. Meanwhile our hearts go in this darkest hour to the bereaved widow. We offer our deepest sympathy and expression of condolence in her great affliction.[4]

DR. SCOTT'S EULOGY

At a meeting of the Bombay Student's Brotherhood held at the Prarthana Samaj recently, Dr. R. Scott said:

We meet for the second time in one year to deplore the loss of an eminent public leader. Two such men have passed away from us, neither leaving a successor. Sir Pherozeshah Mehta was the foremost citizen of Bombay. Anywhere he would have been an outstanding man. He possessed strong intellect, wide culture, unfaltering moral courage, a firm grasp of constitutional principle, a clear insight into complex practical questions, a commanding eloquence and a personal authority or leadership over men. A lawyer by profession he was by choice a public servant. He did not direct his ambitions towards the Bench, nor did he endeavour to accumulate wealth; but he gave to his profession only so much time as to secure for him a competence while he devoted the greater part of his energies to the service of his country. For more than a generation he has been prominent in our midst tending the growth of the city and growing therewith. The Municipal Corporation was one in sphere in which very varried activities were exercised; and you remember that after he had already thrice been President when the King announced a visit to his Eastern Empire, Sir Pherozeshah wast at once chosen for a fourth term of office in order that the City might be represented by its leading citizen when it welcomed its Sovereign. The University was another sphere, and there I have watched his unequalled influence and have particularly observed his insistence on constitutional law and practice—a foundation principle on which encroachments are more frequent than is supposed. It is a matter of gratification that he received the headship of that Institution, though, as formerly in the case of Telang, his period of office has been cut short. Again he was a leading member of the Legislative Council: and his power was felt in every department of the State. Sir Pherozeshah's mind was formed on the lines of the old robust liberalism which prevailed in England in the third quarter of the nineteenth century and was then expounded by various philosophical thinkers. Some points of that creed such as the non-interference of Government with public institutions or social movements, are now absolute in Europe, and there will always be diversities of opinion where there are changing conditions of life. But where is the man who with equal wisdom and capacity will wear the mantle of our departed leader? He has fallen in the fulness of his powers, while he still seemed to have the promise of year; and all we can now do is to commend a great example while we record our sense of an irreparable loss.[5]

References

1. Tribute by V.S. Srinivasa Sastri in *The Indian Review*, November 1915.
2. *Ibid.*
3. Tribute by D.E. Wacha in *Ibid.*
4. *Ibid.*
5. Views expressed by Dr. R. Scott in *Ibid.*
6. The Surat Convention.
7. Views on expansion of Councils.

energies to the service of his country. For more than a generation he has been prominent in ... the city ... ever ... Tha ... was one ... sphere in which very ... we ... remember that after the ... President ... the King announced ... the British Empire Sir Pherozeshah was at once ... of office ... that ... might ... leading ... welcomed as Secretary ... another sphere, and there I have ... influence and have particularly ... constitutional ... practice ... which ... fundaments ...

... matter of gratification that ... that institution ... upon ... period of office has been ... member of the Legislative Council ... was felt in every department of the State. Sir ... was ... on the lines of the old ... in England ... the ... was expounded by various ... points of that school such as the ... with public institutions ... social movements ... in Europe, and there will always be ... these ... changing conditions of ... who with equal wisdom and capacity ... our departed Leader. He has fallen ... walk ... he still seemed ... the ... can ... is to command a great example ... sense of an irreparable loss.

References

1. Tribute by V.S. Srinivasa Sastri in The Indian Review ... 1915.
2. Ibid.
3. Tribute by D.E. Wacha in Ibid.
4. Ibid.
5. Views expressed by D. R. Scott in Ibid.
6. The Surat Convention.
7. Views on expansion of Councils.

Bibliography

Primary Sources

Speeches of Pherozeshah Mehta
Debates, Municipal Corporation, Bombay
Debates, Bombay Legislative Council
Debates, Imperial Legislative Council
Reports of Annual Sessions of Indian National Congress

Secondary Works

Banerjea, Surendranath, *A Nation in Making*, London, 1925.

Das, C.R., *India for Indians*, Madras, 1921.

Ghose, Aurobindo, *On National Problems*, Calcutta, 1950.

Gokhale, Gopal Krishna, *Speeches*, Madras, 1916.

Jeejeebhoy, J.R.B., *Some Unpublished and Later Speeches and Writings of The Hon. Sir Pherozeshah Mehta*, Bombay, 1918.

Mody, H.P., *Sir Pherozeshah Mehta: A Political Biography*, Bombay, 1921.

Pal, B.C., *His Life and Utterances*, Madras, 1910.

Rai, Lala Lajpat, *The Political Future of India*, New York, 1919.

Tilak, Bal Gangadhar, *Speeches and Writings*, Madras, 1922.

Wedderburn, William, *Speeches and Writings*, Madras, 1918.

Index